WORKBOOK C

HOLT

MIDDLE SCHOOL
HANDBOOK

HOLT, RINEHART AND WINSTON
Harcourt Brace & Company

Austin • New York • Orlando • Chicago • Atlanta • San Francisco • Boston • Dallas • Toronto • London

NOTE TO THE STUDENT: **Excerpted Literary Works Used in** *Holt Middle School Handbook: Workbook C*

The following excerpt was used to illustrate a point of grammar:
  from "O Captain! My Captain!" by Walt Whitman, 23

The following excerpts were used to illustrate capitalization:
  quotation by Yogi Berra on the 1973 National League pennant race, 115
  from "Sonnet 29," by William Shakespeare, 115
  from *Alaska Fragment,* by John Muir, 115

Requests for permission to make copies of any part of the work should be mailed to: Permissions Department, Holt, Rinehart and Winston, Inc., 6277 Sea Harbor Drive, Orlando, Florida 32887-6777.

Some material in this work was previously published in ELEMENTS OF WRITING, Pupil's Edition, Second Course, copyright © 1993 by Holt, Rinehart and Winston, Inc.; ELEMENTS OF WRITING, Teacher's ResourceBank™, Second Course, copyright © 1993 by Holt, Rinehart and Winston, Inc.; and ENGLISH COMPOSITION AND GRAMMAR, Teacher's Resource Book, Second Course, copyright © 1988 by Harcourt Brace & Company. All rights reserved.

Printed in the United States of America

ISBN 0-03-098485-8

6 7 8 082 00 99

Table of Contents

WRITER'S QUICK REFERENCE

Worksheet 1 Common Usage Problems A...1
Worksheet 2 Common Usage Problems B..2
Worksheet 3 Common Usage Problems C..3
Worksheet 4 Common Usage Problems D..4
Worksheet 5 Common Usage Problems E..5
Worksheet 6 Common Usage Problems F..6
Worksheet 7 Common Usage Problems G...7
Worksheet 8 The Double Negative..8
Worksheet 9 Review...9

GRAMMAR AND USAGE

CHAPTER 1 PARTS OF SPEECH

Worksheet 1 Types of Nouns A...11
Worksheet 2 Types of Nouns B...12
Worksheet 3 Types of Pronouns A..13
Worksheet 4 Types of Pronouns B..14
Worksheet 5 Adjectives A..15
Worksheet 6 Adjectives B..16
Worksheet 7 Noun, Pronoun, or Adjective?...17
Worksheet 8 Action Verbs and Linking Verbs...18
Worksheet 9 Transitive Verbs and Intransitive Verbs...19
Worksheet 10 Verb Phrases..20
Worksheet 11 Adverbs That Modify Verbs...21
Worksheet 12 Adverbs That Modify Adjectives and Adverbs..22
Worksheet 13 Prepositions and Their Objects..23
Worksheet 14 Conjunctions...24
Worksheet 15 Interjections..25
Worksheet 16 Determining Parts of Speech...26
Worksheet 17 Review..27

CHAPTER 2 AGREEMENT

Worksheet 1 Singular and Plural..29
Worksheet 2 Agreement of Subject and Verb A..30
Worksheet 3 Agreement of Subject and Verb B..31
Worksheet 4 Agreement with Indefinite Pronouns..32
Worksheet 5 Agreement with Compound Subjects...33
Worksheet 6 Other Problems in Agreement A..34
Worksheet 7 Other Problems in Agreement B..35

Worksheet 8   Agreement of Pronoun and Antecedent A 36
Worksheet 9   Agreement of Pronoun and Antecedent B 37
Worksheet 10   Review 38

CHAPTER 3 USING VERBS

Worksheet 1   Regular Verbs..41
Worksheet 2   Irregular Verbs A...42
Worksheet 3   Irregular Verbs B 43
Worksheet 4   Verb Tense..44
Worksheet 5   Consistency of Tense..45
Worksheet 6   Commonly Confused Verbs 46
Worksheet 7   Review 47

CHAPTER 4 USING PRONOUNS

Worksheet 1   Case Forms 49
Worksheet 2   Nominative Case 50
Worksheet 3   Objective Case A 51
Worksheet 4   Objective Case B 52
Worksheet 5   Who and Whom 53
Worksheet 6   Other Pronoun Problems 54
Worksheet 7   Review 55

CHAPTER 5 USING MODIFIERS

Worksheet 1   Comparison of Modifiers 57
Worksheet 2   Regular Comparison 58
Worksheet 3   Uses of Comparative and Superlative Forms 59
Worksheet 4   Irregular Comparison 60
Worksheet 5   Double Comparison and Double Negative 61
Worksheet 6   Misplaced Prepositional Phrases..62
Worksheet 7   Misplaced and Dangling Participial Phrases 63
Worksheet 8   Misplaced Adjective Clauses 64
Worksheet 9   Review 65

PHRASES, CLAUSES, SENTENCES

CHAPTER 6 PHRASES

Worksheet 1   Prepositional Phrases..67
Worksheet 2   Adjective Phrases..68
Worksheet 3   Adverb Phrases..69
Worksheet 4   Participles and Participial Phrases..70
Worksheet 5   Gerunds and Gerund Phrases...71
Worksheet 6   Infinitives and Infinitive Phrases..72
Worksheet 7   Appositives and Appositive Phrases 73
Worksheet 8   Review 74

CHAPTER 7 CLAUSES

Worksheet 1 Independent and Subordinate Clauses 77
Worksheet 2 Subjects and Verbs in Independent Clauses..78
Worksheet 3 Subjects and Verbs in Subordinate Clauses..79
Worksheet 4 The Adjective Clause 80
Worksheet 5 The Adverb Clause..81
Worksheet 6 The Noun Clause 82
Worksheet 7 Review 83

CHAPTER 8 SENTENCES

Worksheet 1 Sentences and Sentence Fragments 85
Worksheet 2 Subject and Predicate..86
Worksheet 3 Complete Subject and Simple Subject...87
Worksheet 4 Complete Predicate and Simple Predicate 88
Worksheet 5 The Verb Phrase 89
Worksheet 6 Compound Subjects and Compound Verbs...90
Worksheet 7 Review 91

CHAPTER 9 COMPLEMENTS

Worksheet 1 Recognizing Complements 93
Worksheet 2 Direct Objects...94
Worksheet 3 Indirect Objects 95
Worksheet 4 Predicate Nominatives and Predicate Adjectives.......................................96
Worksheet 5 Review 97

CHAPTER 10 KINDS OF SENTENCES

Worksheet 1 Simple Sentences...99
Worksheet 2 Compound Sentences...100
Worksheet 3 Simple or Compound Sentence?...101
Worksheet 4 Complex Sentences..102
Worksheet 5 Compound-Complex Sentences 103
Worksheet 6 Classifying Sentences by Purpose 104
Worksheet 7 Review 105

CHAPTER 11 WRITING EFFECTIVE SENTENCES

Worksheet 1 Sentence Fragments 107
Worksheet 2 Run-on Sentences 108
Worksheet 3 Combining Sentences by Inserting Words and Phrases................................109
Worksheet 4 Combining by Using *And, But,* or *Or*..110
Worksheet 5 Combining by Using a Subordinate Clause..111
Worksheet 6 Stringy Sentences and Wordy Sentences..112
Worksheet 7 Review 113

MECHANICS

CHAPTER 12 CAPITAL LETTERS

Worksheet 1 Using Capital Letters A..115
Worksheet 2 Using Capital Letters B..116
Worksheet 3 Using Capital Letters C..117
Worksheet 4 Using Capital Letters D..118
Worksheet 5 Using Capital Letters E..119
Worksheet 6 Review..120

CHAPTER 13 PUNCTUATION

Worksheet 1 Using End Marks..121
Worksheet 2 Using Commas A..122
Worksheet 3 Using Commas B..123
Worksheet 4 Using Commas C..124
Worksheet 5 Using Commas D..125
Worksheet 6 Using Commas E..126
Worksheet 7 Using Semicolons..127
Worksheet 8 Using Colons...128
Worksheet 9 Review..129

CHAPTER 14 PUNCTUATION

Worksheet 1 Underlining (Italics)..131
Worksheet 2 Direct and Indirect Quotations...132
Worksheet 3 Setting Off Direct Quotations...133
Worksheet 4 Punctuating Dialogue...134
Worksheet 5 Other Uses of Quotation Marks..135
Worksheet 6 Review..136

CHAPTER 15 PUNCTUATION

Worksheet 1 Using Apostrophes to Show Possession.................................137
Worksheet 2 Using Apostrophes in Contractions.......................................138
Worksheet 3 Using Contractions and Possessive Pronouns........................139
Worksheet 4 Using Apostrophes in Plurals..140
Worksheet 5 Using Hyphens..141
Worksheet 6 Using Parentheses and Dashes...142
Worksheet 7 Review..143

CHAPTER 16 SPELLING AND VOCABULARY

Worksheet 1 Improving Your Spelling..145
Worksheet 2 Roots..146
Worksheet 3 Prefixes...147
Worksheet 4 Suffixes...148
Worksheet 5 Spelling Rules A...149

Worksheet 6   Spelling Rules B..150
Worksheet 7   Plurals of Nouns A 151
Worksheet 8   Plurals of Nouns B 152
Worksheet 9   Spelling Numbers..153
Worksheet 10 Using Context Clues A 154
Worksheet 11 Using Context Clues B 155
Worksheet 12 Choosing the Right Word...156
Worksheet 13 Review 157

COMPOSITION

CHAPTER 17 THE WRITING PROCESS

Worksheet 1   Freewriting...159
Worksheet 2   Brainstorming 160
Worksheet 3   Clustering...161
Worksheet 4   Asking Questions 162
Worksheet 5   Reading and Listening..163
Worksheet 6   Purpose and Audience 164
Worksheet 7   Arranging Ideas 165
Worksheet 8   Using Visuals A..166
Worksheet 9   Using Visuals B 168
Worksheet 10 Writing a First Draft 170
Worksheet 11 Self-Evaluation..171
Worksheet 12 Peer Evaluation 172
Worksheet 13 Revising 173
Worksheet 14 Proofreading and Publishing 175
Worksheet 15 The Aim and Process of Writing 176

CHAPTER 18 PARAGRAPH AND COMPOSITION STRUCTURE

Worksheet 1   The Paragraph's Main Idea 177
Worksheet 2   The Topic Sentence..178
Worksheet 3   Using Sensory Details 179
Worksheet 4   Using Facts and Examples 180
Worksheet 5   Unity in Paragraphs...181
Worksheet 6   Coherence in Paragraphs A...182
Worksheet 7   Coherence in Paragraphs B 183
Worksheet 8   Description: Using Spatial Order 184
Worksheet 9   Narration: Using Chronological Order 185
Worksheet 10 Classification: Using Logical Order 186
Worksheet 11 Evaluation: Using Order of Importance 187
Worksheet 12 Planning a Composition 188
Worksheet 13 Early Plans 189
Worksheet 14 Formal Outlines 190
Worksheet 15 The Introduction 191
Worksheet 16 The Body 192
Worksheet 17 Unity and Coherence in a Composition 193
Worksheet 18 The Conclusion..194

CHAPTER 19 THE RESEARCH REPORT

Worksheet 1 Choosing a Subject 195
Worksheet 2 Narrowing a Subject 196
Worksheet 3 Thinking About Audience and Purpose 197
Worksheet 4 Making an Early Plan and Asking Questions 198
Worksheet 5 Finding and Evaluating Sources...199
Worksheet 6 Listing Sources and Taking Notes..200
Worksheet 7 Organizing and Outlining Information......................................201
Worksheet 8 Writing a First Draft 202
Worksheet 9 Evaluating and Revising 203
Worksheet 10 Proofreading and Publishing 204

RESOURCES

Worksheet 1 The Dewey Decimal System 205
Worksheet 2 The Card Catalog 206
Worksheet 3 The Parts of a Book 207
Worksheet 4 Using Reference Materials...208
Worksheet 5 Using the Newspaper 209
Worksheet 6 Using the Dictionary A...210
Worksheet 7 Using the Dictionary B...211
Worksheet 8 Using the Dictionary C...212
Worksheet 9 Using the Dictionary D...213
Worksheet 10 Personal Letters 214
Worksheet 11 Social Letters...215
Worksheet 12 The Parts of a Business Letter...216
Worksheet 13 Types of Business Letters 217
Worksheet 14 Addressing Envelopes and Completing Printed Forms 218
Worksheet 15 Manuscript Style A...219
Worksheet 16 Manuscript Style B...220
Worksheet 17 Manuscript Style C...221
Worksheet 18 Review..222

APPENDIX: DIAGRAMING SENTENCES

Worksheet 1 Diagraming Subjects and Verbs..225
Worksheet 2 Diagraming Compound Subjects and Verbs 226
Worksheet 3 Diagraming Adjectives and Adverbs 227
Worksheet 4 Diagraming Direct Objects and Indirect Objects......................228
Worksheet 5 Diagraming Subject Complements 229
Worksheet 6 Diagraming Prepositional Phrases and Verbal Phrases 230
Worksheet 7 Diagraming Subordinate Clauses 231
Worksheet 8 Diagraming Sentences Classified by Structure.........................232

Name _____ Date _____ Class _____

 **WORKSHEET 1** *Common Usage Problems A*

The following guidelines will help you avoid errors in usage.

accept, except   *Accept* is a verb that means "to receive." *Except* may be either a verb or a preposition. As a verb, *except* means "to leave out" or "to exclude"; as a preposition, *except* means "other than" or "excluding."

advice, advise   The noun *advice* means "a recommendation about a course of action." The verb *advise* means "to give advice."

affect, effect   *Affect* is a verb meaning "to influence." As a noun, *effect* means "the result of some action."

ain't   Avoid this word in speaking and writing; it is nonstandard English.

altar, alter   The noun *altar* means "a table for a religious ceremony." The verb *alter* means "to change."

anywheres, everywheres, nowheres, somewheres   Use these words without the final *s.*

at   Do not use *at* after *where.*

Exercise A   Underline the word or expression in parentheses that is correct according to standard usage.

1. According to an old Korean saying, you are never out of sight of mountains (anywheres, anywhere) in Korea.

2. The 1988 Olympic games in Seoul had a dramatic (affect, effect) on Korea's image.

3. I looked on a map to find out where Korea's Lotte World (is, is at).

4. In 1446, King Sejong the Great required the Korean people to use a new alphabet, which scholars and government officials readily (accepted, excepted).

5. Even if you (ain't, aren't) interested in dancing, take my (advice, advise) and go to see the lively Korean folk dancers.

Exercise B: Proofreading   Most of the following sentences contain errors in usage. If a sentence contains an error, cross out the error, and write the correct word on the line provided. If a sentence is correct, write C.

EXAMPLE: 1. Will you ~~except~~ my invitation? *accept*

1. "You simply cannot alter the facts," argued the lawyer.   _____

2. Whose advise are you taking, and how will it affect your plans?   _____

3. In the 1984 presidential election, Ronald Reagan carried every state accept Minnesota.   _____

4. How does standing on your head effect the flow of blood and oxygen to your brain?   _____

5. The coach advices us to stick to the training rules.   _____

Name _____ Date _____ Class _____

Common Usage Problems B

The following guidelines will help you avoid errors in usage.

bad, badly   *Bad* is an adjective. *Badly* is an adverb.

between, among   Use *between* when referring to two things at a time, even though they may be part of a group containing more than two (*the wire ran* between *telephone poles*). Use *among* when referring to a group rather than to separate individuals or items (*the weeds grew* among *the flowers*).

bust, busted   Avoid using these words as verbs. Use a form of either *burst* or *break*.

clothes, cloths   The noun *clothes* means "wearing apparel." The noun *cloths* means "pieces of fabric."

complement, compliment   The noun *complement* means "something that completes." As a verb, *compliment* means "to praise someone." As a noun, it means "praise."

consul, council, counsel   The noun *consul* refers to a representative of a government in a foreign country. *Council* refers to a group of people who meet together. Used as a noun, *counsel* means "advice." Used as a verb, *counsel* means "to give advice."

could of   Do not write *of* with the helping verb *could*. Write *could have*. Also avoid *ought to of, should of, would of, might of,* and *must of*.

Exercise A   Underline the word in parentheses that is correct according to standard usage.

1. The student (council, counsel) voted for "A Night on the Nile" as its dance theme.

2. Many shoppers at Egyptian markets wear Western (clothes, cloths).

3. Some Egyptians, however, wear traditional garments, including (clothes, cloths) called *kaffiyehs* wrapped around their heads.

4. The American (consul, council) in Cairo welcomed the vice president to Egypt.

5. In Cairo, the confused tourists looked to their tour director for (council, counsel).

Exercise B: Proofreading   The following sentences contain errors in usage. If a sentence contains an error, cross out the error, and write the correct word(s) on the line provided.

EXAMPLE: 1. Use the dust ~~clothes~~ that are in the closet. *cloths*

1. Among the two of them, Earlene was the faster runner; she made the perfect complement for the relay team.   _____

2. The public-address system sounds badly and needs repair.   _____

3. No, we can't play; my little brother busted the video game.   _____

4. I don't know how you could of done such a thing!   _____

5. Neil blushed at her complements.   _____

Writer's Quick Reference

Common Usage Problems C

The following guidelines will help you avoid errors in usage.

councilor, counselor   The noun *councilor* refers to a member of a council. The noun *counselor* means "one who advises."

de´sert, desert´, dessert´   The noun *de´sert* means "a dry, sandy region." The verb *desert´* means "to abandon" or "to leave." The noun *dessert´* means "the final course of a meal."

doesn't, don't   *Doesn't* is the contraction of *does not*. *Don't* is the contraction of *do not*. Use *doesn't* (not *don't*) with *he, she, it, this, that*, and singular nouns.

fewer, less   *Fewer* is used with plural words. *Less* is used with singular words. *Fewer* tells "how many"; *less* tells "how much."

formally, formerly   *Formally* means "with dignity" or "according to strict rules or procedures." *Formerly* means "previously" or "in the past."

good, well   *Good* is always an adjective. Never use *good* as an adverb. Instead, use *well*. Although *well* is usually an adverb, *well* may also be used as an adjective to mean "healthy."

had ought, hadn't ought   Unlike other verbs, *ought* is not used with *had*.

Exercise: Proofreading   Most of the following sentences contain errors in usage. If a sentence contains an error, cross out the error and, when necessary, write the correct word on the line provided. If a sentence is correct, write *C*.

EXAMPLE: 1. He ~~hadn't ought~~ to have told my secret. *ought not*

1. Camels didn't dessert their owners when they crossed the desert. _____

2. Figs, grapes, and dates are often served for desert at that restaurant. _____

3. Before the club takes up new business, the secretary formally reads the minutes of the previous meeting. _____

4. Navajo blankets look extremely well hanging on a wall. _____

5. My mother told me that our new neighbor, Mr. Brown, was formally a colonel in the U.S. Army. _____

6. You had ought to get out of those wet clothes before you catch cold. _____

7. We need less comments and more action. _____

8. No, this parakeet don't ever bite unless, of course, she's angry. _____

9. Do you always follow the advice of your councilor at school? _____

10. Delicate plants like these don't do good in full sun. _____

Writer's Quick Reference

WORKSHEET 4 | *Common Usage Problems D*

The following guidelines will help you avoid errors in usage.

hardly, scarcely   The words *hardly* and *scarcely* convey negative meanings. They should never be used with another negative word.

he, she, they   Avoid using a pronoun along with its antecedent as the subject of a verb. This error is called the *double subject*.

hear, here   The verb *hear* means "to perceive sounds by ear." The adverb *here* means "in this place."

hisself   *Hisself* is nonstandard English. Use *himself*.

how come   In informal situations, *how come* is often used instead of *why*. In formal situations, *why* should always be used.

its, it's   *Its* is a personal pronoun in the possessive form. *It's* is a contraction of *it is* or *it has*.

kind, sort, type   The words *this, that, these*, and *those* should agree in number with the words *kind(s), sort(s)*, and *type(s)*.

Exercise A   Underline the word in parentheses that is correct according to standard usage.

1. If you don't wait (hear, here), we may lose you in the crowd.

2. According to Ethan's map, (its, it's) a long way from (hear, here) to the park.

3. (Its, It's) too bad that the oak tree has lost (its, it's) leaves.

4. Didn't you (hear, here) me, Charlotte? Come over (hear, here) now!

5. Put everything in (its, it's) place before you leave.

Exercise B: Revising   The following sentences contain errors in usage. On the lines provided, write the corrected sentences.

EXAMPLE: 1. Speak up; I can't here you. *Speak up; I can't hear you.*

1. How come the moon seems to become smaller as it rises?

_____

2. Mom! The baby's got jam all over hisself!

_____

3. These kind of dogs make excellent pets for young children.

_____

4. The passengers they could do nothing but wait for the next flight.

_____

5. Its so dark that we can't scarcely see the footpath.

_____

Writer's Quick Reference

 **WORSHEET 5** | *Common Usage Problems E*

The following guidelines will help you avoid errors in usage.

kind of, sort of   In informal situations, *kind of* and *sort of* are often used to mean "somewhat" or "rather." In formal English, *somewhat* or *rather* is preferred.

lead, led   *Lead* is the present tense form of the verb *lead*. It rhymes with *feed* and means "to go first" or "to be a leader." *Led* is the past tense form of the verb *lead*. The noun *lead* rhymes with *red*. It means "a heavy metal" or "graphite used in pencils."

learn, teach   *Learn* means "to gain knowledge." *Teach* means "to instruct" or "to show how."

like, as if, as though   In informal situations, the preposition *like* is often used for the compound conjunctions *as if* or *as though*. In formal situations, *as if* or *as though* is preferred.

of   Do not use *of* with other prepositions such as *inside*, *off*, and *outside*.

principal, principle   As a noun, *principal* means "the head of a school." As an adjective, it means "main or most important." The noun *principle* means "a rule of conduct" or "a main fact or law."

quiet, quite   The adjective *quiet* means "still and peaceful" or "without noise." The adverb *quite* means "wholly or entirely" or "to a great extent."

Exercise A   Underline the word in parentheses that is correct according to standard usage.

1. The ancient Chinese, Greeks, and Romans used (lead, led) in their coins.

2. Steffi Graf (lead, led) in the first game of the tennis match.

3. The summer was not (quiet, quite) over before school began.

4. This is a well-known (principal, principle) in mathematics.

5. Have you heard that the new (principal, principle) used to be a student here?

Exercise B: Proofreading   The following sentences contain errors in usage. Cross out each error and, when necessary, write the correct word(s) on the line provided.

EXAMPLE: 1. Sacagawea ~~lead~~ them through the mountain pass.   _led_

1. The man looked like he was guilty, but he was found innocent.   _____

2. Mother lions learn their cubs how to hunt.   _____

3. Abraham Lincoln was rather a quite man; his most famous speech, "The Gettysburg Address," is a very short one.   _____

4. Suddenly, the owl swooped off of its perch and flew away.   _____

5. When the publisher misunderstood two of the lines in her latest poem, the poet was sort of disappointed.   _____

QUICK REFERENCE

Name _____ Date _____ Class _____

Common Usage Problems F

The following guidelines will help you avoid errors in usage.

real   In informal situations, *real* is often used as an adverb meaning "very" or "extremely." In formal situations, *very* or *extremely* is preferred.

reason . . . because   In informal situations, *reason . . . because* is often used instead of *reason . . . that*. In formal situations, use *reason . . . that*, or revise your sentence.

shone, shown   *Shone* is the past tense form of the verb *shine*. It means "gleamed" or "glowed." *Shown* is the past participle form of the verb *show*. It means "revealed." Another meaning of *shine* is "to polish," but the preferred past tense form for this meaning is *shined,* not *shone*.

some, somewhat   Do not use *some* for *somewhat* as an adverb.

stationary, stationery   The adjective *stationary* means "in a fixed position." The noun *stationery* means "writing paper."

to, too, two   *To* is a preposition. It is also part of an infinitive, a verbal. *Too* is an adverb that means "also" or "overly." *Two* is the number equal to one plus one.

try and   In informal situations, *try and* is often used instead of *try to*. In formal situations, *try to* should be used.

Exercise   Underline the word or expression in parentheses that is correct according to standard usage.

1. A documentary about the tunnels through the Alps will be (shone, shown) at the library.

2. Staring at my saddle helped me (some, somewhat) when I became nervous riding a mule up the slopes of the Grand Canyon.

3. The reason geese migrate is (that, because) they can't survive in frozen water.

4. Huge exhaust fans were constructed to move the (stationary, stationery) air in the Holland Tunnel in New York.

5. For (to, too, two) travelers on foot, the road (to, too, two) Mexico City was (to, too, two) hot and dusty.

6. The warm sun (shone, shown) bright on the snowy top of Mont Blanc, but in the mountain's tunnel it was dark and chilly.

7. The reason I took the train is (because, that) I am afraid of flying.

8. We had a (real, very) good time during our visit to Niagara Falls.

9. We rode the underground, or subway, into London, where I bought some (stationary, stationery).

10. Whenever the bus got stuck on a back road in Chile, the passengers would (try and, try to) push it out of the mud.

Writer's Quick Reference

WORKSHEET 7   *Common Usage Problems G*

The following guidelines will help you avoid errors in usage.

use to, used to   Be sure to add the *d* to *use*. *Used to* is the past form.

way, ways   Use *way*, not *ways*, in referring to a distance.

when, where   Do not use *when* or *where* incorrectly in writing a definition.

who, which, that   The relative pronoun *who* refers to people only; *which* refers to things only; *that* refers to either people or things.

who's, whose   *Who's* is the contraction of *who is* or *who has*. *Whose* is the possessive form of *who*.

without, unless   Do not use the preposition *without* in place of the conjunction *unless*.

your, you're   *Your* is the possessive form of the pronoun *you*. *You're* is the contraction of *you are*.

Exercise A   Underline the word in parentheses that is correct according to standard usage.

1. (Your, You're) class gets to visit Minnehaha Park in Minneapolis.

2. (Whose, Who's) books are you carrying?

3. (Your, You're) a long (way, ways) off course, Captain.

4. Find out (whose, who's) going if you can.

5. Nobody should try out (without, unless) he or she is willing to rehearse daily.

Exercise B: Proofreading   Most of the following sentences contain errors in usage. If a sentence contains an error, cross out the error and, when necessary, write the correct word on the line provided. If a sentence is correct, write C.

EXAMPLE: 1. If ~~your~~ ready, let's go now. *you're*

1. Old Dog Tray was the faithful dog that Stephen Foster owned.   _____

2. "I'm not use to all this racket," muttered my grandfather.   _____

3. Singing a cappella is when there's singing without musical instruments.   _____

4. Don't go swimming in the ocean without you have someone with you.   _____

5. Only a short ways from the main road, we found a perfect place for a campsite.   _____

QUICK REFERENCE

Writer's Quick Reference

 **WORKSHEET 8** *The Double Negative*

A **double negative** is the use of two negative words to express one negative idea. Avoid using double negatives.

Common Negative Words

barely	never	none	nothing
hardly	no	no one	nowhere
neither	nobody	not (–n't)	scarcely

NONSTANDARD: I hadn't never danced before.
STANDARD: I had never danced before.
STANDARD: I hadn't ever danced before.

NONSTANDARD: The park rangers don't let nobody in at night.
STANDARD: The park rangers don't let anyone in at night.
STANDARD: The park rangers let no one in at night.

NONSTANDARD: She couldn't barely remember that far back.
STANDARD: She could barely remember that far back.

Exercise: Revising   The following sentences contain errors in usage. On the lines provided, write the corrected sentences. Although some sentences may be corrected in more than one way, you need to give only one correction.

EXAMPLE: 1. I couldn't find no books on the Boxer Rebellion.

I could find no books on the Boxer Rebellion.
or
I couldn't find any books on the Boxer Rebellion.

1. Don't use no double negatives!

   _____

2. Neither student knew nothing about the pop quiz.

   _____

3. Hadn't you never heard of Zachary Taylor?

   _____

4. The vegetables can't scarcely grow because of all the weeds.

   _____

5. None of the children could find the last Easter egg nowhere.

   _____

Writer's Quick Reference

WORKSHEET 9 *Review*

Exercise A: Proofreading Most of the following sentences contain errors in usage. If a sentence contains an error or errors, cross out the error(s) and, when necessary, write the correct word(s) on the line provided. If a sentence is correct, write *C*.

EXAMPLE: 1. ~~Between~~ the various Native American peoples, there were many stories about mythological figures. *Among*

1. The Creek people believed that spirits, giants, and little people could effect their lives both bad and well. _____

2. The Micmacs believed that an enormous being named Glooscap created humans and animals everywheres. _____

3. Glooscap's magic is the reason that humans busted into life. _____

4. It seems that the other animals didn't always think well of Glooscap's new creations. _____

5. The Tehuelche people of South America tell the story of Elal, a hero who brought fire to where the people were at. _____

6. When the Mayas heard the thunderous approach of their god Chac, they knew who's power brought rain to their fields. _____

7. The Pawnee couldn't hardly help noticing where the stars were. _____

8. They told stories about Morning Star, who fought good and triumphed over star monsters. _____

9. One sad Tewa story is about Deer Hunter, who had ought to have excepted the death of his wife, White Corn Maiden. _____

10. Her death busted Deer Hunter's heart, causing him to disobey the laws of his people. _____

Exercise B: Proofreading Most of the following sentences contain errors in usage. If a sentence contains an error, cross out the error and, when necessary, write the correct word(s) on the line provided. If a sentence is correct, write *C*.

EXAMPLE: 1. It was pirate Jean Laffite ~~which~~ established an early settlement on Texas's Galveston Island. *who (or that)*

1. Since ancient times, pirates they have terrorized the world's seas. _____

2. Bands of pirates use to build fortified hide-outs from which they attacked ships. _____

3. I once read that Julius Caesar hisself was captured by pirates. _____

4. My history teacher learned my class about pirates who disrupted shipping along the North African coast. _____

QUICK REFERENCE

Writer's Quick Reference, Worksheet 9, continued

5. As you may have seen in movies, these pirates preyed upon African, European, and American ships. _____

6. During the 1600's and 1700's, pirates lived off of the South American coast. _____

7. One of these pirates, Sir William Kidd, was a real dangerous cutthroat on the Caribbean Sea. _____

8. You may be surprised to learn that two other fearsome pirates were women. _____

9. Anne Bonny and Mary Read lead their crews on many attacks on ships in the Caribbean. _____

10. You may think that piracy is a thing of the past, but its still going on in some parts of the world. _____

Exercise C: Revising   Most of the following sentences contain errors in usage. On the lines provided, write the corrected sentences. If a sentence is correct, write C.

EXAMPLE: 1. Alex Haley has had an affect on many Americans.
Alex Haley has had an effect on many Americans.

1. When young Alex Haley heard stories about his ancestors, he wanted to know more about his roots, and not nothing would stop him.

_____

_____

2. Neither he nor anyone else might have guessed then that his life's work had begun.

_____

_____

3. He talked to family members, but he hadn't scarcely started the search that would take him to Africa.

_____

_____

4. There he would be embraced by family long lost, though he couldn't understand none of their words.

_____

_____

5. Now, there ain't scarcely a person in the United States who hasn't never heard of Alex Haley's roots.

_____

_____

Chapter 1: Parts of Speech

WORKSHEET 1   *Types of Nouns A*

A **noun** is a word used to name a person, a place, a thing, or an idea.

PERSONS: Danny Glover, actor, students, Native American

PLACES: stadium, theater, beach, Kansas, kitchen, Central Park

THINGS: *The Outsiders*, 1492, tamales, football, World War II

IDEAS: justice, equality, love, happiness, security

A **compound noun** is two or more words used together as a single noun. The parts of a compound noun may be written as one word, as separate words, or as a hyphenated word. When you are not sure how to write a compound noun, look in a dictionary.

COMPOUND NOUNS: basketball, *Don Quixote*, self-confidence, Ms. Chen

Exercise   Underline all of the nouns in each of the following sentences. Underline compound nouns twice.

EXAMPLE: 1. Many Native American <u>chiefs</u> are known for their <u>courage</u> and <u>wisdom</u>.

1. Chief Joseph of the Nez Perce was a wise leader whose Native American name means "thunder traveling over the mountains."

2. He was an educated man and wrote that his people believed they should speak only the truth.

3. Satanta, a Kiowa chief, wore a silver medal with the profile of President James Buchanan on it.

4. He wore the medal during a famous peace council at Medicine Lodge Creek in Kansas.

5. In a moving speech, Satanta described the love that his people had for the Great Plains and the buffalo.

6. *The Autobiography of Black Hawk* is an interesting book by the Sauk chief who fought for lands in the Mississippi Valley.

7. Sitting Bull's warriors soundly defeated General George A. Custer and his troops at the Battle of the Little Big Horn.

8. After years of leading the Sioux in war, Sitting Bull toured with Buffalo Bill and his Wild West Show.

9. Red Cloud of the Oglala Sioux and Dull Knife of the Cheyenne were other important chiefs.

10. Chief Washakie received praise for his leadership of the Shoshones; he was also a noted singer and craftsperson.

GRAMMAR/USAGE

Chapter 1: Parts of Speech

Types of Nouns B

A **collective noun** is a word that names a group.

> COLLECTIVE NOUNS: troop, clan, audience, senate, herd

A **common noun** is a general name for a person, a place, a thing, or an idea. A **proper noun** names a particular person, place, thing, or idea. Proper nouns always begin with a capital letter. Common nouns are capitalized only when they begin a sentence or a line of poetry, or when they are in a title.

> COMMON NOUNS: statue, boy, country, ship, anger

> PROPER NOUNS: *The Thinker*, Lucknow, India, Yarmoth Castle

A **concrete noun** names a person, place, or thing that can be perceived by one or more of the senses (sight, hearing, taste, touch, or smell). An **abstract noun** names an idea, a feeling, a quality, or a characteristic.

> CONCRETE NOUNS: president, school, bakery, smile

> ABSTRACT NOUNS: democracy, education, peace, contentment

Exercise A   Write *C* for each common noun and *P* for each proper noun. Then write *CON* if the noun is concrete or *ABS* if the noun is abstract.

> EXAMPLES: <u>*P, CON*</u>   1. Ben Franklin
> <u>*C, ABS*</u>   2. honesty

_____ 1. Philadelphia

_____ 2. wisdom

_____ 3. eagle

_____ 4. First Continental Congress

_____ 5. freedom

_____ 6. Thomas Jefferson

_____ 7. Declaration of Independence

_____ 8. Potomac River

_____ 9. law

_____ 10. happiness

Exercise B   Underline the collective nouns in the following sentences.

> EXAMPLE: 1. Members of the <u>jury</u> have been dismissed from duty.

1. My sister-in-law and her family lived on a houseboat on Lake Ontario.

2. After the performance, the cast took bow after bow as the audience continued to cheer.

3. A half block away, you could hear the voices of the congregation as they sang.

4. During the long nights, a pack of wolves had been preying on the sheep.

5. How proud we were of John when he directed the orchestra!

Chapter 1: Parts of Speech

Types of Pronouns A

A **pronoun** is a word used in place of one noun or more than one noun. The word that a pronoun stands for is called its **antecedent**. Sometimes the antecedent is not stated.

> The new student is named **Daroab,** and **he** comes from Iran. [*Daroab* is the antecedent of *he*.]
>
> **She** is a good athlete. [The antecedent of *she* in this sentence is not stated.]

A **personal pronoun** refers to the one speaking *(first person)*, the one spoken to *(second person)*, or the one spoken about *(third person)*.

> FIRST PERSON: Give **me** a hand.
>
> SECOND PERSON: Do **you** have any change?
>
> THIRD PERSON: **They** left an hour ago.

A **reflexive pronoun** refers to the subject and directs the action of the verb back to the subject. An **intensive pronoun** emphasizes a noun or another pronoun. Notice that reflexive and intensive pronouns have the same form.

> REFLEXIVE PRONOUN: I promised **myself** that I would save my money.
>
> INTENSIVE PRONOUN: George and Lian built the cabin **themselves**.

Exercise Underline the pronouns in the following sentences, and above each pronoun write *PER* if it is personal, *REF* if it is reflexive, or *INT* if it is intensive. Then, on the line provided, write the antecedent of each pronoun. If a pronoun does not refer to a specific antecedent, write *unidentified*.

>   *PER*
>
> EXAMPLE: 1. Italian explorer Marco Polo traveled to China, where <u>he</u> and Emperor Kublai Khan became friends. *Marco Polo*

1. We watched the movie about Robert O'Hara Burke's trip across Australia in the 1800's. _____

2. Queen Isabella of Spain herself gave approval for the famous voyages of Christopher Columbus. _____

3. Matthew Henson prided himself on being the first person actually to reach the North Pole. _____

4. I myself just read about Dutch explorer Abel Tasman's voyages on the South Seas. _____

5. Mrs. Welch told us about Samuel de Champlain's founding of the colony of Quebec. _____

GRAMMAR/USAGE

Chapter 1: Parts of Speech

WORKSHEET 4 — Types of Pronouns B

A **demonstrative pronoun** points out a person, a place, a thing, or an idea.

That is the World Trade Center. **These** are the oldest rocks on earth.

An **interrogative pronoun** introduces a question.

Who discovered DNA? **Whose** are the gloves on the table?

A **relative pronoun** introduces a subordinate clause.

The book **that** I read is by Nobel Prize winner Nadine Gordimer, **who** writes about life in South Africa.

An **indefinite pronoun** refers to a person, a place, or a thing that is not specifically named.

Everyone here has read the assignment. **Something** is bothering me.

Many indefinite pronouns can also serve as adjectives.

INDEFINITE PRONOUN: **Some** of the apples were ripe.

ADJECTIVE: **Some** apples were ripe.

Exercise Underline the demonstrative, indefinite, interrogative, and relative pronouns in the following sentences. On the line provided, identify each with the abbreviation *DEM*, *IND*, *INT*, or *REL*.

EXAMPLE: 1. Which of you has heard of *The Mustangs of Las Colinas*, a sculpture that is located in Irving, Texas? *INT; REL*

1. As anyone who has seen it can testify, the sculpture is larger than life. _____

2. The nine mustangs that make up the work appear to gallop across Williams Square in the Las Colinas Urban Center. _____

3. The horses, whose images are cast in bronze, form the world's largest equestrian (horse) sculpture. _____

4. That is one of the most amazing sights! _____

5. What is the name of the sculptor who created the mustangs? _____

6. Robert Glen, who was born in Kenya, is the artist whom you mean. _____

7. Anybody who has seen this work can tell how much time Glen has spent studying horses. _____

8. The Mustang sculpture exhibit, which is located near the statue, provides more information about Glen and the mustangs. _____

9. Who told me mustangs are descended from horses brought to the Americas by the Spanish? _____

10. Horses like those in Glen's sculpture roamed wild over many of the western states in the 1800's. _____

Chapter 1: Parts of Speech

 **Adjectives A**

An **adjective** is a word used to modify a noun or a pronoun. To *modify* a word means to describe the word or to make its meaning more definite. An adjective modifies a word by telling *what kind*, *which one*, *how much*, or *how many*.

WHAT KIND: **Chinese** art   HOW MUCH: **more** wood

WHICH ONE: **eighth** grade   HOW MANY: **several** A's

The most frequently used adjectives are *a*, *an*, and *the*. These adjectives are called **articles**. *A* and *an* are **indefinite articles**. They indicate that a noun refers to someone or something in general. *A* is used before a word beginning with a consonant sound. *An* is used before a word beginning with a vowel sound. The adjective *the* is a **definite article**. It indicates that the noun refers to someone or something in particular.

Since they were camping on **an** island, they had to sail **an** hour to reach **a** store.

The screwdrivers are in **the** garage.

Exercise A   Underline the articles in the following sentences. Above each article write *D* if it is definite or *I* if it is indefinite.

                              D   *I*

           EXAMPLE: 1. <u>The</u> Shoshone woman Sacagawea was <u>a</u> famous guide.

1. She led the explorers Lewis and Clark through a large portion of the West.

2. Lewis and Clark had been given an assignment by Thomas Jefferson.

3. They were to explore the uncharted lands west of the Mississippi River.

4. Sacagawea joined them as a guide and an interpreter of native languages.

Exercise B: Revising   Revise the following sentences, replacing the italicized questions with adjectives that answer them.

           EXAMPLE: 1. They sold *how many?* tickets for the *which one?* show.

                     They sold fifty tickets for the first show.

1. Even though we had run *how many?* laps around the track, we still had to run *how many?* more.

_____

2. *Which one?* weekend, *how many?* hikers went on a *what kind?* trip to the *what kind?* park.

_____

3. We rode in a *what kind?* van that carried *how many?* people and drove *how many?* miles to the game.

_____

4. There was *how much?* time left when I started the *which one?* question on the test.

_____

Chapter 1: Parts of Speech

 *Adjectives B*

An adjective may come before or after the word it modifies.

His **short** but **interesting** report fascinated us.

Short but **interesting,** the report fascinated us.

The report was **short** but **interesting**.

The report, **short** but **interesting,** was on virtual reality.

A **proper adjective** is formed from a proper noun and begins with a capital letter. Notice that some proper nouns, such as *Rio Grande,* do not change spelling when they are used as adjectives.

PROPER NOUNS: Asia, Thomas Jefferson, Hebrew, Florida

PROPER ADJECTIVES: **Asian** elephants, **Jeffersonian** ideals, **Hebraic** law, **Florida** oranges

Exercise A   Underline each adjective in the following paragraph, and draw an arrow to the word it modifies. Do not include *a, an,* and *the*.

EXAMPLE: [1] Many fishers considered the old man unlucky.

[1] For eighty-four days, Santiago, an old Cuban fisher, had not caught a single fish.

[2] Despite his bad luck, he remained hopeful. [3] On the eighty-fifth day, he caught a ten-pound albacore. [4] Soon after this catch, he hooked a huge marlin. [5] For nearly two days, the courageous fisher struggled with the mighty fish and finally harpooned it.

[6] Exhausted but happy, Santiago sailed toward shore. [7] Within an hour, however, his bad luck returned. [8] What happened to the old fisher and his big catch? [9] Does the story have a happy ending? [10] You can find the answers in Ernest Hemingway's novel *The Old Man and the Sea*.

Exercise B   Underline the proper adjectives in the following sentences.

EXAMPLE: 1.   In recent years many American tourists have visited the Great Wall in China.

1. The early Spanish explorers built several forts along the Florida coast.

2. The professor of African literature gave a lecture on the novels of Camara Laye, a writer who was born in Guinea.

3. Which Arthurian legend have you chosen for your report?

4. The program about the Egyptian ruins was narrated by an English scientist and a French anthropologist.

5. Marian McPartland, a jazz pianist from New York City, played several Scott Joplin songs.

Name _____ Date _____ Class _____

WORKSHEET 7 · *Noun, Pronoun, or Adjective?*

This, *that*, *these*, and *those* can be used both as adjectives and as pronouns. When they modify a noun or a pronoun, these words are called **demonstrative adjectives**. When they are used alone, they are called **demonstrative pronouns**.

DEMONSTRATIVE ADJECTIVE: **That** movie isn't very funny.

DEMONSTRATIVE PRONOUN: **That** isn't very funny.

A noun that modifies another noun or a pronoun is considered an adjective.

NOUN: On the **Fourth of July,** we're having a picnic.

ADJECTIVE: Our **Fourth of July** picnic was a huge success.

Exercise On the line provided, identify the italicized word in each sentence of the following paragraph as a *noun*, a *pronoun*, or an *adjective*.

EXAMPLE: [1] Don't let *anyone* tell you that the age of exploration is over.

1. *pronoun*

[1] Two brothers, Lawrence and Lorne Blair, went on an amazing *adventure* that began in 1973. [2] For ten years they traveled among the nearly 14,000 *islands* of Indonesia. [3] *Each* of them returned with remarkable tales about the people, animals, and land. [4] Their *adventure* story began when some pirates guided them through the Spice Islands. [5] There, they located *one* of the world's rarest and most beautiful animals—the greater bird of paradise. [6] Another *island* animal that the brothers encountered was the frightening Komodo dragon. [7] *Some* Komodo dragons are eleven feet long and weigh more than five hundred pounds. [8] *Each* day brought startling discoveries, such as flying frogs and flying snakes. [9] On *one* island, Borneo, they found a group of people thought to be extinct. [10] To *some*, the brothers' stay with the cannibals in western New Guinea is the strangest part of their trip.

1. _____   6. _____

2. _____   7. _____

3. _____   8. _____

4. _____   9. _____

5. _____   10. _____

GRAMMAR/USAGE

Chapter 1: Parts of Speech

Action Verbs and Linking Verbs

A **verb** is a word used to express action or a state of being. Every sentence must have a verb. The verb says something about the subject.

Bitter cold winds **swept** the streets and alleyways. Soon, the streets **were** empty.

An **action verb** may express physical action or mental action.

PHYSICAL ACTION: laugh, speak, bounce, fly, sing

A steamroller **pressed** the new road flat.

MENTAL ACTION: dream, know, hope, fear, expect

She **wants** another chance.

A **linking verb** links, or connects, the subject with a noun, a pronoun, or an adjective in the predicate. The most commonly used linking verbs are *appear, become, feel, grow, look, remain, seem, smell, sound, stay, taste, turn*, and forms of the verb *be*.

He **is** my brother. [he = brother]

The puppy **seemed** lonely. [puppy = lonely]

Geography **was** easy for me. [geography = easy]

All the linking verbs except the forms of *be* and *seem* may also be used as action verbs. Whether a verb is used to link words or to express action depends on its meaning in a sentence.

ACTION VERB: The judges **tasted** each entry in the chili contest.

LINKING VERB: The chili **tasted** delicious! [chili = delicious]

NOTE: The verb *be* does not always link the subject with a noun, pronoun, or adjective in the predicate. *Be* can express a state of being and be followed by words or word groups that tell *when* or *where*.

The rehearsal **is** tonight.   Your letters **are** here.

Exercise   On the line provided, write the subject and verb in each of the following sentences. If the verb is a linking verb, identify also the word that the verb links to the subject.

EXAMPLE: 1. Chili cook-offs throughout the Southwest appear popular with chili fans. *cook-offs appear—popular*

1. Real fans grow hungry at the mention of any dish with chili peppers and chili powder.

_____

2. These are important ingredients in Mexican cooking. _____

3. Chili varies from somewhat spicy to fiery hot. _____

4. You also find many recipes for chili without meat. _____

5. Regardless of the other ingredients in a batch of chili, the chili powder smells wonderful to

chili fans. _____

Name _____ Date _____ Class _____

WORKSHEET 9

Transitive Verbs and Intransitive Verbs

A **transitive verb** is an action verb that expresses an action directed toward a person or thing. With transitive verbs, the action passes from the doer (the subject) to the receiver of the action. Words that receive the action of a transitive verb are called **objects**.

Margarita **read** her new book. [The action of *read* is directed toward *book. Book* is the object of the verb *read*.]

An **intransitive verb** expresses action (or tells something about the subject) without passing the action to a receiver.

The boys **left**. [The action of *left* is not directed to an object.]

A verb may be transitive in one sentence and intransitive in another.

TRANSITIVE: The boys **left** their notebooks.

INTRANSITIVE: The boys **left** early.

INTRANSITIVE: The boys **left** in a hurry.

Exercise   Above each italicized verb in the following paragraph, write *T* for a transitive verb or *I* for an intransitive verb. Then circle the object of each transitive verb.

EXAMPLE: Whether you [1] *know* (it) or not, about 20 percent of America's
                cowboys were African Americans.

During the years following the Civil War, thousands of African American cowboys

[1] *rode* the cattle trails north from Texas. They [2] *worked* alongside Mexican, Native

American, and white trail hands. All the members of a cattle drive [3] *slept* on the same

ground, [4] *ate* the same food, and performed the same hard jobs. When day was done, they

[5] *enjoyed* each other's company as they swapped stories and [6] *sang* around the campfire.

When they finally [7] *reached* their destinations with their herds, they all [8] *celebrated* by

having rodeos, parades, and shooting contests. Nat Love, one of the most famous African

American cowboys, [9] *wrote* a book about his experiences on the range. In his book, he

[10] *recalls* the times that he and his trail mates looked out for one another, regardless of

skin color.

GRAMMAR/USAGE

Chapter 1: Parts of Speech

 **WORKSHEET 10** *Verb Phrases*

A **helping verb (auxiliary verb)** helps the main verb to express an action or a state of being.

FORMS OF *BE:*   am, be, being, was, are, been, is, were

FORMS OF *DO:*   do, does, did

FORMS OF *HAVE:*   have, has, had

OTHER HELPING VERBS: can, may, must, should, would, could, might, shall, will

A **verb phrase** consists of a main verb preceded by at least one helping verb.

She **is enjoying** Galarza's poetry. [The main verb is *enjoying*. The helping verb is *is*.]

You **should have been practicing** for the game. [The main verb is *practicing*. The helping verbs are *should, have,* and *been*.]

Some helping verbs may also be used as main verbs.

I **have** an appointment with the dentist.

Sometimes the verb phrase is interrupted by another part of speech. In most cases, the interrupter is an adverb. In a question, however, the subject often interrupts the verb phrase.

Environmental activists **do** not **agree** with the plan.

Can this computer **read** this disk?

Exercise   Underline the verb phrases in the sentences in the following paragraph. Some sentences contain more than one verb phrase.

EXAMPLE: [1] What unusual jobs <u>can</u> you <u>name</u>?

[1] Many people are earning their livings at unusual jobs. [2] Even today people can find positions as shepherds, inventors, and candlestick makers. [3] It might seem strange, but these people have decided that ordinary jobs have become too boring for them. [4] Some people have been working as messengers. [5] You may have seen them when they were wearing costumes such as gorilla suits and clown makeup. [6] Other people have been finding work as mimes. [7] They can be seen performing at public fairs and festivals. [8] People can still call chimney sweeps to clean their chimney flues. [9] Some chimney sweeps may even wear the traditional, old-time clothes of the trade. [10] With a little imagination, anyone can find an unusual job.

Chapter 1: Parts of Speech

Adverbs That Modify Verbs

An **adverb** is a word used to modify a verb, an adjective, or another adverb. An adverb tells *where, when, how,* or *to what extent (how much* or *how long).*

WHERE: We traveled **there** by train.   HOW: Handle the kittens **carefully**.

WHEN: Write **soon**!   TO WHAT EXTENT: The tiny sailboat sailed **far**.

Adverbs may appear at various places in a sentence. Adverbs may come before, after, or between the verbs they modify.

   Yesterday, I could **not** see the problem **clearly**.

Adverbs are sometimes used to ask questions.

   When was the Parthenon built?   **How** have you been?

NOTE: The word *not* is an adverb. When *not* is part of a contraction like *hadn't*, the *–n't* is an adverb.

Exercise   On the lines provided, identify the adverbs and the verbs they modify in the following sentences.

              EXAMPLE: 1. How can I quickly learn to take better pictures?
                        How—can learn; quickly—can learn

1. You can listen carefully to advice from experienced photographers, who usually like to share their knowledge.

   _____

2. Nobody always takes perfect pictures, but some tips can help you now.

   _____

3. You should stand still and hold your camera firmly.

   _____

4. Some photographers suggest that you keep your feet apart and put one foot forward.

   _____

5. A good photographer automatically thinks about what will be in a picture and consequently avoids disappointment afterward.

   _____

GRAMMAR/USAGE

Chapter 1: Parts of Speech

WORKSHEET 12

Adverbs That Modify Adjectives and Adverbs

An adverb may be used to modify an adjective.

An **especially** quiet crew works on board a submarine. [The adverb *especially* modifies the adjective *quiet*, telling how quiet the crew is.]

An adverb may be used to modify another adverb.

The submarine dove **rather slowly**. [The adverb *rather* modifies the adverb *slowly*, telling how slowly or to what degree the submarine dove slowly.]

Many adverbs end in –ly: *quietly, briefly, calmly*. However, some words that end in –ly are adjectives: *friendly, lonely, timely*. If you're not sure whether a word is an adjective or an adverb, ask yourself what it modifies. If a word modifies a noun or a pronoun, it's an adjective. If a word modifies a verb, an adjective, or an adverb, then it's an adverb.

Exercise A   On the lines provided, identify the adverbs and the adjectives they modify in the following sentences.

EXAMPLE: 1. Because so many bicycles have been stolen, the principal hired a guard. *so—many*

1. The team is extremely proud of its record.   _____

2. All frogs may look quite harmless, but some are poisonous.   _____

3. The class was unusually quiet today.   _____

4. The Mardi Gras celebration in New Orleans is very loud and colorful.   _____

5. The coach said we were too careless when we made the routine plays.   _____

Exercise B   Each of the following sentences contains an adverb that modifies another adverb. On the line provided, write the adverb and the adverb that it modifies.

EXAMPLE: 1. Condors are quite definitely the largest living birds.

quite—definitely

1. The California condor and the Andean condor are almost entirely extinct.   _____

2. Only a few California condors exist today, and very nearly all of them live in captivity.   _____

3. Andean condors are slightly more numerous, and more of them can still be seen in the wild.   _____

4. Some people think that condors are most assuredly the ugliest birds.   _____

5. Yet, once in the air, condors soar so gracefully that they actually can look beautiful.   _____

Chapter 1: Parts of Speech

Prepositions and Their Objects

A **preposition** is a word used to show the relationship of a noun or a pronoun to another word.

> The roots are **under** the ground.

A preposition is always followed by a noun or a pronoun. This noun or pronoun following the preposition is called the **object of the preposition**. A preposition may have more than one object. All together, the preposition, its object(s), and the modifiers of the object are called a **prepositional phrase**.

> A package has come **for you and Etta**. [*You* and *Etta* are the objects of the preposition *for*.]

Prepositions that consist of more than one word, such as *in front of,* are called **compound prepositions**.

> The trip was canceled **on account of** hail and sleet.

Some words may be used as either prepositions or adverbs. To tell an adverb from a preposition, remember that a preposition is always followed by a noun or pronoun object.

ADVERB: Come **inside**.

PREPOSITION: Come **inside the house**.

NOTE: Be careful not to confuse a prepositional phrase that begins with *to* (*to town, to her club*) with a verb form that begins with *to* (*to run, to be seen*).

Exercise   Underline the prepositional phrase or phrases in each sentence in the following paragraph. Then circle each preposition. Be sure to include all parts of a compound preposition.

EXAMPLE: [1] Walt Whitman wrote the moving poem "O Captain! My Captain!" (about) Abraham Lincoln.

[1] In Whitman's poem, the captain directs his ship toward a safe harbor. [2] The captain represents Abraham Lincoln, and the ship is the ship of state. [3] The captain has just sailed his ship through stormy weather. [4] This voyage across rough seas symbolizes the Civil War. [5] On the shore, people joyfully celebrate the ship's safe arrival. [6] One of the ship's crew addresses his captain, "O Captain! my Captain! rise up and hear the bells." [7] Sadly, everyone except the captain can hear the rejoicing. [8] The speaker in the poem says that the captain "has no pulse nor will." [9] The captain has died during the voyage, just as Lincoln died at the end of the Civil War. [10] According to many people, "O Captain! My Captain!" is one of Whitman's finest poems.

GRAMMAR/USAGE

Chapter 1: Parts of Speech

 **WORKSHEET 14** *Conjunctions*

A **conjunction** is a word used to join words or groups of words.

Coordinating conjunctions connect words or groups of words used in the same way.

> We celebrate birthdays, weddings, **and** national holidays. [The word *and* connects things we celebrate.]

When *for* is used as a conjunction, it connects groups of words that are sentences, and it is always preceded by a comma. On all other occasions, *for* is used as a preposition.

> CONJUNCTION: I couldn't read the article, **for** I had misplaced my glasses.
> PREPOSITION: Would you look **for** my glasses?

Correlative conjunctions are pairs of conjunctions that connect words or groups of words used in the same way.

> Their family celebrated **not only** birthdays **but also** name days. [The words *not only . . . but also* link *birthdays* and *name days*.]

Exercise   Circle the coordinating and correlative conjunctions in the following sentences. Then underline the words or groups of words connected by the conjunctions.

> EXAMPLE: 1. Have you seen men (or) women wearing African clothes?

1. African clothing is fashionable today for both men and women in the United States.

2. People wear not only clothes of African design but also Western-style clothes made of African materials.

3. American women have worn modified African headdresses for years, but nowadays men are wearing African headgear, too.

4. Men and women sometimes wear *kufi* hats, which originated with Muslims.

5. Both women's dresses and women's coats are especially adaptable to African fashions.

6. Many women wear African jewelry or scarves.

7. Clothes made of such materials as *kente* cloth from Ghana, *ashioke* cloth from Nigeria, and *dogon* cloth from Mali have become quite popular.

8. These fabrics are decorated either with brightly colored printed designs or with stripes.

9. African-inspired clothes usually fit in whether you are at work or at play.

10. African styles are popular, for they show appreciation for ancient cultures.

Chapter 1: Parts of Speech

Interjections

An **interjection** is a word used to express emotion. It does not have a grammatical relation to other words in the sentence. Usually an interjection is followed by an exclamation point. Sometimes an interjection is set off by a comma.

Wow! That show was great!

Well, I learned a lot about the ocean floor.

Exercise A   Some fairy-tale characters are meeting to discuss their images. They're worried that the familiar fairy tales make them look stupid or silly. Underline the ten interjections used in the dialogue.

EXAMPLE: [1] "Hooray! We're finally getting a chance to tell our side of the stories!"

[1] "Beans! It's not fair what they say. I knew I was taking a giant step that day."

[2] "Well, it's not fair what they say about us, either. Don't you think Papa and Mama saw that little blonde girl snooping around our house?"

[3] "Yeah! And don't you think I intended to buy magic beans, anyway?"

[4] "You guys don't have it as bad as I do. Ugh! How dumb do people think I am? Of course I'd know my own grandmother when I saw her."

[5] "Pooh! I think your cloak was over your eyes, but how about me? I didn't go near those three pigs."

[6] "Right! Next you'll probably tell me that I didn't see your brother at Grandmother's house."

[7] "Humph! I don't know what you really saw. It's difficult to tell sometimes in the woods."

[8] "Aw, let's not argue. We've got to put our best feet forward—all the way up the beanstalk if need be."

[9] "Yes! And I want to give people the real story about that kid who broke my bed."

[10] "Great! I'm ready to squeal on those three pigs!"

Exercise B   Fill in each blank below with an interjection of your choice.

1. _____ , did you see that shooting star?

2. _____ ! I left my homework at home.

3. Janell said, "_____ ! My watch has stopped."

4. _____ ! We won the contest!

GRAMMAR/USAGE

Chapter 1: Parts of Speech

 ## Determining Parts of Speech

The part of speech of a word is determined by the way the word is used in a sentence. Many words can be used as more than one part of speech.

PRONOUN: **Some** of these waters have not been charted.

ADJECTIVE: **Some** areas have not been charted.

ADVERB: The cat had never seen a monkey **before**.

PREPOSITION: The cat had never seen a monkey **before** today.

NOUN: Can you give me a **ride** on your bike?

VERB: **Ride** your own bike!

INTERJECTION: **Well,** you certainly look pleased with yourself.

ADVERB: I did quite **well** on my English test.

Exercise   On the line provided, identify the part of speech of the italicized word in each of the following sentences.

EXAMPLE: 1. Heck! I *forgot* my raincoat. *Verb*

1. "*So!* You've been swimming in the pond again!" Mona scolded the dog. _____

2. That wasn't *so* hard. _____

3. One of the wheels is loose on my *skate*. _____

4. Lots of people *skate* here in the winter. _____

5. As we stood at the stoplight, three ambulances sped *past*. _____

6. Go *past* the mall and turn right. _____

7. Is this the *right* way to Omaha? _____

8. I have a *right* to my own opinion. _____

9. *Many* of the drivers were dissatisfied with their hours. _____

10. Currently, they work on *many* weekends. _____

Chapter 1: Parts of Speech

WORKSHEET 17 *Review*

Exercise A On the lines provided, identify the part of speech of each italicized word or group of words in the following paragraphs.

> EXAMPLES: Dancing may be [1] *easy* for [2] *some*, but I have [3] *always* had [4] *two* left [5] *feet*.
>
> 1. _adjective_   3. _adverb_   5. ___noun___
> 2. _pronoun_   4. _adjective_

[1] *Yesterday* after [2] *school*, one of my friends [3] *tried* to teach [4] *me* some new dance steps. [5] *Well*, I was [6] *so* embarrassed I could have hidden [7] *in* the [8] *closet*. My feet [9] *seem* to have [10] *minds* of [11] *their* own [12] *and* do [13] *not* do what I want them to.

"You're [14] *too* tense when you dance, [15] *or* you're trying too hard. [16] *You* should [17] *relax* more," my friend told me.

[18] *"Hey!* [19] *How* can I relax?" I groaned. [20] *"No one* [21] *can relax* with a body that goes [22] *left* and feet that go right!" At that point, I [23] *decided* to give up, but I know I'll try [24] *again* [25] *another* day.

1. _____   8. _____   15. _____   22. _____
2. _____   9. _____   16. _____   23. _____
3. _____   10. _____   17. _____   24. _____
4. _____   11. _____   18. _____   25. _____
5. _____   12. _____   19. _____
6. _____   13. _____   20. _____
7. _____   14. _____   21. _____

Exercise B On the line provided, identify each italicized word or words as a linking verb *(LV)*, action verb *(AV)*, or helping verb *(HV)*. Then identify each action verb as transitive *(T)* or intransitive *(I)*.

_____ 1. The car of the future *might be* powered by batteries.

_____ 2. It *must* look very tiny to you.

_____ 3. Today's cars *seem* huge by comparison.

_____ 4. You *program* the car of the future to take you to a destination.

_____ 5. Computers in the car *monitor* everything.

_____ 6. The car *will* not drive by itself, however.

_____ 7. The exterior *appears* sleek, shiny, and inviting.

_____ 8. Yet, the design *is* practical and efficient.

_____ 9. Today's designers *are* very clever.

_____10. Their imaginations *soar*.

Exercise C   Each of the following sentences contains an italicized word that is used twice. This word may function as more than one part of speech. On the line provided, indicate the part of speech for each use of this word. Use the following abbreviations:

N = noun   ADV = adverb
P = pronoun   PREP = preposition
ADJ = adjective   CON = conjunction
V = verb   INT = interjection

1. *My!* _____ You certainly look nice in *my* _____ parka.

2. *This* _____ will be the one-thousandth time that I'll read *this* _____ story to the twins.

3. The cat jumped *off* _____ the windowsill and ran *off* _____ .

4. Put the contents of the biscuit *mix* _____ in a bowl and *mix* _____ well.

5. I arrived at the bus stop on time, *but* _____ no one was there *but* _____ me.

Exercise D   Each of the following sentences contains either one or two words or word groups of the kind specified before the sentence. Find these words, and write them on the lines provided. Base your answers on the way each word or word group is used in the sentence. Do not include the words *a*, *an*, or *the* in your answers.

EXAMPLE: 1. *noun*   Charles Drew was an American doctor.

Charles Drew, doctor

1. *pronoun*   Charles Drew developed techniques that are used in the separation and preservation of blood.   _____

2. *adjective*   During World War II, Dr. Drew was the director of donation efforts for the American Red Cross.   _____

3. *pronoun*   He established blood bank programs.   _____

4. *preposition* His research saved many lives during the war.   _____

5. *verb*   Dr. Drew set up centers in which blood could be stored.   _____

6. *adjective*   The British government asked him to develop a storage system in England.   _____

7. *adverb*   Shortly before the beginning of World War II, Dr. Drew became a professor of surgery at Howard University.   _____

8. *preposition* After the war, he was appointed chief surgeon at Freedman's Hospital.   _____

9. *conjunction* This physician and researcher made important contributions to medical science.   _____

10. *verb*   Many people who have needed blood owe their lives to his methods.   _____

Chapter 2: Agreement

 **WORKSHEET 1** ## Singular and Plural

Number is the form of a word that indicates whether the word is singular or plural. When a word refers to one person, place, thing, or idea, it is **singular** in number. When a word refers to more than one, it is **plural** in number.

SINGULAR: bone	dish	man	I	she	each
PLURAL: bones	dishes	men	we	they	few

Exercise A On the line provided, write *S* if the word is singular or *P* if the word is plural.

EXAMPLE: ___*S*___ 1. cat

_____ 1. rodeos   _____ 11. mice

_____ 2. telephone   _____ 12. children

_____ 3. they   _____ 13. woman

_____ 4. I   _____ 14. data

_____ 5. many   _____ 15. both

_____ 6. igloo   _____ 16. troops

_____ 7. geese   _____ 17. datum

_____ 8. we   _____ 18. tooth

_____ 9. it   _____ 19. each

_____ 10. friends   _____ 20. anyone

Exercise B On the line provided, write *S* if the subject is singular or *P* if the subject is plural.

EXAMPLE: ___*S*___ 1. The class sings.

_____ 1. The lion yawns.

_____ 2. The cubs play.

_____ 3. No one stays.

_____ 4. The refugees arrive.

_____ 5. She wins.

_____ 6. The play opens.

_____ 7. Everyone goes.

_____ 8. All applaud.

_____ 9. They lead.

_____ 10. Several agree.

GRAMMAR/USAGE

Name _____ Date _____ Class _____

Agreement of Subject and Verb A

A verb agrees with its subject in number. A subject and verb agree when they have the same number. Singular subjects take singular verbs. Plural subjects take plural verbs.

The **balloon floats** in the air. [The singular verb *floats* agrees with the singular subject *balloon*.]

The **answers are** clear. [The plural verb *are* agrees with the plural subject *answers*.]

The first auxiliary (helping) verb in a verb phrase must agree with its subject.

Zachary has been taking piano lessons. [singular]

They have been taking piano lessons. [plural]

NOTE: Generally, nouns ending in –s are plural (*candles, ideas, neighbors, horses*), and verbs ending in –s are singular (*sees, writes, speaks, carries*). However, verbs used with the singular pronouns *I* and *you* do not end in –s.

Exercise A   Underline the form of the verb in parentheses that agrees with the subject.

EXAMPLE: 1. it (<u>is</u>, are)

1. this (costs, cost)

2. Chinese lanterns (glows, glow)

3. the swimmer (dives, dive)

4. we (considers, consider)

5. the men (was, were)

6. she (asks, ask)

7. these (needs, need)

8. those tacos (tastes, taste)

9. that music (sounds, sound)

10. lessons (takes, take)

Exercise B: Proofreading   Most of the following sentences contain errors in subject-verb agreement. If a verb does not agree with its subject, cross out the verb. Then write the correct form of the verb on the line provided. If a sentence is correct, write *C*.

EXAMPLE: 1. Next week we i̶s̶ reading *Great Expectations*. _are_

1. In the book, Charles Dickens tell the strange story of Pip.   _____

2. Yet, this author's own life were almost equally extraordinary.   _____

3. His childhood experiences was often painful.   _____

4. Readers sees the result of both Dickens's hardships and his success in his books.   _____

5. This book overflows with interesting people from all walks of life.   _____

Chapter 2: Agreement

WORKSHEET 3

Agreement of Subject and Verb B

The number of a subject is not changed by a prepositional phrase following the subject.

NONSTANDARD: Those birds in the tree is finches.

STANDARD: Those **birds** in the tree **are** finches.

NONSTANDARD: The book on ancient legends are interesting.

STANDARD: The **book** on ancient legends **is** interesting.

Exercise A Underline the form of the verb in parentheses that agrees with the subject.

EXAMPLE: 1. The houses on my block (has, <u>have</u>) two stories.

1. My favorite collection of poems (is, are) *Where the Sidewalk Ends.*

2. People in some states (observes, observe) the fourth Friday in September as Native American Day.

3. The starving children of the world (needs, need) food and medicine.

4. The cucumbers in my garden (grows, grow) very quickly.

5. Koalas in the wild and in captivity (eats, eat) only eucalyptus leaves.

Exercise B Underline the subject in each sentence. Then underline the form of the verb in parentheses that agrees with the subject.

EXAMPLE: 1. <u>Homes</u> throughout the world (is, <u>are</u>) quite different.

1. Millions of people (live, lives) in large cities.

2. Transportation in cities (include, includes) subways and buses.

3. Many people in the world (live, lives) in villages.

4. Areas outside a city (is, are) called suburbs.

5. Some villages in Greece (has, have) very narrow roads.

6. Some houses in Amsterdam (is, are) very tall and narrow.

7. Some houses on the Atlantic shore (has, have) been built on stilts.

8. A typical apartment house in southern Spanish towns (is, are) bright white.

9. Huts of mud (is, are) found in Afghanistan.

10. Some lighthouses on the coast (has, have) not been occupied for years.

GRAMMAR/USAGE

Name _____ Date _____ Class _____

Agreement with Indefinite Pronouns

Some pronouns do not refer to a definite person, place, thing, or idea and are therefore called **indefinite pronouns**.

The following indefinite pronouns are singular: *anybody, anyone, each, either, everybody, everyone, neither, nobody, no one, one, somebody,* and *someone*.

> **One** of the mice **was** black and white.

The following indefinite pronouns are plural: *both, few, many,* and *several*.

> **Few** of the visitors **have seen** a giant jellyfish before.

> **Many** of the ocean's creatures **look** strange to us.

The following indefinite pronouns may be either singular or plural: *all, any, most, none,* and *some*. The number of the subject *all, any, most, none,* or *some* is determined by the number of the object in the prepositional phrase following the subject. If the subject refers to a singular object, the subject is singular. If the subject refers to a plural object, the subject is plural.

> **All** of the sea monsters **were** frightening. [*All* refers to the plural object *monsters*.]

> **Some** of the window **was** frost-covered. [*Some* refers to the singular object *window*.]

Exercise   On the line provided, write the subject of each of the following sentences. Then underline the form of the verb in parentheses that agrees with the subject.

> EXAMPLE: 1. Each of the marchers (<u>was</u>, were) carrying a sign protesting apartheid. *Each*

1. All of my friends (has, have) had the chickenpox.   _____

2. Everyone at the party (likes, like) the hummus dip.   _____

3. Both of Fred's brothers (celebrates, celebrate) their birthdays in July.   _____

4. Some of my baseball cards (is, are) valuable.   _____

5. None of those rosebushes ever (blooms, bloom) in February.   _____

6. Several of those colors (do, does) not appeal to me.   _____

7. Many of Mrs. Taniguchi's students (speaks, speak) fluent Japanese.   _____

8. Nobody in the beginning painting classes (has, have) displayed work in the annual art show.   _____

9. Most of the appetizers on the menu (tastes, taste) delicious.   _____

10. One of Georgia O'Keeffe's paintings (shows, show) a ram's skull.   _____

Name _____ Date _____ Class _____

Agreement with Compound Subjects

Subjects joined by *and* usually take a plural verb.

Plants, flowers, and **soil were** interesting to George Washington Carver. [Three things were interesting.]

A compound subject that names only one person or thing takes a singular verb.

A famous **professor** and **scientist** at Tuskegee Institute was George Washington Carver. [One person was a professor and scientist.]

When subjects are joined by *or* or *nor*, the verb agrees with the subject nearer the verb.

Neither the local **farmers** nor Carver's closest **friend was** interested in his ideas at first. [The verb agrees with the nearer subject, *friend*.]

Exercise A   On the line provided, indicate whether the compound subject in each of the following sentences is *singular* or *plural*. Then underline the form of the verb in parentheses that agrees with the compound subject.

EXAMPLE: 1. Cleon and Pam (is, <u>are</u>) here. *plural*

1. My mother and the mechanic (is, are) discussing the bill.   _____

2. Monica Seles and Jennifer Capriati (plays, play) in the finals today.   _____

3. Red beans and rice (is, are) my favorite Cajun dish.   _____

4. English and science (requires, require) hours of study.   _____

5. Our star and winner of the track meet (is, are) here.   _____

Exercise B   Choose the form of the verb in parentheses that agrees with the compound subject in each of the following sentences.

EXAMPLE: 1. Neither Theo nor Erin (<u>has</u>, have) learned the Jewish folk dance *Mayim, Mayim.*

1. Neither my sister nor my brother (mows, mow) the lawn without protesting.

2. Our guava tree and our fig tree (bears, bear) more fruit than our entire neighborhood can eat.

3. Tuskegee Institute or Harvard University (offers, offer) the best courses in Francine's field.

4. Sarah's report on Booker T. Washington and Sam's report on Quanah Parker (sounds, sound) interesting.

5. Either Franco or his teammates (calls, call) the plays.

GRAMMAR/USAGE

Chapter 2: Agreement

Other Problems in Agreement A

A **collective noun** is singular in form but names a group of persons, animals, or things. Collective nouns may be either singular or plural. A collective noun takes a singular verb when the noun refers to the group as a unit. A collective noun takes a plural verb when the noun refers to the individual parts or members of the group.

> The **committee is** in charge of the reception. [The committee as a unit is in charge of the reception.]

> The **committee have been** unable to decide where to hold the reception. [The members of the committee have different opinions.]

A verb agrees with its subject, not with its predicate nominative.

>   S   V   PN
> The main **problem is insecticides**.

>   S   V   PN
> **Insecticides are** the main **problem**.

When the subject follows the verb, find the subject and make sure the verb agrees with it. The subject usually follows the verb in sentences beginning with *here* or *there* and in questions.

> There **are** many old **castles** in Scotland. Where **is** the **moat**?

NOTE: When the subject of a sentence follows the verb, the word order is said to be *inverted*. To find the subject of a sentence with inverted order, restate the sentence in usual word order.

Exercise   Choose the form of the verb in parentheses that agrees with the subject in each of the following sentences.

> EXAMPLE: 1.   There (is, <u>are</u>) many new students this year.

1. The audience (loves, love) the mime performance.

2. Four tickets to Orlando (was, were) the first prize.

3. The club (sponsors, sponsor) a carwash each March.

4. Andy's gift to Janelle (was, were) two roses.

5. Here (is, are) the letters I have been expecting.

6. The public (differs, differ) in their opinions on the referendum.

7. (Do, Does) you want the last two rolls?

8. The tennis team usually (plays, play) every Saturday morning.

9. His legacy to us (was, were) words of wisdom.

10. Where (is, are) the limericks you wrote?

Chapter 2: Agreement

Other Problems in Agreement B

The contractions *don't* and *doesn't* must agree with their subjects. Use *don't* with plural subjects and with the pronouns *I* and *you*. Use *doesn't* with other singular subjects.

The helmets don't fit.

I don't feel comfortable in this helmet.

Doesn't it look like rain?

The contractions *here's*, *there's*, and *where's* contain the verb *is* and should be used only with singular subjects.

Here's my umbrella.   **Where are** my boots?

Words stating amounts are usually singular.

Two dollars is a lot to pay for a pencil.

The title of a book or the name of an organization or country, even when plural in form, usually takes a singular verb.

A Tale of Two Cities **is** being shown in English today.

A few nouns, though plural in form, are singular and take singular verbs.

Physics requires a good imagination.

Some nouns that end in *–s* and name a *pair* (such as *pants*) take a plural verb even though they refer to a singular item.

Those **scissors need** sharpening.

Exercise A   Choose the form of the word or words in parentheses that agree with the subject in each of the following sentences.

1. Lawson Industries (has, have) been in this location for fifty years.

2. (Here's, Here are) the Natalie Cole tapes I borrowed.

3. Three teaspoons of sugar (is, are) too much for me.

4. (There's, There are) no easy answer to that question.

5. The map shows that (there's, there are) seven countries in Central America.

Exercise B   Complete each sentence by inserting the correct contraction, *doesn't* or *don't*.

EXAMPLE: 1. _Don't_ they go to our school?

1. _____ anyone in the class know who Susan B. Anthony is?

2. They _____ have enough people to form a softball team.

3. _____ the Japanese celebrate spring with a special festival?

4. Hector _____ win every track meet; sometimes he places second.

5. He _____ know the shortest route from Dallas to Peoria.

GRAMMAR/USAGE

Name _____ Date _____ Class _____

Agreement of Pronoun and Antecedent A

A pronoun usually refers to a noun or another pronoun that comes before it, called its **antecedent**. Whenever you use a pronoun, make sure that it agrees in number and gender with its antecedent. Masculine pronouns (*he, him,* and *his*) refer to males. Feminine pronouns (*she, her,* and *hers*) refer to females. Neuter pronouns (*it* and *its*) refer to things (neither male nor female) and sometimes to animals.

> **Jeremy** has **his** ticket.   **Sara** has met **her** match.   The **cat** lost **its** tag.

To determine the gender of a personal pronoun that refers to an indefinite pronoun, look in the phrase that follows the indefinite pronoun.

> **Each** of the boys took **his** place at the starting line.

Some antecedents may be either masculine or feminine. When referring to such antecedents, use both the masculine and the feminine forms.

> **Everybody** in the club wanted **his or her** name card.

A singular pronoun is used to refer to *anybody, anyone, each, either, everybody, everyone, neither, nobody, no one, one, someone,* or *somebody.* A plural pronoun is used to refer to *both, few, many,* or *several.* Either a singular or a plural pronoun may be used to refer to *all, any, more, most, none,* or *some.*

> **No one** on the girls' team likes **her** new uniform.
> **Several** in the audience had left **their** seats.
> **Most** of the movie was entertaining, but **it** was not very logical.
> **Most** of my friends have not chosen **their** careers.

Exercise: Proofreading   For each sentence below, underline the antecedent, cross out the incorrect pronoun form, and write the correct pronoun on the line provided.

> EXAMPLE: 1. <u>Everyone</u> has to give ~~their~~ oral report on Friday. *his or her*

1. None of the boys have given his report yet. _____

2. Several of us, including me, volunteered to give mine first. _____

3. Everybody else in class wanted to put off giving their report. _____

4. Each of the boys has fears about their own public-speaking abilities. _____

5. I am surprised that more of the students didn't volunteer to give his or her reports first. _____

6. Has someone volunteered to be third to give their report? _____

7. Some are trying to get out of giving his or her reports. _____

8. However, Ms. Wu said that anyone who does not give an oral report will get an "incomplete" as their course grade. _____

9. Most of us wish that he or she did not have to give an oral report. _____

10. But Ms. Wu says it will help all of us overcome his or her shyness. _____

Chapter 2: Agreement

WORKSHEET 9

Agreement of Pronoun and Antecedent B

A plural pronoun is used to refer to two or more antecedents joined by *and*. A singular pronoun is used to refer to two or more singular antecedents joined by *or* or *nor*.

Jaime and Fernando are cleaning **their** room.

Either **Helena or Wilma** will bring **her** notes.

Either a singular or a plural pronoun may be used with a collective noun.

The **orchestra** played **its** first song. [The orchestra as a unit played the song.]

The **orchestra** took **their** seats. [The members of the orchestra sat.]

The title of a book or the name of an organization or a country, even when plural in form, usually takes a singular pronoun.

The **Bahamas** prizes **its** vacation industry.

A few nouns, though plural in form, are singular and take singular pronouns.

Next semester, **civics** will make **its** first appearance on my schedule.

Words stating amounts usually take singular pronouns.

Fifty pounds is a lot to carry, especially when **it** is packed in cumbersome suitcases.

Exercise   For each of the following sentences, insert the pronoun that correctly completes the sentence.

EXAMPLE: 1. Yes, I have read *Many Moons*; in fact, I wrote a report on _____it_____ .

1. My sister has the measles, but luckily I haven't caught _____ .

2. When we moved to Fair Valleys, I didn't like _____ at first.

3. Either Don or Buddy will give _____ speech next.

4. Two teaspoons of almond extract is not mentioned in the recipe, so _____ must be a secret ingredient.

5. Next month, Congress will begin _____ discussion of new taxes.

6. Julio and Claire brought _____ science project to the auditorium.

7. Should the team bring _____ own equipment?

8. I don't suppose you have an extra three dollars. Could I borrow _____ until Friday?

9. The Crafts Club will be showing _____ creations at the recreation center on Saturday.

10. Did Lena or Sally leave _____ raincoat here?

GRAMMAR/USAGE

Chapter 2: Agreement

WORKSHEET 10 **Review**

Exercise A: Revising   If the subject and the verb in each of the following sentences do not agree, write the sentence correctly on the line provided. In the new sentence, underline the subject once and the verb twice. Remember that subjects and verbs can be compound. If the subject and verb agree, write C on the line below.

> EXAMPLE: 1. Was you and Carlo doing the report on China?
>
> *Were you and Carlo doing the report on China?*

1. Does you know the most important food crop in China?

   _____

2. Rice and wheat are basic, or staple, foods around the world.

   _____

3. People in the United States eat wheat in the form of bread.

   _____

4. Many kinds of rice is grown in China.

   _____

5. There is more rice eaters in the world than wheat eaters.

   _____

6. All of the world's people eats grain.

   _____

7. Other kinds of grain includes oats, barley, rye, and corn.

   _____

8. Most of the people of Indonesia eats rice.

   _____

9. Wheat and rice doesn't grow in the same climate.

   _____

10. Cold weather or little rainfall stop the growth of rice.

    _____

Exercise B: Proofreading   Most of the following sentences contain errors in agreement of subject and verb. If a sentence is correct, write C. If a sentence contains an error in agreement, write the correct form on the line provided.

> EXAMPLE: 1. There is a man and a woman here to see you. *are*

1. Leilani and Yoshi doesn't know how to swim. _____

Chapter 2, Worksheet 10, continued

2. Carrots are my favorite vegetable. _____

3. The Seminoles of Florida sews beautifully designed quilts and
jackets. _____

4. Here's the sweaters I knitted for you. _____

5. Today, each of these ten-speed bicycles cost more than one hundred
dollars. _____

6. The soccer team always celebrate each victory with a pizza party. _____

7. The wheelchair division of the six-mile race was won by Randy
Nowell. _____

8. The flock of geese fly over the lake at dawn. _____

9. Doesn't that Thai dish with chopped peanuts taste good? _____

10. Where's the bus schedule for downtown routes? _____

Exercise C Complete each of the following sentences by inserting a pronoun that
agrees with its antecedent. On the line provided, identify the antecedent.

EXAMPLE: 1. Ann and Margaret wore _their_ cheerleader uniforms.
Ann and Margaret

1. The trees lost several of _____ branches in the
storm. _____

2. Each of the early Spanish missions in North America took pride

in _____ church bell. _____

3. Anthony, do you know whether anyone else has turned in

_____ paper yet? _____

4. Many in the mob raised _____ voices in protest. _____

5. The creek and the pond lost much of _____
water during the drought. _____

6. One of my uncles always wears _____ belt
buckle off to one side. _____

7. No person should be made to feel that _____
is worth less than someone else. _____

8. None of the dogs had eaten all of _____ food. _____

9. A few of our neighbors have decided to fence

_____ backyards. _____

10. Magic Johnson talked about _____ award
from the National Basketball Association. _____

Exercise D: Proofreading   Many of the following sentences contain errors in agreement of pronoun and antecedent. Underline the antecedent. Then cross out the incorrect pronoun form, and write the correct form of the pronoun on the line provided. If the sentence is correct, write C.

> EXAMPLE: 1. <u>Each</u> of the president's Cabinet officers gave ~~their~~ advice about what to do. _his or her_

1. All of the nation's presidents have had his own Cabinets, or groups of advisers.   _____

2. Shortly after taking office, presidents appoint the members of their Cabinets.   _____

3. Everyone appointed to the Cabinet is an expert in their field.   _____

4. George Washington and John Adams met regularly with his advisers.   _____

5. Neither had more than five people in their Cabinet.   _____

6. The Cabinet received its name from James Madison, the fourth president.   _____

7. Congress and the president have used their power over the years to create new government agencies.   _____

8. In 1979, Shirley M. Hufstedler took their place on the Cabinet as the first Secretary of Education.   _____

9. Did either President Reagan or President Bush create a new post in their Cabinet?   _____

10. The Cabinet's meeting room now has more than fifteen chairs around their large table.   _____

Chapter 3: Using Verbs

 **Regular Verbs**

The four basic forms of a verb are called the **principal parts** of the verb. The principal parts of a verb are the **base form**, the **present participle**, the **past**, and the **past participle**. To form the past and past participle of a **regular** verb, add *–d* or *–ed* to the base form.

Base Form	Present Participle	Past	Past Participle
cook	(is) cooking	cooked	(have) cooked

Avoid the following common errors when forming the past or past participle of regular verbs.

1. leaving off the *–d* or *–ed* ending

   NONSTANDARD: He is suppose to be here.

   STANDARD: He is **supposed** to be here.

2. adding unnecessary letters

   NONSTANDARD: The ship was attackted.

   STANDARD: The ship was **attacked**.

Exercise For each of the following sentences, write the correct form (past or past participle) of the verb in parentheses.

   EXAMPLE: 1. Some experts say that Stone Age surgeons in Peru
      (operate) *operated* on the brain.

1. Carlos has (bake) _____ the Christmas pie every year for three years now.

2. The barber has (comb) _____ my hair, and now he will cut it.

3. The journalists (want) _____ to get an interview yesterday with the award-winning teacher.

4. In March 1836, about one hundred eighty Texas soldiers (die)

_____ in battle at an old fort called the Alamo.

5. We have (look) _____ for that library book for weeks, but we can't locate it.

6. The carpenter has (saw) _____ the oak panels for the playroom, and now she will varnish the wood.

7. Abraham Lincoln's parents (live) _____ in Kentucky when Abe was born.

8. Many years ago, Jane Addams (start) _____ Hull House, a place for underprivileged people in Chicago.

9. The child (kiss) _____ her baby brother and took his hand.

10. The chairperson has (call) _____ a special meeting for this afternoon.

GRAMMAR/USAGE

Chapter 3: Using Verbs

 **WORKSHEET 2** *Irregular Verbs A*

An **irregular verb** forms its past and past participle in some other way than by adding *–d* or *–ed* to the base form. The past and past participle of an irregular verb is formed by changing vowels or consonants, changing vowels and consonants, or making no change.

Base Form	Present Participle	Past	Past Participle
draw	(is) drawing	drew	(have) drawn
think	(is) thinking	thought	(have) thought
put	(is) putting	put	(have) put

Exercise A   For each of the following sentences, write the correct form (past or past participle) of the verb in parentheses.

EXAMPLE: 1. Tani (swim) *swam* forty laps three times this week.

1. The bean seedlings and the herbs have (freeze) _____ in the garden.

2. After she won the race, she (drink) _____ two glasses of water.

3. He (tell) _____ me that *waffle, coleslaw,* and *cookie* are words that came from Dutch.

4. We had (drive) _____ all night to attend my sister's college graduation.

5. Marianne (sit) _____ quietly throughout the discussion.

Exercise B   For each of the following sentences, underline the verb form that correctly completes the sentence.

EXAMPLE: 1. The children (brought, brang) their new notebooks to school.

1. Ray Charles (has written, has wrote) many popular songs.

2. Leigh (did, done) everything the instructions said.

3. She (knowed, knew) the best route to take.

4. Maria Tallchief (chose, chosen) a career as a dancer.

5. He (ate, eaten) chicken salad on whole-wheat bread for lunch.

6. The dog (stealed, had stolen) the newspaper from the neighbor's porch.

7. Felipe and Tonya (singed, sang) a duet in the talent show.

8. The turtle (came, comed) closer to me to reach the lettuce I was holding.

9. The Spaniards (have rode, have ridden) horses for more than a thousand years.

10. The eagle (spread, spreaded) its wings and swooped into the canyon.

Chapter 3: Using Verbs

 **WORKSHEET 3** *Irregular Verbs B*

Avoid the following common errors when forming the past or past participle of irregular verbs.

1. using the past form with a helping verb

   NONSTANDARD: Kyle has took the books back to the library.

   STANDARD: Kyle **took** the books back to the library.

2. using the past participle form without a helping verb

   NONSTANDARD: We done our best.

   STANDARD: We **have done** our best.

3. adding *–d* or *–ed* to the base form

   NONSTANDARD: No one knowed about the new regulation.

   STANDARD: No one **knew** about the new regulation.

Exercise: Proofreading   For each of the following sentences, cross out any error in verb form. Then, on the line provided, write the correct form of the verb. If a sentence is correct, write C.

EXAMPLE: 1. Have you ~~readed~~ about the Underground Railroad? _read_

1. Mr. Tucker, our history teacher, writed the words *Underground Railroad* on the chalkboard. _____

2. Then he drawed black lines on a map to show us where the Underground Railroad ran. _____

3. What strange tracks this railroad must have had! _____

4. The lines even runned into the Atlantic Ocean. _____

5. As you may imagine, this map leaved the class very confused. _____

6. But then Mr. Tucker explained that no one actually had rode on an underground railroad. _____

7. The railroad was really a secret network to help slaves who runned away. _____

8. Between 1830 and 1860, thousands of slaves had gain their freedom by traveling along the routes marked on this map. _____

9. The name *Underground Railroad* come from the use of railroad terms as code words. _____

10. Mr. Tucker said that hiding places were called stations and that people who helped slaves were called conductors. _____

GRAMMAR/USAGE

Chapter 3: Using Verbs

WORKSHEET 4 *Verb Tense*

The **tense** of a verb indicates the time of the action or state of being expressed by the verb. Every verb has six tenses: **present, past, future, present perfect, past perfect,** and **future perfect**.

PRESENT: walks
PAST: walked
FUTURE: will walk
PRESENT PERFECT: have walked
PAST PERFECT: had walked
FUTURE PERFECT: will have walked

Exercise A In the items below, write *P* if the italicized verb is in the past tense. Write *PR* if the verb is in the present tense. Write *F* if the verb is in the future tense.

EXAMPLE: __PR__ 1. I *enjoy* selling houses.

_____ 1. Susan and John Rieger *will buy* the bungalow on University Boulevard.

_____ 2. The Riegers *looked* for a house all last year.

_____ 3. The couple *saw* the little bungalow last month for the first time.

_____ 4. They *inspected* the house yesterday.

_____ 5. Now they *are* very happy and excited.

Exercise B: Revising Rewrite each of the following sentences, using the verb tense indicated in parentheses.

EXAMPLE: 1. Tulips lined the sidewalk. (present) *Tulips line the sidewalk.*

1. Sara Luisa lives in Lima, Peru. (past) _____

_____

2. Every day, Colin reads all of London's daily newspapers. (past) _____

_____

3. We climbed Mount Monadnock. (future) _____

_____

4. Today, we will meet the former president of the United States. (present) _____

_____

5. I run three miles every day after school. (future) _____

_____

Chapter 3: Using Verbs

 **Consistency of Tense**

Do not change needlessly from one tense to another. When writing about events that take place in the present, use verbs in the present tense. Similarly, when writing about events that occurred in the past, use verbs in the past tense.

INCONSISTENT: When the weather was good, we ride the horses. [*Was* is past tense, and *ride* is present tense.]

CONSISTENT: When the weather **is** good, we **ride** the horses. [Both *is* and *ride* are present tense.]

CONSISTENT: When the weather was good, we rode the horses. [Both *was* and *rode* are past tense.]

Exercise: Revising   On the line provided, revise each of the following sentences for consistency of verb tense. Some sentences may be revised in two ways; however, you need give only one correct revision.

EXAMPLE: 1. Then the robot reaches out and took the next piece on the assembly line.

Then the robot reached out and took the next piece on the assembly line.

1. The duck flies across the lake and landed in the tall grass near the bank.

   _____

2. Before we moved here, we live in Oregon.

   _____

3. So I take the note and gave it to Mr. Gilman.

   _____

4. When I gave the signal, you open the gate.

   _____

5. The story is dull, but the illustrations were wonderful.

   _____

GRAMMAR/USAGE

Chapter 3: Using Verbs

 **WORKSHEET 6** *Commonly Confused Verbs*

Base Form	Present Participle	Past	Past Participle
sit	(is) sitting	sat	(have) sat
set	(is) setting	set	(have) set
lie	(is) lying	lay	(have) lain
lay	(is) laying	laid	(have) laid
rise	(is) rising	rose	(have) risen
raise	(is) raising	raised	(have) raised

sit, set The verb *sit* means "to rest in an upright seated position." *Sit* seldom takes an object. The verb *set* means "to put (something) in a place." *Set* usually takes an object. Notice that *set* has the same form for the base form, past, and past participle.

lie, lay The verb *lie* means "to rest," "to recline," or "to be in a place." *Lie* never takes an object. The verb *lay* means "to put (something) in a place." *Lay* usually takes an object.

rise, raise The verb *rise* means "to go up" or "to get up." *Rise* seldom takes an object. The verb *raise* means "to lift up" or "to cause (something) to rise." *Raise* usually takes an object.

Exercise Some sentences in the following paragraph contain incorrect forms of the verbs *sit* and *set*, *lie* and *lay*, and *rise* and *raise*. If the sentence is correct, write C on the line provided. If the sentence has an incorrect verb form, write the correct form.

> EXAMPLES: [1] We rose early for our journey to Havasu Canyon. [2] I laid awake for hours thinking about the trip.
>
> 1. __*C*__
> 2. __*lay*__

[1] I helped Dad sit our bags in the car, and we headed for Havasu Canyon. [2] The canyon, which lies in northern Arizona, is home of the Havasupai Indian Reservation. [3] At the canyon rim, a Havasupai guide helped me up onto a horse and rose the stirrups so that I could reach them.

[4] After we rode horses eight miles to the canyon floor, I was tired from setting. [5] Yet I knew I must sit a good example for my younger brother and not complain. [6] The trail we took was fairly narrow and lay along the side of a steep, rocky wall. [7] We watched the sun raise high and hot as we rode through this beautiful canyon. [8] I thought about laying down when we reached the village of Supai. [9] Still, I quickly raised my hand to join the next tour to Havasu Falls. [10] When we arrived, I was ready to lay under the spray of the waterfall.

1. _____
2. _____
3. _____
4. _____

5. _____
6. _____
7. _____
8. _____

9. _____
10. _____

Chapter 3: Using Verbs

 **WORKSHEET 7** *Review*

Exercise A   Each of the following sentences has at least one pair of verbs in parentheses. Choose the correct verb from each pair.

EXAMPLE: 1. Josh (catched, <u>caught</u>) seven fish this morning.

1. Buffy Sainte-Marie has (sang, sung) professionally for more than twenty years.

2. Have you (began, begun) your Scottish bagpipe lessons yet?

3. Cindy Nicholas was the first woman who (swam, swum) the English Channel both ways.

4. When the trainer (rose, raised) her voice, the dogs (knew, knowed) it was time to behave.

5. After we had (saw, seen) all of the exhibits at the county fair, we (ate, eat) a light snack and then (went, go) home.

6. The egg (burst, bursted) in the microwave oven.

7. He (lay, laid) his lunch money on his desk.

8. The loud noise (breaked, broke) my concentration.

9. We (sat, set) through the movie three times because it is so funny.

10. We had (rode, ridden) halfway across the desert when I began to wish that I had (brought, brung) more water.

Exercise B: Proofreading   Some of the following sentences contain incorrect verb forms. If the sentence has an incorrect verb form, write the correct form on the line provided. If the sentence is correct, write C.

EXAMPLES: 1. Mario has lent me his copy of *Journey to the Center of the Earth.* __C__

2. I thinked I had a copy of this famous novel. *thought*

1. During the 1800's, Jules Verne wrote many scientific adventure tales.   _____

2. Back then, readers founded his stories amazing.   _____

3. Some people believe that he seen into the future.   _____

4. For example, in some novels he telled about space exploration and boats that traveled underwater.   _____

5. These books fascinated readers in the days before space travel and submarines.   _____

6. Verne lead a quiet life but had incredible adventures in his imagination.   _____

7. He gived the world some wonderful stories.   _____

GRAMMAR/USAGE

8. Some inventors of modern rockets have said that they read Verne's stories.

_____

9. Some of his books, such as *20,000 Leagues Under the Sea*, have been made into great movies.

_____

10. People have gave Verne the title "the father of modern science fiction."

_____

Exercise C   Each of the following sentences has at least one pair of verbs in parentheses. Choose the correct verb from each pair.

> EXAMPLE: 1. (Sit, <u>Set</u>) the groceries on the table while I start dinner.

1. Since I have grown taller, I have (rose, raised) the seat on my bicycle.

2. Mr. DeLemos (lay, laid) the foundation for the new Vietnamese Community Center.

3. The crane (rose, raised) the steel beam and carefully (sat, set) it into place.

4. Will you (lie, lay) the towels on the sand so that we can (lie, lay) on them?

5. When the sun (rises, raises), I often have trouble (sitting, setting) aside my covers and getting up.

Exercise D: Revising   On the line provided, revise each of the following sentences for consistency of verb tense and correct verb form. Some sentences may be revised in two ways; however, you need give only one correct revision.

> EXAMPLE: 1. Carmen gives me a menu to her mom's new restaurant, so I asked my dad if we could go.
>
> *Carmen gave me a menu to her mom's new restaurant, so I asked my dad if we could go.*

1. When we arrived at the restaurant, I run ahead of everyone to tell the hostess we needed three seats.

_____

2. We sit down, and the waiter brought our menus.

_____

3. I chose the refried beans and rice, and my sister picks the *enchiladas verdes*.

_____

4. My dad wants to try a bite of my beans; then he asked to try my sister's enchiladas.

_____

5. Dad told Carmen's mom that the food is delicious.

_____

Chapter 4: Using Pronouns

 **Case Forms**

Case is the form of a noun or a pronoun that shows how it is used. There are three cases: *nominative*, *objective*, and *possessive*.

> NOMINATIVE: That **author** is my favorite. [subject]
>
> OBJECTIVE: I recommended my favorite **author**. [direct object]
>
> I gave **him** a recommendation. [indirect object]

The possessive case of a noun is usually formed by the addition of an apostrophe and an *s*.

> POSSESSIVE: I have read many of that **author's** books.

Unlike nouns, most personal pronouns have different forms for all three cases.

		Nominative	Objective	Possessive
SINGULAR	FIRST PERSON	I	me	my, mine
	SECOND PERSON	you	you	your, yours
	THIRD PERSON	he, she, it	him, her, it	his, her, hers, its
PLURAL	FIRST PERSON	we	us	our, ours
	SECOND PERSON	you	you	your, yours
	THIRD PERSON	they	them	their, theirs

Exercise A On the line provided, write *O* if the italicized noun is in the objective case, *N* if it is in the nominative case, or *P* if it is in the possessive case.

> EXAMPLE: __O__ 1. The adventurer planned her *journey*.

_____ 1. The *explorer* went to the bottom of the ocean.

_____ 2. Near the shore, she saw a *shelf* of land.

_____ 3. This *shelf's* name is the continental shelf.

_____ 4. A *shelf* can slope many fathoms underwater.

_____ 5. These shelves attract many *explorers*.

Exercise B On the line provided, write *O* if the italicized personal pronoun is in the objective case, *N* if it is in the nominative case, or *P* if it is in the possessive case.

> EXAMPLE: __N__ 1. Yesterday, *I* read "The Lady or the Tiger?" by Frank R. Stockton.

_____ 1. It is the most famous tale written by *him*.

_____ 2. It didn't fit *my* idea of a typical short story.

_____ 3. First published in 1882, *it* fired the imaginations of readers all over the country.

_____ 4. *They* held many debates about its ending.

_____ 5. In fact, the story still puzzles *us* today.

GRAMMAR/USAGE

Name _____ Date _____ Class _____

Nominative Case

A **subject of a verb** is in the nominative case.

> SUBJECT: **I** use my computer.
>
> COMPOUND SUBJECT: **Ke** and **I** play computerized chess.

To help in choosing the correct pronoun in a compound subject, try each form of the pronoun separately.

> EXAMPLE: Elena and (I, me) went to the computer store.
>
> *I* went to the computer store.
>
> *Me* went to the computer store.
>
> ANSWER: Elena and **I** went to the computer store.

A **predicate nominative** is in the nominative case. A predicate nominative follows a linking verb and explains or identifies the subject of the verb. A personal pronoun used as a predicate nominative follows a form of the verb *be* (*am, is, are, was, were, be,* or *been*).

The first one there was **he**. [*He* follows the linking verb *was* and identifies the subject *one.*]

The winners of the contest were Kele and **I**. [*Kele* and *I* follow the linking verb *were* and identify the subject *winners.*]

NOTE: Expressions such as *It's me, That's her,* and *It was them* are accepted in everyday speaking. In writing, however, such expressions are considered nonstandard.

Exercise   Each sentence in the following paragraph contains a pair of personal pronouns in parentheses. Underline the correct pronoun form in each pair. Then, on the line provided, identify the underlined pronoun as a subject *(S)* or a predicate nominative *(PN).*

> EXAMPLE: [1] (We, Us) think of Leonardo da Vinci mostly as an artist. __*S*__

[1] (Me, I) think you probably have seen some paintings by this Italian Renaissance master. _____ [2] (Him, He) painted two works that are particularly famous. _____ [3] The *Mona Lisa* and *The Last Supper* are (they, them). _____ [4] In science class (we, us) were surprised by what our teacher said about Leonardo. _____ [5] (Her, She) said that he was also a brilliant inventor. _____ [6] My friend Jill and (me, I) were amazed to hear that Leonardo invented a flying machine that looked like a helicopter. _____ [7] We could see the propellers on the flying machine that (he, him) drew in 1488. _____ [8] (Me, I) was also impressed by his drawing of a spring-driven car. _____ [9] The inventor of the diving bell and the battle tank was (him, he), too. _____ [10] Scientists have studied Leonardo's ideas, and (them, they) have made models of many of his drawings. _____

Chapter 4: Using Pronouns

Objective Case A

A **direct object** is in the objective case. A direct object follows an action verb and tells *who* or *what* receives the action of the verb.

The guide described **it** as a desert. [*It* tells *what* the guide described.]

To help in choosing the correct pronoun in a compound direct object, try each form of the pronoun separately in the sentence.

EXAMPLE: He also guided Mai and (him, he).

He guided *he*.

He guided *him*.

ANSWER: He guided Mai and **him**.

An **indirect object** is in the objective case. An indirect object comes between an action verb and a direct object and tells *to whom* or *to what* or *for whom* or *for what*.

Sam gave **us** water. [*Us* is the indirect object, telling *to whom* Sam gave water.]

To help in choosing the correct pronoun in a compound indirect object, try each form of the pronoun separately in the sentence.

EXAMPLE: My mother gave Katherine and (I, me) a bouquet.

My mother gave *I* a bouquet.

My mother gave *me* a bouquet.

ANSWER: My mother gave Katherine and **me** a bouquet.

Exercise Choose appropriate pronouns for the blanks in the following sentences. Use a variety of pronouns, but do not use *you* or *it*. Then, identify the pronoun you chose as a direct object *(DO)* or an indirect object *(IO)*.

EXAMPLE 1. The teacher helped *us—DO* with the assignment.

1. All five judges have chosen _____ and

   _____ as the winners.

2. Kyle drew _____ a picture of his new puppy.

3. Did you know Jarvis and _____ ?

4. The guide directed _____ to New York City's Little Italy.

5. Yesterday, Mr. Finn showed _____ a shortcut.

6. Augie took _____ and _____ fishing.

7. Please order _____ a set of colored pencils, too.

8. Grandfather made _____ a table for Christmas.

9. Would you please give _____ a hand with these groceries?

10. They asked Ms. Shore and _____ for permission.

GRAMMAR/USAGE

Chapter 4: Using Pronouns

WORKSHEET 4 *Objective Case B*

An **object of a preposition** is in the objective case. The object of a preposition is a noun or a pronoun that follows a preposition. Together with any of the object's modifiers, the preposition and its object make a prepositional phrase.

> with her   for me   next to us   beside him   between you and me

A pronoun used as the object of a preposition should always be in the objective case.

> How did Mary present the gift **to her**? [*Her* is the object of the preposition *to*.]
>
> The teacher shared the paper **with her and him**. [*Her* and *him* are the objects of the preposition *with*.]

To help in choosing the correct pronoun when the object of a preposition is compound, try each form of the pronoun separately in the sentence.

> EXAMPLE: The car was coming directly at Mara and (I, me).
>
> The car was coming directly at *I*.
>
> The car was coming directly at *me*.
>
> ANSWER: The car was coming directly at Mara and **me**.

Exercise A   Choose appropriate pronouns for the blanks in the following sentences. Use a variety of pronouns, but do not use *you* or *it*.

> EXAMPLE: 1. We could not find all of _them_ .

1. The teacher read to André and _____ a saying by Confucius about friendship.

2. I made an appointment for _____ and you.

3. There are some seats behind Lusita and _____ .

4. No one except Patrice and _____ was studying.

5. I couldn't have done it without you and _____ .

Exercise B: Proofreading   Most of the following sentences contain errors in pronoun usage. Cross through each incorrect pronoun, and on the line provided, write the correct form. If a sentence is correct, write *C*.

> EXAMPLE: 1. The letter was addressed to both Bill and I. _me_

1. The safari continued without he and I. _____

2. We stood beside their families and them during the ceremony. _____

3. Do you have any suggestions for Jalene or we? _____

4. With the help of Juan and he, we built a fire and set up camp. _____

5. Did you speak Chinese with Ms. Tan and her? _____

Chapter 4: Using Pronouns

 **Who *and* Whom**

The pronoun *who* has different forms in the nominative and objective cases. *Who* is the nominative form; *whom* is the objective form.

When you are choosing between *who* and *whom* in a subordinate clause, follow these steps:

STEP 1: Find the subordinate clause.

STEP 2: Decide how the pronoun is used in the clause—as subject, predicate nominative, object of the verb, or object of a preposition.

STEP 3: Determine the case of the pronoun according to the rules of standard English.

STEP 4: Select the correct form of the pronoun.

EXAMPLE: Do you know (who, whom) he is?

STEP 1: The subordinate clause is *(who, whom) he is.*

STEP 2: In this clause, the subject is *he,* the verb is *is,* and the pronoun is the predicate nominative: *he is (who, whom).*

STEP 3: As a predicate nominative, the pronoun should be in the nominative case.

STEP 4: The nominative form is *who.*

ANSWER: Do you know **who** he is?

Exercise Underline the correct pronoun form in parentheses.

EXAMPLE: 1. (Who, Whom) taught you sign language?

1. To (who, whom) should I address my question?

2. Taro is the one (who, whom) gave me the letter.

3. Judge O'Connor, (who, whom) I admire, is on the Supreme Court.

4. Do you know (who, whom) is on the committee?

5. I don't know to (who, whom) this address book belongs.

6. The dedication page tells for (who, whom) the book was written.

7. Aborigines are the only people (who, whom) live in some parts of Australia.

8. We need a business leader (who, whom) can speak Japanese.

9. (Who, Whom) did he ask for a date?

10. Coretta Scott King is a woman (who, whom) I respect.

GRAMMAR/USAGE

Name _____ Date _____ Class _____

 *Other Pronoun Problems*

Sometimes a pronoun is followed directly by a noun that identifies the pronoun. Such a noun is called an **appositive**. To help in choosing which pronoun to use before an appositive, omit the appositive and try each form of the pronoun separately.

EXAMPLE: (We, Us) bowlers play every Saturday. [*Bowlers* is the appositive identifying the pronoun.]

We play every Saturday. *or* *Us* play every Saturday.

ANSWER: **We** bowlers play every Saturday.

Reflexive pronouns (such as *myself* and *himself*) can be used as objects. A reflexive pronoun should be used only when the pronoun *refers* to the subject, never *as* a subject.

STANDARD: Ed had left **himself** wide open to be tackled.

NONSTANDARD: No one knew the answer but Ellen and myself.

STANDARD: No one knew the answer but Ellen and **me**.

NONSTANDARD: Cindy and myself mow lawns in the summer.

STANDARD: Cindy and **I** mow lawns in the summer.

Do not use the nonstandard forms *hisself* and *theirselves* in place of *himself* and *themselves*.

Exercise A   Underline the correct pronoun form in parentheses in the sentences that follow. Then, on the line provided, tell how each pronoun is used. Write *S* for subjects, *DO* for direct objects, *IO* for indirect objects, or *OP* for object of a prepositions.

EXAMPLE: _____S_____ 1. This weekend, (we, us) Scouts are going camping.

_____ 1. Shelby sent (we, us) children boots for the winter.

_____ 2. (We, Us) dancers practice every day.

_____ 3. Lione presented the trophy to (we, us) gymnasts.

_____ 4. Mr. González gave (we, us) runners encouragement at the meet.

_____ 5. The dance company sent (we, us) tap-dancers to New York City.

Exercise B: Proofreading   Most of the following sentences contain errors in the use of reflexive pronouns. Draw a line through each incorrect pronoun, and write the correct form above it. If a sentence is correct, write *C* on the line provided.

EXAMPLE: _____ 1. Won't you give him and ~~myself~~ *me* another chance?

_____ 1. I'll leave the honor of washing dishes to Vince and yourself.

_____ 2. Don't let your little brother hurt hisself!

_____ 3. My father and myself enjoy studying African culture.

_____ 4. Worried about forgetting the appointment, Karen wrote a note to herself.

_____ 5. They must get theirselves in shape before the hike.

Chapter 4: Using Pronouns

WORKSHEET 7 *Review*

Exercise A   For each sentence below, underline the correct pronoun form in parentheses.

EXAMPLE: 1. Say hello to (she, <u>her</u>) and Anna.

1. Tulips surround (we, us) during May in Holland, Michigan.

2. The audience clapped for Rudy and (he, him).

3. The best singer in the choir is (she, her).

4. The officer gave (we, us) girls a ride home.

5. I wrote a short story about my great-grandpa and (he, him) last week.

6. Daniel and (me, I) read a book about Pelé, the great soccer player.

7. Last year's winner was (he, him).

8. To (who, whom) did you send invitations?

9. Please tell me (who, whom) the girl in the yellow dress is.

10. (We, Us) sisters could help Dad with the dishes.

Exercise B   Each sentence in the following paragraph contains at least one personal pronoun. On the numbered lines provided after the paragraph, write the personal pronouns. Then tell whether each is used as a subject *(S)*, a predicate nominative *(PN)*, a direct object *(DO)*, an indirect object *(IO)*, or an object of a preposition *(OP)*.

EXAMPLE: [1] I enjoy watching Edward James Olmos in movies and on TV because he always plays such interesting characters.

1. *I—S; he—S*

[1] He is a cowboy in the movie *The Ballad of Gregorio Cortez*. [2] In the movie, he plays an innocent man hunted by Texas Rangers. [3] The film will give you a good idea of Olmos's acting talents. [4] After I saw him in this movie, I wanted to know more about him. [5] A librarian gave me a book of modern biographies. [6] I read that Olmos's father came from Mexico but that the actor was born in Los Angeles. [7] Growing up, Olmos faced the problems of poverty and gang violence, but he overcame them. [8] Before becoming a successful actor, he played baseball, sang in a band, and moved furniture. [9] In 1978, Olmos's role in the play *Zoot Suit* gave him the big break he needed in show business. [10] Later, the movie *Stand and Deliver*, in which he played math teacher Jaime Escalante, earned him widespread praise.

1. _____   6. _____

2. _____   7. _____

3. _____   8. _____

4. _____   9. _____

5. _____   10. _____

Chapter 4, Worksheet 7, continued

Exercise C   On the lines provided, write the correct pronoun form, *who* or *whom*.

1. People _____ live in large cities must learn to get along with one another.

2. For _____ were you waiting yesterday at the gallery?

3. Give this task to the one _____ has the least work now.

4. _____ do you know in Los Angeles?

5. I respect those _____ think deeply.

Exercise D   In each of the sentences below, a pronoun is used with an appositive. Underline the correct pronoun form in parentheses.

1. The first people on the program were (we, us) twirlers.

2. (We, Us) brothers were known as the Great Beninos.

3. The teacher called (we, us) students up to the stage.

4. Nurse Anthony gave a plaque to (we, us) volunteers.

5. (We, Us) boys plan to help with the park cleanup.

Exercise E: Proofreading   Cross out the incorrect pronouns in the following sentences, and write the correct forms on the lines provided. If a sentence is correct, write C.

EXAMPLE: 1. I gave ~~me~~ a present. *myself*

1. We saved seats for Paul and yourself.   _____

2. For hisself, he chose a pair of red Western boots.   _____

3. Do you ever talk to yourself?   _____

4. The home economics class divided the leftovers among theirselves.   _____

5. The jobs sound right for Niko and myself.   _____

Name _____ Date _____ Class _____

 **WORKSHEET 1** *Comparison of Modifiers*

A **modifier** is a word, a phrase, or a clause that describes or limits the meaning of another word. Two kinds of modifiers—**adjectives** and **adverbs**—may be used to compare things. The three degrees of comparison of modifiers are **positive, comparative,** and **superlative**.

	Adjectives
POSITIVE	Jill is a **fast** runner. [no comparison]
COMPARATIVE	Jill is a **faster** runner than Vicente is. [one compared with another]
SUPERLATIVE	Jill is the **fastest** runner on the team. [one compared with many others]
	Adverbs
POSITIVE	Jill runs **quickly**. [no comparison]
COMPARATIVE	Jill runs **more quickly** than Vicente does. [one compared with another]
SUPERLATIVE	Of all of us, Jill runs **most quickly**. [one compared with many others]

Exercise   On the line provided, write *P* if the italicized modifier is in the positive degree. Write *C* if it is in the comparative degree. Write *S* if it is in the superlative degree. Then write *1, 2,* or *3 or more* to tell how many things are being described or compared.

EXAMPLE: 1. Who is *taller*—you or your brother? __C–2__

1. You should not play your trumpet *more loudly* than he plays his saxophone. _____

2. That was the *fastest* fire drill that we've ever had. _____

3. Walk *slowly*. _____

4. These shoes are *tighter* than the other ones. _____

5. Of all the cars, this one is the *most efficient.* _____

6. I feel *happier* today than I did yesterday. _____

7. Of all the days this week, the sun was *brightest* on Tuesday. _____

8. She seems to understand biology *more easily* than I do. _____

9. I'm telling you *honestly* that I don't know where your jacket is. _____

10. Marcelle was the *most timid* of the swimmers from the beginners' class. _____

Name _____ Date _____ Class _____

 **Regular Comparison**

In comparisons, adjectives and adverbs take different forms. The specific form that is used depends on how many syllables the modifier has and how many things are being compared. Most one-syllable modifiers form their comparative and superlative degrees by adding *–er* and *–est*. Some two-syllable modifiers form their comparative and superlative degrees by adding *–er* and *–est*. Other two-syllable modifiers form their comparative and superlative degrees by using *more* and *most*. Modifiers that have three or more syllables form their comparative and superlative degrees by using *more* and *most*.

	Modifiers with One Syllable		Modifiers with Two Syllables		Modifiers with Three or More Syllables	
POSITIVE	big	low	happy	calmly	rapidly	confident
COMPARATIVE	bigger	lower	happier	more calmly	more rapidly	more confident
SUPERLATIVE	biggest	lowest	happiest	most calmly	most rapidly	most confident

To show decreasing comparisons, all modifiers form their comparative and superlative degrees with *less* and *least*.

POSITIVE:	clear	wildly	near
COMPARATIVE:	less clear	less wildly	less near
SUPERLATIVE:	least clear	least wildly	least near

NOTE: When you are not sure how a two-syllable modifier forms its degrees of comparison, look up the word in a dictionary.

Exercise   On the lines provided, write the comparative and superlative degrees of each modifier below.

POSITIVE   COMPARATIVE   SUPERLATIVE

EXAMPLE: 1. small *smaller, less small*   *smallest, least small*

1. quick _____   _____

2. suddenly _____   _____

3. quietly _____   _____

4. small _____   _____

5. furious _____   _____

6. surely _____   _____

7. simply _____   _____

8. weary _____   _____

9. old _____   _____

10. sheepish _____   _____

Name _____ Date _____ Class _____

Uses of Comparative and Superlative Forms

Use the comparative degree when comparing two things. Use the superlative degree when comparing more than two.

COMPARATIVE: These vegetables are **fresher** than those.

Of the two speakers, he spoke **more confidently**.

SUPERLATIVE: What is the **brightest** star in the sky?

Of the three guard dogs, this one barked **most loudly**.

Avoid the common mistake of using the superlative degree to compare two things.

NONSTANDARD: Of the two shirts, this one is the most expensive.

STANDARD: Of the two shirts, this one is the **more expensive**.

Include the word *other* or *else* when comparing a member of a group with the rest of the group.

NONSTANDARD: Edmund sings better than anyone in school. [Edmund is one of the students in school and cannot sing better than himself.]

STANDARD: Edmund sings better than anyone **else** in school.

Exercise: Proofreading Some sentences in the following paragraph contain incorrect uses of comparative and superlative forms. On the line provided, write the incorrect form and then the correct form. If a sentence is correct, write C.

EXAMPLE: [1] My family spends the most time preparing for Cinco de Mayo than our next-door neighbors.

1. *the most—more*

[1] My parents work harder than anyone in the family to prepare for the holiday. [2] But I get more excited than they do about the parade and festivals. [3] I think Cinco de Mayo is the better holiday of the year. [4] At least it's the more lively one in our San Antonio neighborhood. [5] Of all the speakers each year, my father always gives the more stirring speech about the history of the day. [6] Cinco de Mayo celebrates Mexico's most important victory over Napoleon III of France. [7] For me, the better part of the holiday is singing and dancing in the parade. [8] I get to wear the beautifulest dresses you've ever seen. [9] They're fancier than any dress I own. [10] Although my other clothes are certainly pretty, they are less colorful than my special Cinco de Mayo dresses.

1. _____   6. _____

2. _____   7. _____

3. _____   8. _____

4. _____   9. _____

5. _____   10. _____

GRAMMAR/USAGE

Name _____ Date _____ Class _____

 **WORKSHEET 4** *Irregular Comparison*

Some modifiers form their comparative and superlative degrees irregularly.

Positive	Comparative	Superlative
bad	worse	worst
far	farther	farthest
good	better	best
well	better	best
many	more	most
much	more	most

Exercise A   For each of the following sentences, underline the correct form of the modifier in parentheses.

EXAMPLE: 1. Of your teammates, whose home is (farther, <u>farthest</u>) from school?

1. Who collected (more, the most) newspapers—your class or hers?

2. The craft show was (more, most) successful than it was last year.

3. This painting costs (more, most) money than that one.

4. I think the green paint looks (worse, worst) on the wall than the blue did.

5. Of the three grocery stores, which is (farther, farthest) away?

Exercise B   For each of the following sentences, write in the blank provided the correct form of the modifier given in parentheses.

EXAMPLE: 1. We danced _*better*_ than anyone else at the recital. (well)

1. Melba ran her _____ time in her third race. (good)

2. I had the _____ meal of my life at that diner. (bad)

3. Miriam played the role _____ than the professional actor I saw on television. (well)

4. I ran _____ on the field than Malcolm did. (far)

5. I gave directions as _____ as I could. (well)

6. My memory is not as _____ as it used to be. (good)

7. Bagels always taste _____ to him than toast does. (good)

8. My sore throat is _____ than it was yesterday. (bad)

9. Would it be a _____ thing for you to share your grapes with your brother? (bad)

10. Of all your hobbies, which do you like _____ ? (well)

Name _____ Date _____ Class _____

Double Comparison and Double Negative

A **double comparison** is the use of both *–er* and *more (less)* or both *–est* and *most (least)* with a modifier. A comparison should be formed in only one of these two ways, not both.

> NONSTANDARD: This pony is more wilder than that one.

> STANDARD: This pony is **wilder** than that one.

A **double negative** is the use of two negative words to express one negative idea. Below are some common negative words.

barely	never	not (–n't)
hardly	no	nothing
neither	nobody	scarcely

Use only one negative word to express a negative idea.

> NONSTANDARD: I don't have no mail today.

> STANDARD: I **don't** have **any** mail today.

> STANDARD: I have **no** mail today.

Exercise: Proofreading   Most of the following sentences contain incorrect forms of comparison. Cross out each error, and write the correct form above it if needed. If a sentence is correct, write *C* on the line provided.

> EXAMPLE: _____ 1. Nobody in our class knew ~~nothing~~ *anything* about the pop quiz.

_____ 1. It's the most homeliest dog in the world.

_____ 2. We never have no shoe polish in our house.

_____ 3. That modern sculpture is the most strangest I've ever seen.

_____ 4. This morning was more sunnier than this afternoon.

_____ 5. Neither of my friends had no extra paper.

_____ 6. Don't say nothing about it to Yolanda.

_____ 7. That was the most luckiest thing that ever happened to me.

_____ 8. Class hadn't hardly started when lightning struck.

_____ 9. Never go nowhere without telling me first.

_____ 10. I have never seen anything cuter than my puppy.

GRAMMAR/USAGE

Chapter 5: Using Modifiers

WORKSHEET 6

Misplaced Prepositional Phrases

A **prepositional phrase** consists of a preposition, a noun or a pronoun called the object of the preposition, and any modifiers of that object. A prepositional phrase may be used as an adjective or as an adverb.

> ADJECTIVE PHRASE: We found a cat **with a sore foot**. [modifies *cat*]
>
> ADVERB PHRASE: Al and I found an injured cat **in the park**. [modifies *found*]

A prepositional phrase used as an adjective should be placed directly after the word it modifies.

> MISPLACED: The woman wrote a play about a dog in the red dress. [Is the dog in the red dress?]
>
> CLEAR: The woman **in the red dress** wrote a play about a dog.

A prepositional phrase used as an adverb should be placed near the word it modifies.

> MISPLACED: I saw a movie about spiders in my science class.
>
> CLEAR: **In my science class,** I saw a movie about spiders.
>
> CLEAR: I saw **in my science class** a movie about spiders.

Avoid placing a prepositional phrase in such a way that it appears to modify either of two words. Place the phrase so that it clearly modifies the word you intend it to modify.

> MISPLACED: Uncle Roberto told me on Tuesday we will visit you. [Does the phrase modify *told* or *will visit*?]
>
> CLEAR: **On Tuesday,** Uncle Roberto told me that we will visit you.
>
> CLEAR: Uncle Roberto told me that we will visit you **on Tuesday**.

Exercise: Revising Find the misplaced phrases in the following sentences. On the line provided, revise each sentence, placing the phrase near the word it modifies.

> EXAMPLE: 1. I read that a satellite was launched in the news today.
>
> *I read in the news today that a satellite was launched.*

1. The nature photographer told us about filming a herd of water buffalo in class today.

   _____

2. I met a girl who owns a toy chihuahua in school.

   _____

3. My aunt promised me on Saturday she will take me to the symphony.

   _____

4. That man bought the rare painting of Pocahontas with the briefcase.

   _____

5. We saw the trapeze artist swinging dangerously through our field binoculars.

   _____

Name _____ Date _____ Class _____

 **WORKSHEET 7** ## *Misplaced and Dangling Participial Phrases*

A **participial phrase** consists of a verb form—either a present participle or a past participle—and its related words. A participial phrase modifies a noun or a pronoun.

> **Turning the corner,** I ran into Jack. [modifies *I*]

> **Addressed incorrectly,** your letter may become lost. [modifies *letter*]

Like a prepositional phrase, a participial phrase should be placed as close as possible to the word it modifies.

> MISPLACED: Buried in the yard, the dog dug up a bone.

> CLEAR: The dog dug up a bone **buried in the yard**.

A participial phrase that does not clearly and sensibly modify any word in the sentence is a dangling participial phrase. To correct a dangling phrase, supply a word that the phrase can modify, or add a subject and a verb to the dangling modifier.

> DANGLING: Planning a picnic, the rain made us sad.

> CLEAR: **Planning a picnic,** we were saddened by the rain.

> CLEAR: Because we were **planning a picnic,** the rain made us sad.

Exercise: Revising   Most of the following sentences contain misplaced or dangling participial phrases. On the line provided, revise each incorrect sentence to eliminate the misplaced or dangling phrase. If a sentence is correct, write *C*.

> EXAMPLE: 1. Dressed in our clown costumes, the police officer waved and smiled.
>
> *Seeing us dressed in our clown costumes, the police officer waved and smiled.*

1. Standing on the dock, the boat didn't look very seaworthy.

   _____

2. Exploring the old house, Janetta and Patty found a secret passageway.

   _____

3. Lions approached our car roaming free on the grounds.

   _____

4. Hanging from the limb of an old oak tree, birds flocked to the bird feeder.

   _____

5. Having locked the cabin door, our fear of the hungry bear lessened.

   _____

GRAMMAR/USAGE

Chapter 5: Using Modifiers

WORSHEET 8 *Misplaced Adjective Clauses*

A **clause** is a group of words that contains a verb and its subject and is used as a part of a sentence. An **adjective clause** modifies a noun or a pronoun. Most adjective clauses begin with a relative pronoun, such as *that, which, who, whom,* or *whose.*

The bike **that I want** is on sale this week. [modifies *bike*]

I have an uncle **who lives in Hungary**. [modifies *uncle*]

Like phrases, clauses should be placed as close as possible to the word or words they modify.

MISPLACED: He gave a turtle to his sister that had a spotted shell. [Did his sister have a spotted shell?]

CLEAR: He gave a turtle **that had a spotted shell** to his sister.

Exercise: Revising Revise each sentence below, placing the clause near the word it modifies.

EXAMPLE: 1. I typed the essay on clean paper which I had corrected.

I typed the essay, which I had corrected, on clean paper.

1. The boy is from my school that won the contest.

   _____

2. We tiptoed over the ice in our heavy boots, which had begun to crack.

   _____

3. The jade sculpture was by a famous Chinese artist that my cousin broke.

   _____

4. We sometimes play soccer in one of the parks on nice days that are near the school.

   _____

5. Did the telethon achieve its goal that ran for thirty-six hours?

   _____

6. Nisei Week is in August, which is celebrated by Japanese Americans in Los Angeles.

   _____

7. A friendly man greeted me, whose name I can't remember.

   _____

8. The sweater belongs to my best friend that has a V-shaped neck.

   _____

9. My married sister has the flu who lives in Ohio.

   _____

10. The documentary was filmed in several countries which will be broadcast in the fall.

   _____

Chapter 5: Using Modifiers

◆ WORSHEET 9 ◆ *Review*

Exercise A: Proofreading   Most of the following sentences contain errors in the use of modifiers. On the line provided, write the incorrect word or words and then the correct word or words. If a sentence is correct, write C.

> EXAMPLE: 1. Of the three programs, the one on Japanese plays was the
> more interesting. *more—most*

1. Before the program, I didn't hardly know anything about Japanese theater.   _____

2. I learned that Japanese theater is much more old than theater in many other countries.   _____

3. *No* and *Kabuki* are the two most best-known kinds of Japanese drama.   _____

4. Dating from the Middle Ages, *No* is different from any form of Japanese theater.   _____

5. *No* plays, which are narrated in an ancient language, are performed more slowly than *Kabuki* plays.   _____

6. *No* plays are seen lesser often than the more modern *Kabuki* plays.   _____

7. In the West, we don't have no theater like Japan's *Bugaku* for the Imperial Court.   _____

8. I was more interested in Japan's puppet theater, the *Bunraku*, than anyone in my class.   _____

9. Puppet-theater performers have a more harder job than other theater performers.   _____

10. I didn't never know that it takes three people to operate one puppet.   _____

Exercise B: Revising   The following sentences contain errors in the use of modifiers. Revise each sentence to eliminate the error.

> EXAMPLE: 1. We don't never stay after school.
> *We never stay after school.*

1. Which did you like best—the book or the movie?

_____

2. Gina has more ideas for the festival than anyone.

_____

3. I can't hardly reason with her.

_____

GRAMMAR/USAGE

4. Of the two singers, he has the best voice.

_____

5. They haven't said nothing to us about it.

_____

Exercise C: Revising   Most of the following sentences contain misplaced or dangling modifiers. Revise each sentence that contains a misplaced or dangling modifier. If a sentence is correct, write C.

EXAMPLE: 1. Living in cold and treeless areas, snow houses are built by some native arctic people.

Living in cold and treeless areas, some native arctic people build snow houses.

1. You've probably seen some pictures of houses built of snow on television.

_____

2. Knowing that these houses are igloos, other facts about them may be new to you.

_____

3. Actually, the word *igloo,* which means "shelter," applies to all types of houses.

_____

4. Only native people build snow houses that live in Canada and northern Greenland.

_____

5. Used only during the winter, large blocks of snow are used in building igloos.

_____

6. Adapting to their environment long ago, snow houses provided protection against the bitter cold.

_____

7. There are three steps in the building of an igloo.

_____

8. First, blocks are cut by the builders of snow.

_____

9. Arranged in a circle about ten feet across, the builder slants the blocks inward.

_____

10. The finished igloo is spiral shaped and has a hole at the top.

_____

Chapter 6: Phrases

Prepositional Phrases

A **phrase** is a group of related words that is used as a single part of speech and does not contain a verb and its subject.

    off base   my sister   going shopping   to see a movie

A **prepositional phrase** includes a preposition, a noun or a pronoun called the **object of the preposition,** and any modifiers of that object.

    The bird **with large, black wings** sat on its perch. [The noun *wings* is the object of the preposition *with*.]

Any modifier that comes between the preposition and its object is part of the prepositional phrase.

    After the roller-coaster ride, I didn't feel too well. [The adjectives *the* and *roller-coaster* modify the noun *ride*.]

An object of a preposition may be compound.

    My aunt likes her tea **with milk and honey**. [Both *milk* and *honey* are objects of the preposition *with*.]

Exercise In the following sentences, underline the prepositional phrase or phrases. Then draw another line under the object of the preposition.

       EXAMPLE: 1. The pitcher threw the ball neatly <u>over home plate</u>.

1. Albert Einstein proved that the speed of light is constant.

2. Although we got a late start, we should be on time for the movie.

3. In an emergency, Frank never loses control of himself.

4. The newscaster looked the governor in the eye and asked the question.

5. Throughout the year, Daria worked hard at her studies.

6. The rivers and lakes thaw during the spring.

7. Elwood is always polite to everyone.

8. Who will volunteer for the job?

9. Renny won the race by only a few inches.

10. I will miss the party because I'm sick with the flu.

SENTENCES

Name _____ Date _____ Class _____

Adjective Phrases

An **adjective phrase** is a prepositional phrase that modifies a noun or a pronoun. An adjective phrase tells *what kind* or *which one*.

> Can a hairstyle be a statement **about politics**? [The phrase *about politics* modifies the noun *statement*. The phrase tells *what kind* of statement.]

More than one adjective phrase may modify the same word.

> Green grass **with tender shoots beside the stream** attracted many deer. [Both phrases modify the noun *grass*.]

An adjective phrase always follows the word it modifies. That word may be the object of another prepositional phrase.

> Some women wore their hair piled **on top of their heads**. [The phrase *of their heads* modifies *top*, which is the object of the preposition *on*.]

NOTE: Be careful not to confuse an infinitive with a prepositional phrase beginning with *to*. A prepositional phrase always has an object that is a noun or pronoun. An infinitive is a verb form that usually begins with *to*.

> INFINITIVE: Flowers have begun **to bloom**.
>
> PREPOSITIONAL PHRASE: Bring the flowers **to me**.

Exercise Each of the following sentences contains one or two adjective phrases. Underline each adjective phrase. Then draw two lines under the word the phrase modifies.

> EXAMPLE: 1. Megan read a book on the origins of words.

1. Mike's sister Tanya, a real terror with a whale of a temper, shouts "Beans!" whenever something goes wrong.

2. Some expressions of anger have their origins in Latin or Greek.

3. Many of us in English class wanted to discuss how people express their anger.

4. Words, gestures, and even art can show expressions of anger and of other emotions.

5. People around the world show emotions similarly.

6. When angry people make a show of teeth, they are copying the gestures of Stone Age humans.

7. Everyone in all of the world has felt angry now and then.

8. When I'm angry, I take a deep breath of air and talk it out.

9. Imagine what would happen if everyone with a bad temper in the city had a bad day.

10. We agreed that the best thing to do is to avoid people with chips on their shoulders.

Chapter 6: Phrases

Adverb Phrases

An **adverb phrase** is a prepositional phrase that modifies a verb, an adjective, or an adverb. An adverb phrase tells *how, when, where, why,* or *to what extent* (that is, *how long, how many,* or *how far*).

An adverb phrase may come before or after the word it modifies.

> Different styles have been popular **throughout the ages**.

> **Throughout the ages,** different styles have been popular.

More than one adverb phrase may modify the same word or words.

> **On Saturday,** we will go **to the fair**. [Both phrases modify the verb phrase *will go*.]

An adverb phrase may be followed by an adjective phrase modifying the object of the adverb phrase.

> The baby feels secure **with the blanket from Grandmother**. [The adverb phrase *with the blanket* modifies the adjective *secure*. The adjective phrase *from Grandmother* modifies the object *blanket*.]

Exercise A   In each of the following sentences, underline the adverb phrase. Then underline twice the word or words the adverb phrase modifies.

> EXAMPLE: 1. The new restaurant <u>was built</u> over a river.

1. The Bali Hai restaurant has opened across the road.

2. The food is fantastic beyond belief!

3. We went to the restaurant last night.

4. At the Bali Hai you can eat exotic food.

5. None of the items on the menu are too expensive for most people.

Exercise B   On the line provided, identify each italicized phrase in the following sentences. Write *ADJ* for an adjective phrase or *ADV* for an adverb phrase.

> EXAMPLE: _ADJ_   1. I like trying foods *from exotic places*.

_____ 1. People *from far and near* enjoy themselves in the friendly atmosphere.

_____ 2. Diners appear happy *with the service*.

_____ 3. *For three weeks* the Bali Hai has been crowded.

_____ 4. When we went there, we were seated on a patio *with beautiful flowers*.

_____ 5. *Off the river* blew a cool breeze.

SENTENCES

Chapter 6: Phrases

Participles and Participial Phrases

A **verbal** is a verb form used as a noun, an adjective, or an adverb. A **participle** is a verbal that can be used as an adjective. There are two kinds of participles—*present participles* and *past participles*.

Present participles end in *–ing*.

The weather was **threatening**. [*Threatening,* the present participle of the verb *threaten,* modifies the noun *weather*.]

Most **past participles** end in *–d* or *–ed*. Others are irregularly formed.

The weather reporter looked **worried**. [The past participle, *worried,* modifies the noun *reporter*.]

The storm, **known** as Hurricane Bob, was forming. [The irregular past participle, *known,* modifies the noun *storm*.]

A **participial phrase** consists of a participle and all of the words related to the participle. The entire phrase is used as an adjective. A participle may be modified by an adverb and may also have a complement, usually a direct object. A participial phrase includes the participle, all of its modifiers, its complement, and modifiers of the complement.

Looking ceaselessly for food, the beast roamed the land. [The participial phrase modifies the noun *beast. Ceaselessly* and *for food* modify *looking*.]

Exercise A   Underline the participles used as adjectives in the following sentences. Draw two lines under the noun or pronoun each participle modifies.

EXAMPLE: 1. We heard the <u>train</u> <u>whistling</u> and <u>chugging</u> in the distance.

1. The records, cracked and warped, were in the old trunk in the attic.

2. Shouting, Carmen warned the pedestrian to look out for the car.

3. The sparkling water splashed in our faces.

4. The papers, aged and yellowed, were found in the bottom of the file cabinet.

5. For centuries the ruins remained there, undiscovered.

Exercise B   Underline the participial phrases in the following sentences. Draw two lines under the word or words that each phrase modifies.

EXAMPLE: 1. Myths are <u>stories</u> <u>passed on from generation to generation</u>.

1. Bathed in radiant light, Venus brought love and joy wherever she went.

2. Observing his path, people said that Ares left blood, ruin, and grief behind him.

3. The Romans, greatly respecting Mars, made him one of their three chief gods.

4. They imagined him dressed in shining armor.

5. Mars, supposed to be the father of Rome's founders, has a planet named after him.

Chapter 6: Phrases

Gerunds and Gerund Phrases

A **gerund** is a verbal ending in *–ing* that is used as a noun.

SUBJECT: **Snorkeling** is a wonderful adventure.

PREDICATE NOMINATIVE: One of the camp's most popular activities is **canoeing**.

OBJECT OF A PREPOSITION: I am looking forward to **fishing**.

DIRECT OBJECT: My father enjoys **camping**.

A **gerund phrase** consists of a gerund and all the words related to the gerund. Because a gerund is a verb form, it may be modified by an adverb and have a complement, usually a direct object. Since a gerund functions as a noun, it may be modified by an adjective. A gerund phrase includes the gerund, its modifiers and complements, and their modifiers.

SUBJECT: **Flying in an airplane** sounds dangerous but is actually quite safe.

PREDICATE NOMINATIVE: A far more dangerous activity is **driving a car**.

OBJECT OF A PREPOSITION: Some motorists endanger others by **recklessly disobeying speed limits**.

DIRECT OBJECT: Many people prefer **traveling by rail or by air**.

Exercise A Underline the gerund phrases in the following sentences. On the line provided, identify each gerund phrase as a *subject*, a *predicate nominative*, a *direct object*, or an *object of a preposition*.

EXAMPLE: 1. After <u>rowing all the way across the lake</u>, we were tired.
object of a preposition

1. Uncle Eli's specialty is barbecuing on the grill. _____

2. Nobody could stand the dog's unceasing whining. _____

3. In-line skating in the park is my favorite hobby. _____

4. Studying every night usually results in higher scores. _____

5. Considering the other choices, Melinda decided on walking to the store.

_____

Exercise B On the line provided, use each of the following gerund phrases in a sentence of your own. Underline the gerund phrase, and identify it as a *subject*, a *predicate nominative*, a *direct object*, or an *object of a preposition*.

EXAMPLE: 1. hiking up the hill

<u>*Hiking up the hill took us all morning.*</u>—*subject*

1. getting up in the morning

_____

2. arguing among themselves

_____

SENTENCES

Chapter 6: Phrases

Infinitives and Infinitive Phrases

An **infinitive** is a verbal that can be used as a noun, an adjective, or an adverb. An infinitive usually begins with *to*.

INFINITIVES AS NOUNS: **To learn** takes time. [*To learn* is the subject of the sentence.]

I like **to dance**. [*To dance* is the direct object of the verb *like*.]

The puppy's goal was **to swim**. [*To swim* is the predicate nominative referring to the subject *goal*.]

INFINITIVE AS ADJECTIVE: The easiest thing **to make** is a mistake. [*To make* modifies the noun *thing*.]

INFINITIVE AS ADVERB: The children were happy **to sing**. [*To sing* modifies the adjective *happy*.]

An **infinitive phrase** consists of an infinitive and its modifiers and complements. An infinitive may be modified by an adjective or an adverb; it may also have a complement, which may have modifiers. The entire infinitive phrase may act as an adjective, an adverb, or a noun.

NOUN: **To eat a proper diet** takes some planning. [The infinitive phrase is the subject of the sentence. The noun *diet* is the direct object of the infinitive *to eat*.]

ADJECTIVE: Raisins and fresh fruit are good snacks **to eat instead of chips**. [The infinitive phrase is an adjective modifying *snacks*. The adverb phrase *instead of chips* modifies the infinitive *to eat*.]

ADVERB: Almost everyone is proud **to maintain a healthy weight**. [The infinitive phrase is an adverb modifying the adjective *proud*. The noun *weight* is the direct object of the infinitive *to maintain*.]

Exercise   Underline the infinitive or infinitive phrase in each sentence in the following paragraphs. On the line provided after each sentence, tell whether the infinitive is used as a noun *(N)*, an adjective *(ADJ)*, or an adverb *(ADV)*.

EXAMPLE: [1] When we met, June and I decided <u>to be friends</u>.   *N*

[1] After school, June and I like to walk home together. _____ [2] Usually, we go to my house or her house to listen to tapes. _____ [3] Sometimes I get up to dance to the music, but June never does. _____ [4] When a good song is playing, it's hard to sit still.

_____ [5] June finally told me that she had never learned to dance. _____

[6] "Do you want to learn some steps?" I asked. _____

[7] "I'm ready to try," she answered. _____

[8] I decided to start with some simple steps. _____ [9] After doing my best to teach her for three weeks, I finally gave up. _____ [10] It's a good thing that June doesn't plan to become a dancer. _____

Name _____ Date _____ Class _____

Appositives and Appositive Phrases

An **appositive** is a noun or a pronoun placed beside another noun or pronoun to identify or explain it.

Appositives are often set off by commas. But if an appositive is needed for meaning or is closely related to the word it refers to, no commas are necessary.

The soldier **Andrew Jackson** was elected president. [The noun *Andrew Jackson* identifies the noun *soldier*. The appositive tells *which soldier*.]

Jackson wanted a new policy for Native Americans, **one** with separate lands for the American Indians. [The pronoun *one* refers to the noun *policy*.]

An **appositive phrase** consists of an appositive and its modifiers. An appositive phrase is always set off by commas.

President Monroe, **an earlier president,** had hoped to establish a similar policy. [The adjectives *an* and *earlier* modify the appositive *president*.]

The Fox people, **one of the Midwestern nations,** fought bravely. [The adjective phrase *of the Midwestern nations* modifies the appositive *one*.]

Exercise   Underline the appositives and appositive phrases in the following sentences.

EXAMPLE: 1. In our own time, more than one hundred years later, we can still see the effects of Jackson's policy.

1. The Battle of Bad Axe, a fight between the Sauk Nation and the U.S. government, took place in 1832.

2. The chief of the Sauks, Black Hawk, led the Indian forces.

3. The Seminole chief, Osceola, also led his people in battle.

4. His fight, the most successful American Indian opposition in the United States, was aided by runaway slaves.

5. Chief Joseph, leader of the Nez Perce, acted with dignity.

6. His force, only three hundred warriors, defended the entire group.

7. On a 1,300-mile trek to Canada, a long and difficult journey, the army attacked.

8. Little Big Horn, the site of Custer's defeat, is famous.

9. A fearless leader of the Sioux, Chief Crazy Horse, was captured.

10. Sitting Bull, another one of the Sioux leaders, fled to Canada.

SENTENCES

Chapter 6: Phrases

◆ WORKSHEET 8 ◆ *Review*

Exercise A   The short blank in each sentence below shows where you can add a prepositional phrase. On the line following each sentence, write a prepositional phrase that could be used to complete the sentence.

EXAMPLE: 1. Young Mateo had always dreamed _____ .
              of having his own horse

1. _____ Mateo's parents bought him a new pony.

   _____

2. The pony had black patches _____ .

   _____

3. So Mateo said _____ ,"Let's call the pony Salt and Pepper."

   _____

4. Mateo's father helped his son into the saddle, and Mateo rode _____ .

   _____

5. Then they led the pony _____ and gave it some fresh hay and a bucket of water.

   _____

Exercise B   Underline each prepositional phrase in the following paragraph. In the space above the line, label each phrase an adjective phrase *(ADJ)* or an adverb phrase *(ADV)*. If a prepostional phrase contains another phrase, identify each phrase separately.

                                      ADV   ADJ
EXAMPLE: [1] Through old journals, we have learned much about the
              pioneers.

[1] Few of us appreciate the determination of the pioneers who traveled west. [2] The word *travel* comes from the French word *travailler,* which means "to work," and the pioneers definitely worked hard. [3] A typical day's journey began long before dawn. [4] On the trip westward, people rode in wagons. [5] During the day the wagon train traveled slowly over the mountains and across plains and deserts. [6] Each evening at dusk, the horses were unhitched from the wagons, and tents were pitched around campfires. [7] The travelers often established a temporary camp down in a valley for protection from the harsh winter weather. [8] Life in these camps was hard—food was often scarce, and many people never recovered from the hardships. [9] The pioneers who did survive by sheer determination usually continued their journey. [10] When the journey ended, these people worked hard to settle an untamed land and make homes for their families.

Chapter 6, Worksheet 8, continued

Exercise C   Each of the following sentences contains at least one verbal or verbal phrase. Underline each verbal or verbal phrase. Then identify it as a *gerund*, a *gerund phrase*, an *infinitive*, an *infinitive phrase*, a *participle*, or a *participial phrase*.

EXAMPLE: 1. <u>Visiting Cahokia Mounds State Historic Site in Illinois</u> is a
wonderful experience. *gerund phrase*

1. The Cahokia were a Native American people who built a highly
developed civilization in North America more than one
thousand years ago.   _____

2. Noting the importance of the Cahokia, the United Nations
Educational, Scientific, and Cultural Organization (UNESCO) set
aside Cahokia Mounds as a World Heritage Site.   _____

3. After studying the site, archaeologists were able to make a sketch
of the ancient city.   _____

4. The city was destroyed long ago, but the remaining traces of it
show how huge it must have been.   _____

5. This thriving community had a population of about twenty
thousand sometime between A.D. 700 and A.D. 1500.   _____

6. The people chose or were required to build their houses mostly
inside the stockade wall.   _____

7. It's still possible to see many of the earthen mounds.   _____

8. The historic site includes about seventy preserved mounds,
which were used mainly for ceremonial activities.   _____

9. Seeing the one-hundred-foot-high Monk's Mound is exciting.   _____

10. The mound was built as the place for the city's ruler to live and
to govern.   _____

Exercise D   Underline all the verbals and appositives in the sentences in the following paragraph. In the space above the line, label each one as an appositive *(APP)*, an infinitive *(INF)*, a gerund *(GER)*, or a participle *(PART)*.

EXAMPLE: 1. My little brother <u>Shawn</u> tried <u>to demonstrate</u> his <u>skating</u>
ability, but his fancy moves put an end to his <u>playing</u> for

a while.

1. Instead of falling on the soft ground, Shawn managed to hit right on the sidewalk.

2. The concrete, broken and crumbling, cut him in several places on his legs and elbows.

3. We heard his piercing wail all the way up at our house, and my mother and I

rushed to see what had happened.

4. By the time we got to him, the cuts had already started bleeding, and he was

struggling to get his skates off.

SENTENCES

Chapter 6, Worksheet 8, continued

5. Bending down, Mom pulled off the skates and dabbed at the seeping red cuts and scrapes.

6. Shawn, a brave little boy usually, could not keep from crying.

7. Mom carried Shawn to the house, and I followed with his skates, scratched and scraped almost as badly as he was.

8. After cleaning Shawn's cuts, Mom decided to take him to the emergency clinic.

9. The doctor, a young intern, said that she would have to close one of the cuts with stitches.

10. When we got home, Mom said that she hoped Shawn had learned to be more careful, but knowing Shawn, I doubt it.

Chapter 7: Clauses

Independent and Subordinate Clauses

A **clause** is a group of words that contains a verb and its subject and is used as part of a sentence. Every clause has a subject and a verb. However, not every clause expresses a complete thought.

SENTENCE: When I come home, I do my chores.

CLAUSE: When **I come** home [incomplete thought]

CLAUSE: **I do** my chores [complete thought]

There are two kinds of clauses: the *independent clause* and the *subordinate clause*. An **independent** (or **main**) **clause** expresses a complete thought and can stand by itself as a sentence.

INDEPENDENT CLAUSE: A hawk flew overhead.

A **subordinate** (or **dependent**) **clause** does not express a complete thought and cannot stand alone as a sentence. A word such as *although, because, since, that, what, which, who*, or *whom* signals the beginning of a subordinate clause.

that I heard   **what** they said   **since** you knew   **whom** you've met

Exercise A   On the line before each sentence, write *IC* if the italicized words form an independent clause. Write *SC* if the italicized words form a subordinate clause.

EXAMPLE: __*SC*__ 1. Do you know *who Sojourner Truth was*?

_____ 1. *She was an African American* who spoke about women's rights in 1852.

_____ 2. Her speech, *which is logical and humorous*, is called "Ain't I a Woman?"

_____ 3. Although she gave her speech unprepared, *Truth defeated arguments for male superiority*.

_____ 4. One man had said that women were inferior *because they always needed men's help*.

_____ 5. Truth pointed out *that she had always worked alongside men without any help*; "Ain't I a woman?" she asked.

Exercise B   On the lines provided, add independent clauses to these subordinate clauses to express complete thoughts.

EXAMPLE: 1. Before my sister was born, <u>we lived in Maine</u> .

1. Because I enjoy reading, _____ .

2. When you meet my mother, _____ .

3. If I could be anything, _____ .

4. Before he could utter another word, _____ .

5. After the plans have been drawn up, _____ .

SENTENCES

Name _____ Date _____ Class _____

Subjects and Verbs in Independent Clauses

An independent clause has a subject and a verb. Two or more independent clauses can appear in a single sentence.

s   v   s   v

In the late 1700's, a **famine hit** Ireland, and many Irish **people moved** to the United States.

Exercise A Draw one line under the subject and two lines under the verb in each independent clause. (Hint: Find the verb first. Remember that the verb may contain a main verb and one or more helping verbs. Then look for the subject of the verb. Ignore prepositional phrases such as *of immigrants*.)

1. The United States is a country of immigrants.

2. Many people have come to the United States from Asia and Latin America.

3. In the eighteenth and nineteenth centuries, thousands came from Scotland and Ireland.

4. The Scots-Irish brought with them their music and their way of speaking.

5. Many settled in the south-central part of the United States.

6. Today, in the hills of Kentucky or West Virginia, you can still hear some of the Scots-Irish songs.

7. One singer of those old ballads is Jeanie Ritchie.

8. Audiences love Ritchie's version of "Barbara Allen," and they love the instruments that she plays—the zither and the dulcimer.

9. Every group of immigrants brings its own special treasures to our shores.

10. Scots-Irish music is just one example.

Exercise B Complete each of the following groups of words by adding an independent clause. Underline the subject of your clause once and the verb or verb phrase twice.

1. Snow can be fun to play in, but _____

2. If I were president for a day, _____

3. When it's rainy outside, _____

4. Cheetahs are fierce, and _____

5. You can get a ride with us, or _____

Chapter 7: Clauses

Subjects and Verbs in Subordinate Clauses

A subordinate clause has a subject and a verb. However, the meaning of a subordinate clause is complete only when the clause is attached to an independent clause. Sometimes the word that begins a subordinate clause is the subject of the clause.

>   S   V
> **If wishes were horses,** then beggars might ride.

>   S   V
> That is a line **that comes from a Mother Goose rhyme.**

Exercise A   Draw a line under the subordinate clause in each of the following sentences. Then circle the subject, and draw a second line under the verb of the subordinate clause.

> EXAMPLE: 1. Did you learn any rhymes when (you) were young?

1. Before the tales of Raffi became popular, English and American children learned Mother Goose rhymes.

2. England is the country where Mother Goose rhymes originated.

3. The people who composed the Mother Goose rhymes lived hundreds of years ago.

4. These stories and rhymes became popular because they were fun and easy to learn.

5. If a rhyme was really funny or interesting, children would sing it.

6. One rhyme that children liked a lot was "Baa, Baa, Black Sheep."

7. Some people think that "Baa, Baa, Black Sheep" was actually a protest against taxes.

8. In the rhyme, the three bags of wool that the sheep produces are given away.

9. Because the sheep had only three bags of wool, he's left with nothing.

10. Since the time that the rhyme was invented, its secret message has been lost.

Exercise B   On the line provided, finish each sentence below by adding a subordinate clause to the independent clause. Draw one line under the subject and two lines under the verb or verb phrase of each clause.

> EXAMPLE: 1. I crossed the street *when the light turned green* .

1. Everyone will be happy _____ .

2. I will give my report today _____ .

3. We will stay for dinner _____ .

4. Can you tell me _____ ?

5. Do you remember _____ ?

SENTENCES

Chapter 7: Clauses

The Adjective Clause

An **adjective clause** is a subordinate clause that modifies a noun or a pronoun. Unlike an adjective or an adjective phrase, an adjective clause contains a verb and its subject. An adjective clause usually follows the word it modifies and tells *which one* or *what kind*.

ADJECTIVE: a **blue** hat

ADJECTIVE PHRASE: the boy **in a blue hat**

ADJECTIVE CLAUSE: the boy **who is wearing a blue hat**

An adjective clause is usually introduced by a **relative pronoun** *(that, which, who, whom, whose)* or a **relative adverb** *(when, where)*. A relative pronoun relates an adjective clause to the word the clause modifies. Sometimes a relative pronoun is preceded by a preposition that is part of the adjective clause. A relative pronoun also has a function in the subordinate (adjective) clause.

Laura was the person **to whom the letter was addressed**. [The relative pronoun *whom* relates the subordinate (adjective) clause to the word *person*.]

This is the question **that interested me**. [*That* functions as the subject of the subordinate (adjective) clause.]

Exercise Underline the adjective clause in each of the following sentences. On the line provided, give the relative pronoun or relative adverb and the word that the pronoun or adverb refers to.

EXAMPLE: 1. Crispus Attucks was an African American patriot <u>who was killed during the Boston Massacre</u>. *who—patriot*

1. Coco Chanel is the woman for whom the perfume is named. _____

2. Here is the concert hall where we heard the great cello player Pablo Casals. _____

3. Tomorrow is the day when we agreed to meet. _____

4. Ella Fitzgerald, who started singing in New York City, is famous throughout the world. _____

5. The English playwright Christopher Marlowe wrote of Helen of Troy, "Was this the face that launched a thousand ships?" _____

6. Anita was one of the sopranos who sang in the chorus. _____

7. In the play *My Fair Lady*, Eliza Doolittle, a poor flower seller, becomes a woman whom everyone admires. _____

8. The Kinderhook was the creek in which we found the shells. _____

9. Janet Flanner, who wrote dispatches from Paris, used the pen name Genêt. _____

10. The astronauts, for whom travel in a space shuttle is always a possibility, must always keep in shape. _____

Chapter 7: Clauses

WORKSHEET 5

The Adverb Clause

An **adverb clause** is a subordinate clause that modifies a verb, an adjective, or an adverb. Unlike an adverb or an adverb phrase, an adverb clause has a subject and a verb.

ADVERB: Call me **soon**.   ADVERB PHRASE: Call me **in ten minutes**.

ADVERB CLAUSE: Call me **as soon as you can**.

An adverb clause tells *where, when, how, why, to what extent,* or *under what condition*.

When the pot boiled over, the cook shrieked. [The adverb clause modifies the verb *shrieked*, telling *when* the cook shrieked.]

The dirt road was muddy **where the trucks had been driving**. [The adverb clause modifies the adjective *muddy*, telling *where*.]

Kim can throw a baseball farther **than I can**. [The adverb clause modifies the adverb *farther*, telling *to what extent*.]

When an adverb clause begins a sentence, the clause is followed by a comma. An adverb clause is introduced by a **subordinating conjunction**—a word that shows the relationship between the adverb clause and the word or words that the clause modifies.

although	because	so that	when	as	if
than	where	as soon as	since	unless	while

Exercise   Underline the adverb clause in each of the following sentences. Draw another line under the subordinating conjunction. On the line provided, write whether the clause tells *when, where, how, why, to what extent,* or *under what condition*.

EXAMPLE: 1. You can learn a lot about sea creatures <u>if you read this book</u>.
          under what condition

1. A lobster fears few enemies because it has a hard, protective shell. _____

2. If an octopus is attacked, it can spray a jet of ink at its opponent. _____

3. When an eel feels threatened, it withdraws into its hiding place. _____

4. The sting of a jellyfish can be dangerous unless the sting is treated. _____

5. A pufferfish blows itself up like a balloon until its attacker swims away. _____

6. A shark can swim faster than a human can. _____

7. Sea turtles don't live as long as they used to. _____

8. At night, a coral reef is more beautiful than you can imagine. _____

9. Although they look similar, sea horses have nothing in common with horses. _____

10. Ice fish live where temperatures often drop below freezing. _____

SENTENCES

Chapter 7: Clauses

The Noun Clause

A **noun clause** is a subordinate clause used as a noun. A noun clause may be used as a subject, a complement (predicate nominative, direct object, indirect object), or an object of a preposition.

SUBJECT: **That the storm did some damage** is an understatement.

PREDICATE NOMINATIVE: The conclusion of the movie was **just what I had expected.**

DIRECT OBJECT: The speaker told us **what could be done about acid rain.**

INDIRECT OBJECT: Leuwana sent **whoever asked her for one** a postcard.

OBJECT OF A PREPOSITION: A prize was offered to **whoever saw land first.**

A noun clause often begins with one of these introductory words: *that, what, whatever, which, whichever, who, whoever, whom,* or *whomever.* The word that introduces a noun clause often has another function within the clause.

No one knows **who discovered America.** [The introductory word *who* is the subject of the verb *discovered.* The entire noun clause is the direct object of the verb *knows.*]

Exercise   Underline the noun clause in each of the following sentences. On the line provided, tell whether the noun clause is a *subject,* a *predicate nominative,* a *direct object,* an *indirect object,* or an *object of a preposition.*

EXAMPLE: 1. We couldn't find <u>what was making the noise in the car.</u>
direct object

1. Whatever you decide will be fine with us. _____

2. We will show whoever wants to go the bats under the bridge. _____

3. Stuart is looking for whoever owns that red bicycle. _____

4. Checking our supplies, we discovered that we had forgotten the flour. _____

5. No, these results are not what we had planned. _____

6. Give whoever wants one a copy of this recipe. _____

7. That I like polar bears is no secret. _____

8. Perform the chores in whatever order you prefer. _____

9. Reading is what I love to do on rainy days. _____

10. Mai realized that she had lost her jacket. _____

Chapter 7: Clauses

WORKSHEET 7 *Review*

Exercise A On the line provided, identify the italicized clause in each of the following sentences. Write *IC* for an independent clause or *SC* for a subordinate clause. Then underline the subject of each italicized clause once and the verb or verb phrase twice.

EXAMPLE: ___SC___ 1. My report is about the plague *that spread across Europe in the fourteenth century*.

_____ 1. *In 1347, trading ships arrived at the Mediterranean island of Sicily from Caffa*, which was a port city on the Black Sea.

_____ 2. *When the sailors went ashore*, many of them carried a strange illness.

_____ 3. No medicine could save the stricken sailors, *who died quickly and painfully*.

_____ 4. *Since it originated in the Black Sea area*, the plague was called the Black Death.

_____ 5. *People* who traveled between cities in Europe *carried the disease with them*.

_____ 6. *Millions of people died* as the plague spread from Sicily across Europe.

_____ 7. On maps, historians trace *how quickly the plague spread*.

_____ 8. The terrified survivors thought *that the world was coming to an end*.

_____ 9. *No one is sure of the total number of people* who died from the dreaded plague.

_____ 10. Since medicine offers new ways for controlling plague, *the spread of this disease is unlikely today*.

Exercise B Underline the adjective clause in each sentence below. Draw another line under the relative pronoun or relative adverb. Then circle the word that the relative pronoun or adverb refers to.

EXAMPLE: 1. One (mountain) that is almost as tall as Mount Everest is K2.

1. The 1960's was a time when great strides were made in civil rights.

2. Every day, the senator rides the train that runs from Delaware to Washington, D.C.

3. Broccoli, which is my favorite vegetable, is high in vitamin A.

4. The mayor, whose car was recently towed, owes a hundred dollars in traffic fines.

5. Mr. Cohen, who conducts the chorus at our school, collects songbooks from the 1800's.

Exercise C Underline the adverb clause in each of the following sentences. Draw a second line under the subordinating conjunction that introduces the clause. On the line provided, write whether the clause tells *how, when, where, why, to what extent,* or *under what condition.*

EXAMPLE: 1. No one has proved the existence of the Loch Ness monster, although many people believe in its existence.

under what condition

SENTENCES

Chapter 7, Worksheet 7, continued

1. When the pot boiled over, the oatmeal spilled onto the stove. _____

2. It has been raining since I arrived. _____

3. Where there is smoke, there is fire. _____

4. Because President Kennedy was killed, Lyndon Johnson was
   sworn in as president. _____

5. While the polar bears walked through the town, the residents
   stayed inside their houses. _____

Exercise D   Underline the noun clause in each of the following sentences. Then draw a
second line under the introductory word.

> EXAMPLE: 1. No one knows <u>who</u> <u>won the election</u>.

1. What the actual story is, is anyone's guess.

2. The traveler was grateful to whoever had put up the road sign.

3. Jessica is whom I would most like to invite.

4. Ms. Desai gave her students what supplies they needed.

5. You can send whomever you choose a card for Valentine's Day.

Exercise E   Each sentence in the following paragraph contains a subordinate clause.
Underline each subordinate clause. On the line provided, identify the clause as an *adjective
clause*, an *adverb clause*, or a *noun clause*.

> EXAMPLE: [1] The Museum of Appalachia, <u>which is in Norris, Tennessee,</u>
>   is a re-created pioneer village.
>
>   1. *adjective clause*

　　　[1] If you've ever wanted to step into the past, you'll like this museum. [2] You
can see many pioneer tools that are still used at the museum. [3] For example,
men split shingles with tools that were used by their fathers. [4] Other men show
how plowing was done before the development of modern equipment. [5] I think
that the 250,000 pioneer tools and other items on display will amaze you.
[6] What some visitors like to do is to tour the village's log buildings and then
take a rest. [7] While they're resting, they can often find some mountain music to
listen to. [8] I noticed the different instruments that the musicians were playing.
[9] The fiddler performed at the museum's Homecoming, which is a yearly fall
event. [10] At Homecoming, you might even meet the museum's founder, John
Rice Irwin, who grew up in the Appalachian Mountains.

1. _____   6. _____

2. _____   7. _____

3. _____   8. _____

4. _____   9. _____

5. _____   10. _____

Chapter 8: Sentences

WORKSHEET 1

Sentences and Sentence Fragments

A **sentence** is a group of words that expresses a complete thought. A sentence begins with a capital letter and ends with a period, a question mark, or an exclamation point.

Whales sing to one another**.**   Listen**.**

Have you heard their songs**?**   How beautiful they sound**!**

When a group of words looks like a sentence but does not express a complete thought, it is a **sentence fragment**.

SENTENCE FRAGMENT: The store on the corner. [This is not a complete thought. What about the store on the corner?]

SENTENCE: The store on the corner has a parrot in the window.

SENTENCE FRAGMENT: Before moving to New York City. [This thought is not complete. Who moved to New York City? What happened before that?]

SENTENCE: Before moving to New York City, we lived in Puerto Rico.

SENTENCE FRAGMENT: Although he had studied law. [The thought is not complete. Although he had studied law, what happened?]

SENTENCE: Although he had studied law, he became an archaeologist.

Exercise   On the line provided, tell whether each group of words is a *sentence* or a *sentence fragment*.

EXAMPLES: [1] One of the best-known women in United States history is Sacagawea. [2] A member of the Lemhi band of the Shoshones.

1. *sentence*
2. *sentence fragment*

[1] She is famous for her role as interpreter for the Lewis and Clark expedition. [2] Which was seeking the Northwest Passage. [3] In 1800, the Lemhis had encountered a war party of the Hidatsa. [4] Who captured some of the Lemhis, including Sacagawea. [5] Later, with Charbonneau, her French Canadian husband, and their two-month-old son. [6] Sacagawea joined the Lewis and Clark expedition in what is now North Dakota. [7] Her knowledge of many languages. [8] Enabled the explorers to communicate with various peoples. [9] Sacagawea also searched for plants that were safe to eat. [10] And once saved valuable instruments during a storm.

1. _____   6. _____

2. _____   7. _____

3. _____   8. _____

4. _____   9. _____

5. _____   10. _____

SENTENCES

Chapter 8: Sentences

 **WORKSHEET 2** *Subject and Predicate*

A sentence consists of two parts: a **subject** and a **predicate**.

    SUBJECT   PREDICATE
    Baton Rouge | is my hometown.

A **subject** tells whom or what the sentence is about. The **predicate** tells something about the subject.

    SUBJECT   PREDICATE
    A pair of doves | sat in the window.

A group of words that doesn't have a subject, doesn't have a verb, or doesn't express a complete thought is a sentence fragment.

    A great white shark. [The verb is missing.]

    Was spotted near the Channel Islands. [The subject is missing.]

    When I was learning about sharks. [This isn't a complete thought.]

Exercise: Revising   Each numbered item below contains two sentence fragments. Each fragment is missing either a subject or a predicate. The first fragment in each item has been corrected for you. Study each correction. Then rewrite the second fragment to make it into a complete sentence.

Fragments	Corrections
1. swimming in the bay	Toshio and his friends went swimming in the bay.
a shark heading toward them	_____
2. the fin on the shark's back	The fin on the shark's back plowed through the water.
the people on the shore	_____
3. opened its terrible jaws	The huge shark opened its terrible jaws.
swam toward shore with all his might	_____
4. Frightened and trembling, the boys	Frightened and trembling, the boys reached the shore.
Realizing that they were safe, the boys	_____
5. closed the beach	The lifeguard closed the beach.
sent the people home	_____

Chapter 8: Sentences

WORKSHEET 3 | Complete Subject and Simple Subject

To find the subject of a sentence, ask *Who?* or *What?* before the predicate.

The balloon suddenly burst. [What burst? The balloon burst. *The balloon* is the subject.]

Usually the subject comes before the predicate. Sometimes, however, the subject may appear elsewhere in the sentence.

At the edge of the forest crouched a wolf. [What crouched at the edge of the forest? A wolf crouched there.]

Last night, Kyle played his new song for us. [Who played a new song? Kyle did.]

Can you dance? [Who can dance? You can.]

The **complete subject** consists of all the words needed to tell whom or what a sentence is about.

A sudden gust of wind | blew the ball out of bounds.

A **simple subject** is the main word in the complete subject.

A sudden **gust** of wind | blew the ball out of bounds.

NOTE: The simple subject of a sentence is *never* part of a prepositional phrase.

Some of the artists use charcoal. [The complete subject is *some of the artists*. The simple subject is *some*. The prepositional phrase *of the artists* modifies *some*.]

Exercise For each of the following sentences, underline the complete subject. Then draw another line under the simple subject.

EXAMPLE: 1. Traditional Eskimo dress includes the parka and mukluks.

1. The long journey would have been impossible without snowshoes.

2. Many of the native people of North America use snowshoes.

3. The study of footwear is Shawn's hobby.

4. The ancient Greeks must have worn sandals with very long laces.

5. These sandals were laced almost up to the knee.

6. Some Native Americans have been wearing moccasins for centuries.

7. The native people of Nepal are often seen in slippers with pointed toes.

8. Cowhands in Argentina have spurs on their leather boots.

9. Some of them are also seen in leather pants.

10. Most of the ancient Egyptians went barefoot.

SENTENCES

Chapter 8: Sentences

Complete Predicate and Simple Predicate

A **complete predicate** consists of a verb and all the words that describe the verb and complete its meaning.

    Amanda **draws beautiful pictures of horses**.

Sometimes the complete predicate appears at the beginning of a sentence.

    On the wall in the dining room hangs one of my favorite paintings.

Part of the predicate may appear on one side of the subject and the rest on the other side.

    In the hall, a large painting of an Arabian stallion **greets visitors**.

A **simple predicate,** or **verb,** is the main word or group of words in the complete predicate.

    Its large, dark eyes **seem** intelligent and almost alive.

    Have you **seen** it?

Exercise For each of the following sentences, underline the complete predicate. Then draw another line under the verb. Keep in mind that parts of the complete predicate may come before and after the complete subject.

          EXAMPLE: 1. A ton and a half of groceries <u>may seem like a big order for a family of five</u>.

1. Such a big order is possible in the village of Pang.

2. This small village lies near the Arctic Circle.

3. The people of Pang receive their groceries once a year.

4. A supply ship visits Pang only during a short time each summer.

5. In spring, families order their year's supply of groceries by mail.

6. A few months later, the huge order arrives in Pang.

7. The people store the groceries in their homes.

8. Frozen food belongs outdoors in this climate.

9. Too costly for most residents is the air-freight charge for shipping groceries to Pang.

10. Villagers also rely on hunting and fishing to obtain much of their food.

Chapter 8: Sentences

WORKSHEET 5 *The Verb Phrase*

A simple predicate may be a one-word verb, or it may be a verb phrase. A **verb phrase** consists of a main verb and its helping verbs.

>The recital **was** wonderful.
>
>**Did** your whole family **attend**?
>
>My sister's performance **had been scheduled** last.
>
>The singers **must have been practicing** all week.

The words *not* and *never*, which are frequently used with verbs, are not part of a verb phrase. Both of these words are adverbs.

>The vegetables **should** not **have been planted** so late.
>
>They **will** never **produce** much in such hot weather.

Exercise   For each of the following sentences, underline the verb or verb phrase.

>EXAMPLE: 1. <u>Have</u> you <u>read</u> any of John Steinbeck's works?

1. He has given us *The Grapes of Wrath*, one of the greatest novels of this century.

2. In his novel Steinbeck describes the lives of farmers during the Great Depression.

3. In one chapter a turtle crossing a road is used as a symbol.

4. Few writers have so ably shown the heroism of ordinary people in extraordinary times as Steinbeck.

5. In fact, the novel was made into a movie.

6. Did you see it?

7. Have you also seen the movie version of Steinbeck's novel *East of Eden*?

8. Perhaps you may have seen an adaptation of Steinbeck's novel *Of Mice and Men*.

9. In the 1950's he was known for writing screenplays.

10. In *Travels with Charley* he has described a trip across country with his pet poodle.

11. These works and more would earn him the 1962 Nobel Prize for literature.

12. Steinbeck did not want to accept the award.

13. To him, the award might signal the end of his writing career.

14. Sure enough, after the award, he would never publish again.

15. Have other writers had this problem?

SENTENCES

Chapter 8: Sentences

WORKSHEET 6 | # Compound Subjects and Compound Verbs

A **compound subject** consists of two or more connected simple subjects that have the same verb. The usual connecting word is *and* or *or*. A **compound verb** consists of two or more verbs that have the same subject. The usual connecting word is *and, or,* or *but*.

> **Vegetables** and whole **grains** are good for your heart.

> Sabrena **swims** or **runs** every other day.

If both the simple subject and the verb are compound, each subject goes with each verb.

> **Larry** and **I had collected** and **stacked** old newspapers for the recycling truck.
> [Larry had collected and stacked, and I had collected and stacked.]

Exercise A   Underline the compound part in each sentence below. Then write *CS* if the compound part is a compound subject or *CV* if the compound part is a compound verb.

> EXAMPLE: ___CS___   1. Are your <u>health</u> and <u>well-being</u> important to you?

_____ 1. According to scientists, fat and cholesterol are both killers.

_____ 2. Hamburgers and milkshakes contain large amounts of both.

_____ 3. Therefore, you shouldn't eat or drink such fast foods too often.

_____ 4. An apple or a carrot is more healthful than these fast foods and just as tasty.

_____ 5. In the future, stop and think about the health effects of your meals.

Exercise B: Revising   Combine each pair of sentences by writing one sentence with a compound subject or a compound verb. When you create a sentence with a compound subject, make sure that the other words in the sentence agree in number with the subject. (Notice that in the example answer below both the verb, *are*, and the common noun, *sites*, agree in number with the plural subject.)

> EXAMPLE: 1. Manassas is a Civil War battle site. Fredericksburg is too.
> *Manassas and Fredericksburg are Civil War battle sites.*

1. Maples grow well in this area. Birches grow well too. _____

_____

2. Rita Moreno sings beautifully. She dances beautifully as well. _____

_____

3. The emu is a flightless bird. So is the kiwi. _____

_____

4. Kwanita designed a new kind of kite. Then she built it. _____

_____

5. Polar bears live in cold climates. Arctic foxes do also. _____

_____

Chapter 8: Sentences

Review

Exercise A: Revising   Read each group of words below. If a word group is a sentence, write *complete sentence* on the line provided. If a word group is a sentence fragment, correct it by adding words to make a complete sentence.

EXAMPLE: 1. Marched for five hours.

The members of the band marched for five hours.

1. Should not be left alone under any circumstances.

_____

2. In the middle of the vacant lot down the street is a basketball court.

_____

3. Pairs of agile dancers in elegant evening clothes.

_____

4. Looked mysterious to us.

_____

5. The best player in the state.

_____

Exercise B   For each of the following sentences, underline the complete subject once and the complete predicate twice.

EXAMPLE: 1. <u>Have</u> <u>you</u> <u>ever seen a laser?</u>

1. The laser can perform many startling operations.

2. It can drill a diamond, carry information, and measure the distance to the moon.

3. Eye surgeons and communications engineers use lasers.

4. Light from a laser is extremely bright.

5. Perhaps in this mysterious beam lies the answer to cheap power.

Exercise C   For each of the following sentences, underline the simple subject once and the verb or verb phrase twice.

EXAMPLE: [1] In Greek mythology, <u>Medusa</u> <u>was</u> a horrible monster.

[1] On Medusa's head grew snakes instead of hair. [2] According to Greek myth, a glance at Medusa would turn a mortal into stone. [3] However, one proud mortal named Perseus went in search of Medusa. [4] Fortunately, he received help from the goddess Athena and the god Hermes. [5] From Athena, Perseus accepted a shiny shield. [6] With Hermes as his guide, Perseus soon found Medusa. [7] He knew about Medusa's power. [8] Therefore, he

SENTENCES

Chapter 8, Worksheet 7, continued

did not look directly at her. [9] Instead, he saw her reflection in the shiny shield. [10] Many

paintings celebrate Perseus' victory over the evil Medusa.

Exercise D Underline each compound part in the following sentences. Underline a
compound subject once. Underline a compound verb twice.

> EXAMPLE: 1. <u>Legends</u> and <u>folk tales</u> <u>have been repeated</u> and
> <u>enjoyed</u> throughout the Americas.

1. The Chorotega people raised families and made their homes in Nicoya, Costa Rica,
   hundreds of years ago.

2. One Chorotega folk tale or legend tells the story of the Chorotegan treasure and
   Princess Nosara.

3. Chireno warriors landed, according to the story, on the Nicoya Peninsula and
   attacked the Chorotegas.

4. The Chorotegan men and women reacted quickly.

5. Princess Nosara grabbed the treasure and ran to her friend's house for help.

6. Nosara and he took a bow and some arrows and fled into the woods.

7. All night, the princess and her friend ran from the enemy and at last reached a
   river.

8. The brave girl dashed into the mountains alone, hid the treasure, and returned to
   the river.

9. Chireno warriors attacked shortly after her return, however, and killed the princess
   and her friend.

10. The murderous Chirenos searched for the treasure but never found it.

Chapter 9: Complements

 **Recognizing Complements**

A **complement** is a word or a group of words that completes the meaning of a verb.

         S   V   C

NOUN: Steve gave a **party**.

         S   V   C

PRONOUN: Helen invited **them**.

         S   V   C

ADJECTIVE: The meeting was **long**.

An adverb is never a complement. A complement is never in a prepositional phrase.

COMPLEMENT: Mia ordered a **burrito** and a **salad**.

ADVERB: Mia ate **quickly**.

OBJECT OF A PREPOSITION: Mia ate in the **cafeteria**.

A sentence may contain more than one complement.

     Rafael told **us** a **joke**.

Exercise A   In each item below, label the subject and verb by writing *S* and *V* above the sentence. Underline the complement.

                   S   V

EXAMPLE: 1.   Sandra Cisneros wrote *The House on Mango Street*.

1. In the book, Esperanza tells us the events in her life.

2. Her name means "hope."

3. Esperanza wants a more exotic name.

4. She would choose "Zeze the X" or "Lisandra."

Exercise B   Write a sentence by adding a complement to each subject-verb set.

         EXAMPLE: 1.   clerk   sold

                  The clerk sold us a new bicycle tire.

1. men   asked

_____

2. days   are

_____

3. Pam   sent

_____

4. runner   seemed

_____

SENTENCES

Chapter 9: Complements

WORKSHEET 2 · *Direct Objects*

A **direct object** is a noun or a pronoun that receives the action of the verb or that shows the result of the action. A direct object tells *what* or *whom* after a transitive verb. A direct object may be compound.

DIRECT OBJECT: She sailed the **boat**. [The noun *boat* receives the action of the transitive verb *sailed* and tells *what* she sailed.]

COMPOUND DIRECT OBJECT: The board elected **Sanford** and **me**. [The compound direct object *Sanford* and *me* tells *whom* the board elected.]

A direct object can never follow a linking verb, such as *be, seem,* or *feel,* because a linking verb does not express action. Also, a direct object is never part of a prepositional phrase.

LINKING VERB: My grandfather **has become** a citizen of the United States. [The verb *has become* does not express action. Therefore, it has no direct object.]

OBJECT OF A PREPOSITION: A mechanic worked on the plane's **engine**. [*Engine* is not the direct object of the verb *worked*. *Engine* is the object of the preposition *on*.]

Exercise A   On the lines provided, identify the direct object in each of the following sentences. If a sentence does not contain a direct object, write *none*.

EXAMPLE: 1. Sweet music poured from his harmonica. *none*

1. The researchers followed the birds' migration from Mexico to Canada.   _____

2. Mr. Ortega has grown a moustache.   _____

3. Thousands of catfish swirled in the holding pond.   _____

4. Did you see her performance on television?   _____

5. Stay there until I come back.   _____

Exercise B   On the line provided, label the verb in each of the following sentences as either a transitive verb *(T)* or a linking verb *(L)*. For each transitive verb, underline its direct object. (Remember, a direct object may be compound.)

EXAMPLE: __*T*__ 1. Did volunteers distribute <u>food</u> to the flood survivors?

_____ 1. The leading man wore a black cape and a hat with a large plume.

_____ 2. Is your mother a judge?

_____ 3. Recycling preserves the environment.

_____ 4. After the game the coach answered questions from the sports reporters.

_____ 5. For thirty years, he remained a sergeant in the Army.

Chapter 9: Complements

Indirect Objects

Another type of complement is the *indirect object*. An **indirect object** is a noun or a pronoun that comes between the verb and the direct object and tells *to what* or *to whom* or *for what* or *for whom* the action of the verb is done. Like a direct object, an indirect object may be compound.

> Grandmother made **Justin** a new coat. [The indirect object telling *for whom* Grandmother made the coat is *Justin*.]

> We gave the **living room** and the **kitchen** a new coat of paint. [The compound indirect object *living room* and *kitchen* tells *to what* we gave a coat of paint.]

Like a direct object, an indirect object helps to complete the meaning of a transitive verb. If a sentence has an indirect object, it always has a direct object also.

> Did you write **him** a **letter**? [The indirect object is *him*. The direct object is *letter*.]

Linking verbs do not have indirect objects. An indirect object, like a direct object, is never in a prepositional phrase.

> LINKING VERB: Gail **was** ready. [The linking verb *was* does not express action.]

> OBJECT OF A PREPOSITION: Gail threw the ball to **her**. [The pronoun *her* is the object of the preposition *to*.]

Exercise For each of the following sentences, underline the indirect object. Draw two lines under the direct object. [Note: Not every sentence has an indirect object.]

> EXAMPLE: 1. They gave us their solemn promise.

1. I gave my dog a bone.

2. Fran told Paco a secret.

3. Carlo bought a birthday gift for his brother.

4. My father told me a really funny joke.

5. Kim told Ertha the news.

6. They sent Tim and me on a wild-goose chase.

7. Gloria mailed the company a check yesterday.

8. The coach praised the students for their school spirit.

9. I gave my cousins some embroidered pillows for their new apartment.

10. Carly and Doreen taught themselves the importance of hard work.

Name _____ Date _____ Class _____

Predicate Nominatives and Predicate Adjectives

A **subject complement** completes the meaning of a linking verb and identifies or describes the subject. There are two kinds of subject complements—the *predicate nominative* and the *predicate adjective*. A **predicate nominative** is a noun or a pronoun that follows a linking verb and identifies the subject or refers to it. Predicate nominatives never appear in prepositional phrases. A predicate nominative may be compound.

> That house **is one** of my father's projects. [The pronoun *one* completes the meaning of the linking verb *is*.]

> He is a skilled **carpenter** and **mason**. [nouns—compound predicate nominative]

A **predicate adjective** is an adjective that follows a linking verb and describes the subject. A predicate adjective may be compound.

> The sky **seems threatening**. [The adjective *threatening* completes the meaning of the linking verb *seems*.]

> The infant got **tired** and **impatient**. [compound predicate adjective]

Some verbs, such as *look, grow,* and *feel,* may be used as either linking verbs or action verbs.

> In a few short years, the tree **grew** tall. [*Grew* links the adjective *tall* to the subject *tree*.]

> Every spring, the tree **grew** many new leaves. [*Grew* is an action verb followed by the direct object *leaves*.]

Exercise   On the lines provided, identify the linking verbs and the subject complements in the following sentences. Then, identify each complement as a predicate nominative *(PN)* or a predicate adjective *(PA)*. (Remember that a subject complement may be compound.)

> EXAMPLE: 1. The raincoat looked too short for me. *looked; short—PA*

1. I am the person who called you yesterday.   _____

2. Many public buildings in the East are proof of I. M. Pei's
   architectural skill.   _____

3. The downtown mall appeared especially busy today.   _____

4. My dog is playful, and he never seems tired.   _____

5. Sally Ride sounded excited and confident during the interview.   _____

6. The package felt too light for a book.   _____

7. These questions seem easier to me than those do.   _____

8. The singer's clothing became a style that her fans imitated.   _____

9. Some poems, such as "The Bells," are highly rhythmical.   _____

10. While the lioness hunted, the cubs remained still.   _____

Chapter 9: Complements

 **WORKSHEET 5** *Review*

Exercise A For the sentences in the following paragraph, underline each indirect object, and draw two lines under each direct object. [Note: Not every sentence has an indirect object.]

EXAMPLE: [1] The spring rodeo gives our <u>town</u> an exciting <u>weekend</u>.

[1] This year Ms. Pérez taught our class many interesting facts about rodeos. [2] She told us stories about the earliest rodeos, which took place more than a hundred years ago. [3] The word *rodeo*, she explained, means "roundup" in Spanish. [4] Ms. Pérez also showed us drawings and pictures of some well-known rodeo performers. [5] The Choctaw roper Clyde Burk especially caught our interest. [6] During Burk's career, the Rodeo Cowboys Association awarded him four world championships. [7] For years Burk entertained audiences with his roping skill. [8] He also bought and trained some of the best rodeo horses available. [9] We saw a picture of Burk on his horse Baldy. [10] The scars on Baldy's legs gave him his name.

Exercise B Each of the following sentences has at least one subject complement. On the lines provided, write each complement and identify it as a predicate nominative *(PN)* or a predicate adjective *(PA)*. (Remember that a subject complement may be compound.)

EXAMPLE: 1. All the food at the Spanish Club dinner was terrific.
terrific—PA

1. The tacos and Juan's fajitas seemed the most popular of the Mexican foods brought to the dinner.   _____

2. The *ensalada campesina*, a chickpea salad of Chile, was Rosalinda's contribution.   _____

3. The Ecuadorian tamales not only looked good but also tasted great.   _____

4. The baked fish fillets from Bolivia were spicy and quite appetizing.   _____

5. Peru is famous for its soups, and the shrimp soup was a winner.   _____

6. The noodles with mushroom sauce were a specialty of Paraguay.   _____

7. The Spanish cauliflower with garlic and onions was a treat but seemed too exotic for some students.   _____

8. However, the pan of *hallacas*, the national cornmeal dish of Venezuela, was soon empty.   _____

SENTENCES

Chapter 9, Worksheet 5, continued

9. *Arroz con coco,* or coconut rice, from Puerto Rico quickly became
the most requested dessert.   _____

10. After dinner all of us felt full and more knowledgeable about
foods from Spanish-speaking countries.   _____

Exercise C   Identify each verb in the following sentences as a transitive verb *(T)* or a
linking verb *(L).* Then identify each complement as a direct object *(DO),* an indirect object
(IO), a predicate nominative *(PN),* or a predicate adjective *(PA).* Remember that a
complement may be compound.

> EXAMPLE: 1. Because they want artistic freedom, many people from
> other countries become United States citizens.
> *want—T; freedom—DO; become—L; citizens—PN*

1. Gilberto Zaldivar's story is a good example.

_____

2. Zaldivar was an accountant and a community theater producer in Havana, Cuba,
in 1961.

_____

3. He became unhappy and frustrated with the Cuban government's control over the arts.

_____

4. So he left his job and his homeland and started a new life in New York City.

_____

5. The change brought Zaldivar many opportunities.

_____

6. It also gave audiences in the United States a new entertainment experience.

_____

7. Zaldivar was a co-founder of the *Repertorio Español* in 1968.

_____

8. This company quickly established a reputation as the country's best Spanish-
language theater troupe.

_____

9. Their productions were fresh and unfamiliar to audiences.

_____

10. Throughout the years, the company has performed numerous Spanish classics and
new plays.

_____

Name _____ Date _____ Class _____

 **WORKSHEET 1** | *Simple Sentences*

Sentences may be classified according to **structure**—the kinds and the number of clauses they contain. A **simple sentence** has one independent clause and no subordinate clauses. A simple sentence may have a compound subject, a compound verb or verb phrase, or both.

     S   S   V
Toy **cars** and **trucks littered** the carpet.

     S   V   V
The **pilot has called** the tower and **has requested** permission for a landing.

            S   S   V   V
More and more **men** and **women speak** and **write** in two languages.

Exercise A In each of the simple sentences below, underline the simple subject(s) once and the verb(s) or verb phrase(s) twice.

          EXAMPLE: 1. <u>Jogging</u> and <u>tennis</u> <u>are</u> fun.

1. Physical fitness is important to everyone.

2. William James, a famous Harvard psychologist, discovered a relationship between muscle tension and the emotions.

3. During World War II, Navy pilots used his technique of voluntary muscle relaxation.

4. Today, athletes and others learn this technique and practice it daily.

5. People have discovered the importance of good health practices.

6. Some have developed personal programs of exercise.

7. Tennis is one of the world's most popular sports.

8. A public park may have several tennis courts.

9. Of course, anyone can see the positive effects of exercise for the body.

10. Exercise also benefits the mind.

Exercise B: Revising Each of the following sentences contains a single subject and a single verb. Rewrite each sentence to make either the subject or the verb compound.

          EXAMPLE: 1. We planted grape hyacinth bulbs in the fall.
              My father and I planted grape hyacinth bulbs in the fall.

1. The colorful flowers had large blossoms.

_____

2. The tulips added color to the yard.

_____

SENTENCES

Chapter 10: Kinds of Sentences

 **WORKSHEET 2** *Compound Sentences*

A **compound sentence** has two or more independent clauses but no subordinate clauses. The independent clauses are usually joined by a coordinating conjunction: *and, but, for, nor, or, so,* or *yet*.

> INDEPENDENT CLAUSE: a **man** with a harmonica **played**
>
> INDEPENDENT CLAUSE: **people danced** in the street
>
> COMPOUND SENTENCE: A **man** with a harmonica **played**, and **people danced** in the street.

Exercise   Each of the sentences below is a compound sentence. For each sentence, draw one line under the simple subject in each clause. Then draw two lines under the verb or verb phrase in each clause. Draw a circle around the conjunction that joins the two clauses.

> EXAMPLE: 1. <u>Herminia Ortega</u> <u>is</u> in my English class at school,⟨and⟩<u>we</u> <u>have become</u> good friends this year.

1. Herminia invited me to the campground with her family, and I had an interesting time.

2. The Ortega family was going to a state park near our town for the weekend, and my parents agreed to the idea.

3. The Ortegas had purchased a new van, and we certainly needed it for all our gear.

4. They did not bring a large tent, for they sleep in the open at campgrounds.

5. On our first night, the others put their sleeping bags out under the stars, but I preferred a small tent.

6. I imagined all kinds of wild creatures, yet the family very kindly did not tease me about my fears.

7. They owned a black Labrador retriever, and it evidently shared my fears.

8. The dog must have been nervous, for it joined me in the tent.

9. In the middle of the night, another problem arose, for the dog left the tent.

10. Later, he bounded into the tent, and it collapsed on top of us both!

Name _____ Date _____ Class _____

Simple or Compound Sentence?

Do not confuse a compound sentence with a simple sentence that contains a compound subject, a compound verb, or both.

                                s   s   v   v

SIMPLE SENTENCE: **Travelers** and their **families met** and **talked** at the airport terminal. [compound subject and compound verb]

                            s   v   s   v

COMPOUND SENTENCE: **I picked** up Uncle Ward's suitcase, and **we walked** to the parking lot. [two independent clauses]

The independent clauses in a compound sentence may also be joined by a semicolon.

    At home, the whole family waited for us; they had not seen him in years.

Exercise A Underline each subject once and each verb or verb phrase twice in the sentences below. On the lines provided, tell whether each sentence is *simple* or *compound*.

EXAMPLES: 1. African American <u>actors</u> and <u>actresses</u> <u>performed</u> in many early Hollywood movies. *simple*

2. <u>Hattie McDaniel</u> <u>made</u> many films, yet <u>she</u> <u>is</u> best <u>known</u> for her role in *Gone with the Wind*. *compound*

1. Over the years, African American performers have earned much acclaim and won a number of Academy Awards. _____

2. Hattie McDaniel, in 1939, and Sidney Poitier, in 1963, were the first black performers to win Oscars. _____

3. Lou Gossett, Jr., and Denzel Washington played military men and won Academy Awards for their performances. _____

4. Another winner, Whoopi Goldberg, first gained fame as a stand-up comic; then she went on to make several hit movies. _____

5. Critics praised her performance in *The Color Purple*, and in 1991, she won an Academy Award for her role in *Ghost*. _____

Exercise B: Revising Rewrite each of the following simple sentences to create a compound sentence.

EXAMPLE: 1. The duck left her nest. *The duck left her nest, and she took her ducklings to the pond.*

1. Jared enjoys swimming. _____

_____

2. He learned only last year. _____

_____

Chapter 10: Kinds of Sentences

WORKSHEET 4 *Complex Sentences*

A **complex sentence** has one independent clause and at least one *subordinate clause*. Like an independent clause, a **subordinate clause** has a verb and a subject. But a subordinate clause does not express a complete thought. A subordinate clause is introduced by a word such as *although, after, as, because, before, that, until, when,* or *who.*

INDEPENDENT CLAUSE: the **bread will be** ready

SUBORDINATE CLAUSE: when the **buzzer sounds**

COMPLEX SENTENCE: When the **buzzer sounds**, the **bread will be** ready.

A subordinate clause can appear at the beginning, in the middle, or at the end of a complex sentence.

When I have free time, I enjoy my hobbies.

The hobby **that I like most** is building model ships.

My best ship is the one **that I made last summer.**

Exercise   In each of the complex sentences below, underline the subordinate clause once and the independent clause twice. Then circle the verb or verb phrase in each clause.

EXAMPLE: 1. When they (returned) from their vacation, they (collected) their mail at the post office.

1. The detective show appeared on television for several weeks before it became popular with viewers.

2. Most of the albums that my parents have from the 1970's are sitting in the corner of the basement behind the broken refrigerator.

3. Richard E. Byrd is but one of the explorers who made expeditions to Antarctica.

4. As studies continued, many important facts about nutrition were discovered.

5. After we have prepared our report on the history of computers, we may go to the basketball game.

6. Although few students or teachers knew about it, a group of sociologists visited our school to study the relationship between classroom environment and students' grades.

7. Although it was a gray, rainy day, Pilar looked forward to her walk in the park with her big shaggy dog, Tiny.

8. When the late spring days were long, the science club went on a field trip to a famous oceanography center.

9. Some who had gone to the museum last month had signed up for art class.

10. When pigs fly, I will go into those woods by myself.

Name _____ Date _____ Class _____

Compound-Complex Sentences

A **compound-complex sentence** has two or more independent clauses and at least one subordinate clause.

                      S   V

INDEPENDENT CLAUSE: **we attended** a lecture on electricity

                      S   V

INDEPENDENT CLAUSE: **we visited** the exhibits

                           S   V

SUBORDINATE CLAUSE: when **we went** to the science museum

COMPLEX SENTENCE: When we went to the science museum, we attended a lecture on electricity, and we visited the exhibits.

Exercise In each of the following sentences, underline the simple subject or subjects in each clause once. Underline the verb(s) or verb phrase(s) in each clause twice. Then circle the introductory word in the subordinate clause or clauses.

        EXAMPLE: 1. (When) Thora Andersen <u>came</u> to this country, <u>she</u> <u>enjoyed</u> her new freedom, but <u>she</u> also <u>worked</u> hard.

1. Cece went to Chile over the winter vacation, but her older brother stayed home because he had made plans with some friends.

2. When Mr. Tolstoi entered the United States, he knew only a few words of English, but his wife was fluent in the language.

3. The two young men had avoided injuries because they had worn their seat belts, but the family in the other car was not as fortunate.

4. Strict vegetarians, who do not eat any animal products, should watch their diets, and they should eat balanced meals.

5. Chip went to his soccer practice, and Ahnawake went to her piano lesson, although they were tired.

6. When I went to the lobby for a drink, there was a long line at the snack counter, but I didn't mind because I didn't like the movie.

7. The two dogs barked at each other constantly until the sun rose, so my mother talked to their owner this morning.

8. Is it true that people get the hiccups because they are afraid, or does fear only cure the hiccups?

9. As we started to leave the library, the rain was pelting down, so we went back inside.

10. When I closed my eyes, I saw that ugly monster with the glaring eyes, and I was afraid again.

SENTENCES

Chapter 10: Kinds of Sentences

WORKSHEET 6

Classifying Sentences by Purpose

In addition to being classified by structure, a sentence is also classified according to its purpose. A **declarative sentence** makes a statement. It is followed by a period.

They trudged along the Trail of Tears**.**

An **interrogative sentence** asks a question. It is followed by a question mark.

Is that the real name of the trail**?**

An **imperative sentence** gives a command or makes a request. It is followed by a period. A strong command is followed by an exclamation point. The subject of an imperative sentence is always *you*. If the word *you* is not stated, it is the "understood" subject.

(You) Ask your librarian**.**   (You) Find out about it for yourself**!**

An **exclamatory sentence** shows excitement or expresses strong feeling. It is followed by an exclamation point.

How tragic the story is**!**

Exercise A   Label each sentence below by purpose. Use *DEC* for declarative, *INT* for interrogative, *IMP* for imperative, and *EXC* for exclamatory. Then add the correct end marks.

EXAMPLE: ___*IMP*___ 1. Aunt Gwen, tell us about the Cherokees⊙

_____ 1. What a proud history the Cherokees have

_____ 2. What did the Cherokees do

_____ 3. They built schools and educated their people to read and write

_____ 4. Where did they live

_____ 5. Look at a map of the Southeast to see

Exercise B: Revising   Rewrite each of the sentences below, following the instructions given in parentheses.

EXAMPLE: 1. I looked at these paintings by George Catlin. (Give a command.) *Look at these paintings by George Catlin.*

1. George Catlin painted portraits of many of the Plains Indians. (Ask a question.)

_____

2. Have you seen his painting of the Seminole chief Osceola? (Make a statement.)

_____

3. I wonder if Osceola really looked as he does in that painting. (Ask a question.)

_____

4. Catlin painted about six hundred portraits of Plains chiefs. (Express strong feeling.)

_____

Name _____ Date _____ Class _____

Review

Exercise A Identify each of the following sentences by structure. If the sentence is simple, write *S*. If the sentence is compound, write *CD*.

EXAMPLE: ___S___ 1. Each year, mystery writers sell thousands of novels.

_____ 1. Suspense novels are extremely popular, and many students enjoy reading them in the summer.

_____ 2. *The Mysterious Affair at Styles* was Agatha Christie's first detective novel.

_____ 3. My favorite mystery is *The Body in the Library*, by Agatha Christie.

_____ 4. Several people are murder suspects, for each has a possible motive.

_____ 5. Miss Marple slowly creates a trap to solve the murders.

Exercise B Identify each of the following sentences by structure. If the sentence is complex, write *CX*. If the sentence is compound-complex, write *CC*.

EXAMPLE: ___CX___ 1. No one could love skateboarding more than I do.

_____ 1. If you skateboard in a competition, you must wear protective pads.

_____ 2. At first, skateboards had roller-skate wheels; however, today's boards have special wheels that are much safer.

_____ 3. When the skater moves his or her weight one way, the board turns in the opposite direction.

_____ 4. I like the bicycle, which is much easier than the skateboard.

_____ 5. If you are a surfer, you may like skateboards, and you may learn to skateboard more quickly because skateboards are similar to surfboards.

Exercise C Underline each independent clause once and each subordinate clause twice in the following sentences. [Not every sentence has a subordinate clause.] Then write *S* if the sentence is simple, *CD* if the sentence is compound, *CX* if the sentence is complex, or *CC* if the sentence is compound-complex.

EXAMPLE: ___CX___ 1. We live in a town <u>where the theater is only open on weekends</u>.

_____ 1. Tyrone and I saw a horror movie together.

_____ 2. When some parts became too scary, I went to the lobby.

_____ 3. Tyrone saw that I was scared.

_____ 4. A few times I did put my hands in front of my eyes, and I didn't even peek unless I had to.

_____ 5. Tyrone got the hiccups, and he rushed out for some water.

SENTENCES

Chapter 10, Worksheet 7, continued

Exercise D   On the lines provided, identify each sentence in the following paragraphs as *S* (simple), *CD* (compound), *CX* (complex), or *CC* (compound-complex).

> EXAMPLE: [1] If he had not practiced, Amleto Monacelli of Venezuela could not have become a champion bowler. __*CX*__

[1] People who are learning a new sport begin by mastering basic skills, and they usually are very eager. _____ [2] After people have practiced basic skills for a while, they usually progress to more difficult moves. _____ [3] At this point a beginner is likely to become discouraged, and the temptation to quit grows strong. _____ [4] One of the most common problems that beginners face is coordination; another is muscular aches and pains. _____ [5] If a beginner is not careful, muscles can be injured, yet the strenuous activity usually strengthens the muscle tissues. _____ [6] When enough oxygen reaches the warmed-up muscles, the danger of injury lessens, and the muscles grow in size. _____ [7] At the same time, coordination grows, along with confidence. _____

[8] The hours of practice that a beginner puts in usually result in rewarding improvements. _____ [9] As a rule, learning something new takes time and work, or it would not seem worthwhile. _____ [10] In sports, as in most activities, persistence and patience often pay off. _____

Exercise E   Add the correct end mark of punctuation to each of the following sentences. On the lines provided, label each sentence as *DEC* (declarative), *IMP* (imperative), *INT* (interrogative), or *EXC* (exclamatory).

> EXAMPLE: __*IMP*__ 1. Turn left at the corner⊙

_____ 1. Alana bought some angelfish for her aquarium

_____ 2. How many times has our track team won the state championship

_____ 3. Imagine a ride in the space shuttle

_____ 4. Because of its ruffled "collar," the frilled lizard looks like a comical monster

_____ 5. Can you give me directions to the post office

_____ 6. How fresh the air feels after a storm

_____ 7. Think about both sides of the problem

_____ 8. Many large museums in the United States display pottery made by Maria Martinez

_____ 9. What teams are playing in the World Series

_____10. What a fantastic world lies beneath the waves

Chapter 11: Writing Effective Sentences

WORKSHEET 1 | *Sentence Fragments*

One of the easiest ways to make your writing more effective is to use complete sentences. A **sentence** is a word group that (a) has a subject, (b) has a verb, and (c) expresses a complete thought. Avoid using sentence fragments. A **sentence fragment** is a part of a sentence that has been punctuated as if it were a complete sentence.

SENTENCE: Lewis Carroll wrote *Alice's Adventures in Wonderland* in the 1860's.

FRAGMENT: Wrote the book *Alice's Adventures in Wonderland*. [The subject is missing. *Who* wrote the book?]

FRAGMENT: Lewis Carroll *Alice's Adventures in Wonderland*. [The verb is missing. *What* did Carroll do?]

FRAGMENT: When Lewis Carroll wrote *Alice's Adventures in Wonderland*. [This group of words has a subject and a verb but does not express a complete thought. *What happened* when Lewis Carroll wrote *Alice's Adventures in Wonderland*?]

Exercise A   On the lines provided, write *S* for each sentence or *F* for each fragment below.

_____ 1. When Alice saw the White Rabbit go down the hole.

_____ 2. She got up and ran after it.

_____ 3. The tiny door at the bottom of the rabbit's hole.

_____ 4. Ate some cake that she found there.

_____ 5. Alice grew so tall that she couldn't see her feet.

_____ 6. When she shrank again.

_____ 7. Almost drowned in a pool of her own tears.

_____ 8. Many very strange and wonderful sights.

_____ 9. A very peculiar cat.

_____10. It disappeared, leaving nothing but its smile.

Exercise B: Revising   On the lines provided, rewrite each fragment below as a complete sentence. Change punctuation and capitalization as needed.

EXAMPLE: 1. When I read.

When I read fairy tales I feel as if I'm in another time.

1. Is one of my favorite books.

_____

2. Another story that I like a lot.

_____

SENTENCES

Name _____ Date _____ Class _____

 **WORKSHEET 2**   *Run-on Sentences*

If you run together two complete sentences as if they were one sentence, you get a **run-on sentence**. Avoid using run-on sentences. There are two ways you can revise run-on sentences. You can make two sentences, or you can use a comma and the coordinating conjunction *and*, *but*, or *or*.

RUN-ON: The octopus is a dangerous foe it preys on many sea creatures.

CORRECT: The octopus is a dangerous foe. **It** preys on many sea creatures.

CORRECT: The octopus is a dangerous foe**, and** it preys on many sea creatures.

NOTE: A comma marks a brief pause in a sentence, but it does not show the end of a sentence. If you use a comma between two sentences, you create a run-on sentence.

Exercise: Revising   On the lines provided, revise each sentence below that is a run-on sentence. If the group of words is correct, write C.

1. The giant octopus is a predator it eats crabs and shellfish.

   _____

2. The octopus usually hunts at night then it carries its prey back to its den.

   _____

3. Octopuses like to be left alone they are often bothered by scuba divers.

   _____

4. Most divers aren't afraid of octopuses, in fact, divers enjoy meeting them.

   _____

5. Octopuses are related to squid these creatures are known as cephalopods.

   _____

6. *Cephalopod* means "head-footed" cephalopods' arms seem to grow out of their heads.

   _____

7. Octopuses have eight arms, but other cephalopods, such as squid, have ten.

   _____

8. The octopus is one of the smartest sea creatures it is about as smart as a cat.

   _____

9. The octopus moves quickly, and it drops to the ocean floor to catch its prey.

   _____

10. An octopus uses the skin between its arms to carry food it can carry a dozen crabs.

   _____

Name _____ Date _____ Class _____

Combining Sentences by Inserting Words and Phrases

Sometimes a short sentence can express your meaning perfectly. But a long, unbroken series of short sentences can make your writing sound choppy. You can combine short sentences by pulling a key word or phrase from one sentence and inserting it into another sentence.

ORIGINAL: A package arrived. It came **today**.

COMBINED: A package arrived **today**.

ORIGINAL: A package arrived today. The package was **from Ohio**.

COMBINED: A package **from Ohio** arrived today.

Exercise A: Revising Combine each of the following sentence pairs by taking the italicized word from the second sentence and inserting it into the first sentence.

EXAMPLE: 1. The cowhand spoke to his horse. He spoke *softly*.
The cowhand spoke softly to his horse.

1. The Santa Fe Trail ran from Independence, Missouri, to Santa Fe, New Mexico. The trail ran *southwest*. _____

_____

2. Traders from Mexico to Missouri used the trail from 1821 until 1880. They used the trail *continually*. _____

_____

3. The trail ran through the home of the Plains Indians. The trail was *long*.

_____

4. The dangers on the trail were thirst, prairie fire, blizzard, and disease. These were the *worst* dangers. _____

_____

Exercise B: Revising Combine each pair of sentences below by inserting the italicized word group from the second sentence into the first sentence. Add commas where needed.

1. Mount Vesuvius is a volcano. Mount Vesuvius is *on the southwest coast of Italy*.

_____

2. The volcano erupted in A.D. 79. It *destroyed the village of Pompeii*. (Hint: Change *destroyed* to *destroying*.) _____

_____

Chapter 11: Writing Effective Sentences

WORKSHEET 4

Combining by Using And, But, *or* Or

You can combine sentences by using the conjunction *and, but,* or *or* to form a compound subject, a compound verb, or a compound sentence.

ORIGINAL: Kam is a writer. Amy is a writer.

COMPOUND SUBJECT: **Kam** and **Amy** are writers.

ORIGINAL: Kam writes songs. Kam composes music.

COMPOUND VERB: Kam **writes** songs and **composes** music.

ORIGINAL: Kam sings the melody. Amy sings the harmony.

COMPOUND SENTENCE: Kam sings the melody, **and** Amy sings the harmony.

Exercise A: Revising   Combine each of the following sentence pairs by forming a compound subject or a compound verb. Make your new subjects and verbs agree in number.

EXAMPLE: 1. Ants create highly organized societies. Bees do too.

Ants and bees create highly organized societies.

1. Janine is from Columbus. Geoff is from Columbus, too.

_____

2. Elgin finished dinner early. He stayed at the table anyway.

_____

3. In February, Teresa visited Puerto Rico. She also toured Florida.

_____

4. Monica Seles played in the tournament. Steffi Graff played, too.

_____

Exercise B: Revising   The sentences in each pair below are closely related. Using a comma and the conjunction *and, but,* or *or*, make each pair into a compound sentence.

EXAMPLE: 1. Paulo wants to go. Ilia wants to stay home.

Paulo wants to go, but Ilia wants to stay home.

1. Fires are common on the California coast. People continue to live there.

_____

2. I can play shortstop today. You can play shortstop tomorrow. _____

_____

3. A Supreme Court justice may serve for a lifetime. A U.S. president can serve only two terms.

_____

4. Leah can go to the puppet show. She can go to the nature center. _____

_____

Chapter 11: Writing Effective Sentences

WORKSHEET 5

Combining by Using a Subordinate Clause

An **independent clause** can stand alone as a sentence. A **subordinate clause** cannot stand alone as a sentence because it doesn't express a complete thought.

INDEPENDENT CLAUSE: the rainstorm was over

SUBORDINATE CLAUSE: when the rainstorm was over

You can make a subordinate clause by replacing the subject of a sentence with *who, which,* or *that.* You can also make a subordinate clause by adding a word that tells time or place.

ORIGINAL: Sandra Cisneros often writes about her childhood. She grew up in Chicago.

COMBINED: Sandra Cisneros, **who grew up in Chicago,** often writes about her childhood. [The word *who* replaced the subject, *she,* in the second original sentence to make a subordinate clause.]

ORIGINAL: The rain ended. We looked for mushrooms.

COMBINED: **When the rain ended,** we looked for mushrooms. [The word *when* has been placed at the beginning of the first original sentence to make a subordinate clause showing time.]

Exercise: Revising Combine each sentence pair by making one of the sentences into a subordinate clause and adding it to the other sentence. The hints in parentheses tell you how to begin the subordinate clause. You may delete word(s) in the second sentence.

EXAMPLE: 1. Paul K. Longmore is a history professor at San Francisco State University. He teaches a class about the history of people with disabilities. (Use *who.*)

Paul K. Longmore is a history professor at San Francisco State University who teaches a class about the history of people with disabilities.

1. When he was seven, Professor Longmore developed polio. The polio caused him to lose the use of his arms. (Use *which.*) _____

   _____

2. Paul Longmore went to Occidental College. He got a degree in history. (Use *where.*)

   _____

3. He finished his bachelor's degree. He wanted to get his doctoral degree in history. (Use *after.*)

   _____

4. The state rehabilitation department got him some special equipment. He was able to write a critically acclaimed book about George Washington. (Use *because.*) _____

   _____

SENTENCES

Chapter 11: Writing Effective Sentences

Stringy Sentences and Wordy Sentences

Stringy sentences have too many independent clauses strung together with words like *and* or *but*. **Wordy sentences** use too many words to say something that can be said simply.

To fix a stringy sentence, you can (a) break the sentence into two or more sentences, or (b) turn some of the independent clauses into phrases or subordinate clauses.

You can revise wordy sentences in three different ways: (1) replace a group of words with one word; (2) replace a clause with a phrase; or (3) take out a whole group of unnecessary words.

Exercise: Revising   Revise the following stringy or wordy sentences using the methods discussed above.

1. Cuzco is a city in the country of Peru, a city way up high in the mountains called the

   Andes that was once the center of the great and mighty Inca Empire. _____

   _____

   _____

2. The Inca were the rulers of the Inca society, and their subjects were peoples from various

   groups, and today Peruvian Indians are called Quechuans. _____

   _____

   _____

3. The Inca were great architects, and they were excellent mathematicians, and they built

   huge stone temples in the mountains. _____

   _____

   _____

4. Builders and scientists today are amazed at the ability of the Inca, and they see how they

   calculated the shapes of stones, and they fitted them perfectly to build huge, solid

   structures on the sides of mountains. _____

   _____

   _____

5. Near the city of Cuzco is the famous and celebrated temple of Machu Picchu, which can be

   reached only by traveling up to it on a train. _____

   _____

   _____

Chapter 11: Writing Effective Sentences

WORKSHEET 7 | *Review*

Exercise A: Revising   Correct the following sentence fragments by making them complete sentences. Write your sentences on the lines provided.

1. George Washington in the Revolutionary War. _____

   _____

2. When Rahshad moved to Toronto. _____

   _____

3. Got out the football equipment. _____

   _____

4. Raked the leaves from the lawn. _____

   _____

5. While you make the posters. _____

   _____

Exercise B: Revising   Correct the following run-on sentences. Write the correct sentences on the lines provided.

1. *The Call of the Wild* is a book by Jack London it is about a dog named Buck who becomes a

   member of a wolf pack in the Yukon. _____

   _____

2. The lawn mower was loud it woke up all the neighbors on Saturday morning.

   _____

3. Insulation keeps buildings warm in winter it keeps them cool in summer, too.

   _____

4. My journal is private I keep it hidden so no one else can read it without my permission.

   _____

5. Thanksgiving was Gilberto's favorite holiday he always made sweet potato pie.

   _____

Exercise C: Revising   Combine the following sentence pairs.

1. *Romeo and Juliet* is a famous play. It is set in Italy. (Use *that*.) _____

SENTENCES

2. The neighborhood kids held a carnival. They held it in the summer. _____

_____

3. Susan can take the bus to school. She can walk to school. _____

_____

4. Manassas is a place in Virginia. One of the Civil War battles was fought there. (Use *where*.)

_____

5. A melody hung in the prince's misty garden. The melody was haunting.

_____

Exercise D: Revising   Revise the following stringy or wordy sentences. Write the revised sentences on the lines provided.

1. The Second World War was a long, drawn-out, terrible war that had its official beginning in the country that is now Poland in September of 1939.

_____

_____

2. Rembrandt was a famous Dutch painter, and his full name was Rembrandt Harmensz van Rijn, but he's widely known by his first name, and he's not so well known by his last name.

_____

_____

3. Clara Barton was born in 1821, and she died in 1912, and she was a battlefield nurse in the Civil War, and she founded the American Red Cross.

_____

_____

4. Raul Julia is an actor, and he has played many dramatic roles, but he is known for playing sympathetic characters, and he is not known for playing villains.

_____

_____

5. Gene Roddenberry was awarded the Purple Heart for his heroism during World War II, and then he became a Los Angeles police officer, and later he created the famous *Star Trek* television series, and he died in 1991.

_____

_____

Name _____ Date _____ Class _____

 **WORKSHEET 1**

Using Capital Letters A

Capitalize the first word in every sentence.

Six days ago, my cousin came for a visit.

The first word of a sentence that is a direct quotation is capitalized even if the quotation begins within a sentence.

Wasn't it Yogi Berra who said, "**It** ain't over till it's over"?

Traditionally, the first word in a line of poetry is capitalized.

For thy sweet love remembered such wealth brings
That then I scorn to change my state with kings.
—William Shakespeare

Capitalize the pronoun *I.*

Ira said that **I** was the best dancer in the show.

Capitalize the interjection *O*, which is often used on solemn or formal occasions and in poetry and songs. It is usually followed by a word in direct address.

Guide and direct us, **O** Lord.

The interjection *oh* requires a capital letter only at the beginning of a sentence.

Oh, I wish I were on a sailboat, floating swiftly out to sea.

Exercise A: Proofreading   Circle the letters that should be capitalized in the following sentences.

EXAMPLE: 1. Ⓡunning and bicycling are more healthful than driving a car is.

1. When i was eight years old, my grandmother came to live with me.

2. She always used to say, "great books need to be read often."

3. my grandmother read many books and poems to me.

4. Sometimes she would say, "o, great bookcase! What have you for us?"

5. then she'd close her eyes and pick the first book that she touched.

Exercise B: Proofreading   The following paragraph contains ten errors in capitalization. Proofread the paragraph, and circle the letters that need to be capitalized.

Last week, i read a book by John Muir. he was the man who founded the Sierra Club. muir loved the wilderness regions and fought hard to protect them. he wrote in his book *Alaska Fragment,* "in God's wildness lies the hope of the world—the great fresh unblighted, unredeemed wilderness." after reading Muir's book, i am eager to hike in the wilderness. oh, it's almost an impossible dream, because the wilderness is so far away. but someday, somehow, i'll make that dream come true.

Name _____ Date _____ Class _____

 **WORKSHEET 2** *Using Capital Letters B*

A **common noun** is a general name for a person, a place, a thing, or an idea. A **proper noun** names a particular person, place, thing, or idea.

A common noun is capitalized only when it begins a sentence or is part of a title. A proper noun is always capitalized.

> COMMON NOUNS: **town, day, structure, writer**
>
> PROPER NOUNS: **Tucson, Monday, Stonehenge, Sandra Cisneros**

Some proper nouns consist of more than one word. In these names, prepositions with fewer than five letters and the articles *a*, *an*, and *the* are not capitalized.

> **Memorial Day**   **Alexander the Great**   **Battle of Bunker Hill**

Capitalize the names of persons and animals.

> **Dorothy West**   **Bessie Smith**   **Flipper**

Capitalize geographical names.

> **San Antonio**   **Norway**   **Lake Michigan**   **Route 66**

NOTE: In a hyphenated street number, the second part of the number is not capitalized: **Forty-sixth Street.** Words such as *north, east,* and *southwest* are not capitalized when they indicate direction.

Capitalize the names of planets, stars, and other heavenly bodies.

> **Mars**   **the Little Dipper**   **Orion**

NOTE: The word *earth* is not capitalized unless it is used along with the names of other heavenly bodies. The words *sun* and *moon* are not capitalized.

Exercise   For each proper noun, give a corresponding common noun. For each common noun, give a proper noun. Use the lines provided.

> EXAMPLES: 1. Jupiter *planet*
>
> 2. city *San Francisco*

1. mountain range _____
2. Oprah Winfrey _____
3. the North Star _____
4. river _____
5. North Dakota _____

6. Ethiopia _____
7. Twenty-first Avenue _____
8. animal _____
9. country _____
10. person _____

Name _____ Date _____ Class _____

 **WORKSHEET 3** *Using Capital Letters C*

Capitalize the names of teams, organizations, businesses, institutions, and government bodies.

    Dallas Cowboys   **Future Teachers of America**   **Central High School**

Capitalize the names of historical events and periods, special events, and calendar items. The name of a season is not capitalized unless it is part of a proper name.

    War of the Roses   **Jazz Age**   **Texas State Fair**   **November**

Capitalize the names of nationalities, races, and peoples.

    Tahitian   **Cherokee**   **Puerto Rican**

Capitalize the names of religions and their followers, holy days, sacred writings, and specific deities.

    Christianity   **Talmud**   **Shiva**

Capitalize the names of buildings and other structures.

    Idaho State Capitol   **Mackinac Bridge**   **Sears Tower**

Capitalize the names of monuments and awards.

    Lincoln Memorial   **Tony Award**   **Best in Show**

Capitalize the names of trains, ships, airplanes, and spacecraft.

    Southwest Chief   **USS** *Arizona*   *Sputnik*

Capitalize the brand names of business products.

    Minolta copiers   **Schwinn** bicycles   **Hyundai** computer

Exercise: Proofreading Circle the letters that should be capitalized in the following sentences.

      EXAMPLE: 1. On (i)ndependence (d)ay I took a vacation.

1. I rode from Atlanta to New York on the train called the *crescent*.

2. I visited my favorite uncle, who lives near the world trade center.

3. He has friends who are korean, indian, african, and lebanese.

4. All of his friends love baseball, and most are new york yankees fans.

5. We went to yankee stadium to see the yankees play the boston red sox.

6. My uncle had a tiny sony TV that he watched the game on, too.

7. The next day, we went to the top of the empire state building.

8. Later we went with a friend to services at an islamic mosque.

9. My uncle said when I come back, we'll go to the statue of liberty.

10. Maybe my whole family can go during thanksgiving vacation.

Chapter 12: Capital Letters

WORKSHEET 4 *Using Capital Letters D*

A **proper adjective** is formed from a proper noun and is almost always capitalized.

PROPER NOUN	PROPER ADJECTIVE
Kansas City	a Kansas City landmark
Mexico	a Mexican artist
William Shakespeare	a Shakespearean play

Do *not* capitalize the names of school subjects, except languages and course names followed by a number.

    After lunch, I go to **French** class, then to **art**, and then to **Algebra II**.

Exercise   On the lines provided, list the proper nouns and proper adjectives in each of the following sentences, adding capital letters as needed.

        EXAMPLE: 1. A finnish architect, eliel saarinen, designed many buildings in detroit. *Finnish, Eliel Saarinen, Detroit*

1. The alaskan wilderness is noted for its majestic beauty. _____

2. The syrian and israeli leaders met in geneva. _____
_____

3. The european cities I plan to visit someday are paris and vienna. _____
_____

4. Our american literature book includes hopi poems and cheyenne legends.
_____

5. The south american rain forests contain many different kinds of plants and animals.
_____

6. Elena has watched two japanese dramas on television. _____

7. Did you see the exhibit of african art at the library? _____
_____

8. Our program will feature irish and scottish folk songs. _____
_____

9. The language most widely spoken in brazil is portuguese. _____
_____

10. In history 101 we discussed early swedish settlements. _____
_____

Name _____ Date _____ Class _____

WORKSHEET 5   *Using Capital Letters E*

Capitalize the title of a person when it comes before a name.

Captain Nemo   **Dr.** Lo   **Professor** Whitig

Capitalize a title used alone or following a person's name only when you want to emphasize the position of someone holding a high office.

CAPITALIZED: The **S**ecretary of **A**griculture gave an important speech.

NOT CAPITALIZED: Lucas is **s**ecretary of the debating club at school.

A title used alone in direct address is usually capitalized.

When will the ship arrive in port, **Captain?**

Capitalize a word showing a family relationship when the word is used before or in place of a person's name. Do not capitalize a word showing a family relationship when a possessive comes before the word.

I know **Mom** wants to see **Uncle** Elmer before he leaves.

Listen to your **uncle** Elmer.

Capitalize the first and last words and all important words in titles of books, magazines, newspapers, poems, short stories, historical documents, movies, television programs, works of art, and musical compositions.

A Jar of Dreams   *Home Alone*   "Old Paint"

NOTE: Most abbreviations, such as *Mr., Ms., U.S., TV,* state names, and organization names, are capitalized.

Exercise: Proofreading   Circle the letters that should be capitalized in the following sentences.

EXAMPLE: 1. Doris Lessing's "A ⓢunrise on the Ⓥeld" was in the Ⓝew Ⓨorker.

1. Lian's mother is a writer for a newspaper, the *philadelphia inquirer*.

2. She interviewed president Clinton when he came to pennsylvania.

3. She later interviewed Warren Christopher, the secretary of state.

4. Lian is president of our journalism club; aunt Katya is our sponsor.

5. We heard a speaker discuss the book *all the president's men*.

6. My uncle Lacon and mr. Torres took me to see *the phantom of the opera*.

7. We saw friends of ours, major Seymour and his wife, there.

8. "What did you think of the play, major?" uncle Lacon asked.

9. "It's good, but I like *les misérables* better," the major said.

10. Then mrs. Seymour said that she liked both plays equally well.

MECHANICS

Chapter 12: Capital Letters

 *Review*

Exercise A: Proofreading Circle the letters that should be capitalized in each of the following sentences.

> EXAMPLE: 1. Our class visited Abraham Lincoln's home in Springfield, Illinois.

1. the federal aviation administration regulates airlines in the united states.

2. the name of the u.s. president's plane is *air force one*.

3. the sacred moslem city of mecca is located in saudi arabia.

4. in chicago, the sears tower and the museum of science and industry attract many tourists.

5. we watched the minnesota twins win the world series in 1991.

6. the valentine's day dance is always the highlight of the winter.

7. my friend bought new shoes at the mall, and oh, was I envious.

8. when i was young i wrote a poem for aunt jessie, who loves birds:
   "o little birds that fly so high
   don't get lost up in the sky."

9. ten of the art students who drew or painted pictures of the jefferson memorial will receive polaroid cameras.

10. our neighbor, sergeant lewis, took astronomy 201 in college and loves to point out venus, mars, and the big dipper on clear nights.

Exercise B: Proofreading Circle the letters that should be capitalized in the following paragraph.

> EXAMPLE: [1] The South African vocal group Ladysmith Black Mambazo sings a capella—that is, without musical instruments.

[1] Ladysmith's music is based on the work songs of south african miners, and most of the songs are sung in zulu, their native language. [2] In a sense, their music is the south African version of the american blues, which grew out of the work songs of african americans. [3] In 1985, ladysmith was featured on two songs on paul simon's album *graceland*. [4] those two songs, "homeless" and "diamonds on the soles of her shoes," helped to make the album an enormous hit; it even won a grammy award. [5] To promote the album, Ladysmith and simon toured the United states, europe, and south America.

Name _____ Date _____ Class _____

 **WORKSHEET 1** | *Using End Marks*

An **end mark** is a mark of punctuation placed at the end of a sentence. The three kinds of end marks are the *period,* the *question mark,* and the *exclamation point.*

Use a period at the end of a statement.

The manatee is also called a sea cow**.**   It is a mammal that lives in the ocean**.**

Use a question mark at the end of a question.

Have you ever seen a manatee**?**   Did it look like a cow to you**?**

Use an exclamation point at the end of an exclamation.

Look how huge it is**!**   That's amazing**!**

Use a period or an exclamation point at the end of a request or a command.

Please read this**.** [request]   Give me that**!** [command]

Use a period after most abbreviations.

PERSONAL NAMES:	Joel H. Fairweather, M. E. Gadski
TITLES USED WITH NAMES:	Mr., Mrs., Ms., Jr., Sr., Dr.
STATES (EXCEPT TWO-LETTER ZIP CODE ABBREVIATIONS):	Ky., Ark., Calif.
ADDRESSES:	Ave., St., Rd., P.O. Box
ORGANIZATIONS AND COMPANIES:	Co., Inc., Corp., Assn.
TIMES:	A.M., P.M., B.C., A.D.

NOTE: Abbreviate most units of measure (except *in.* for *inch*) without periods.

Exercise: Proofreading   Write periods (⊙), question marks (?), and exclamation points (!) where they belong in the following sentences.

EXAMPLE: 1. Where did you see a manatee*?*

1. We took the 11:15 A M flight

2. We flew AmFly, Inc to Ft Myers, Florida, which is on the Gulf coast

3. Do you know where Sanibel Island is

4. Sometimes you can see manatees off its coast

5. They are about 10 ft long, weigh up to 3,500 lbs, and are gray

6. Did you know they are endangered

7. Mrs C Van Dam was crying, "Save the manatee"

8. Please give me that book about endangered species

9. I see it was written by C K Lee, Jr, the famous naturalist

10. What wonderful photos it contains

Chapter 13: Punctuation

WORKSHEET 2   *Using Commas A*

A **comma** is used to separate words or groups of words *within* a complete thought.

Use commas to separate items in a series.

WORDS IN A SERIES: His pocket was full of **pennies, nickels,** and **dimes**. [nouns]

He **sorted, counted,** and **rolled** the coins. [verbs]

The coins were **small, shiny,** and **numerous**. [adjectives]

PHRASES IN A SERIES: **Counting the money, bringing it to the bank,** and **depositing it** took all day. [gerund phrases]

I **have applied** for an account, **have signed** my name, and **have received** a bank book. [verb phrases]

We searched for the lost dollar **under the bed, in the drawers,** and **on the shelves**. [prepositional phrases]

CLAUSES IN A SERIES: Daphne knew **where the bank was, how late it was open,** and **how we could get there**. [subordinate (noun) clauses]

I **counted the money, Daphne put it in the envelope,** and **we left**. [short independent clauses]

If all items in a series are joined by *and* or *or,* do not use commas to separate them.

Walking **or** jogging **or** running is good exercise.

Exercise: Proofreading   Insert commas (˄) where they are needed in the following sentences. If a sentence is correct, make no change.

EXAMPLE: 1. The hikers took food˄water˄and tents.

1. Carlos and Anna and I made a piñata filled it with small toys and hung it up.

2. The four states that have produced the most U.S. presidents are Virginia Ohio Massachusetts and New York.

3. The band instruments include clarinets trumpets tubas saxophones and trombones.

4. Most flutes used by professional musicians are made of sterling silver fourteen-carat gold or platinum.

5. Notice designs in the centers on the sides and in the corners of bills.

6. Squanto became an interpreter for the Pilgrims showed them how to plant corn and stayed with them throughout his life.

7. Sylvia Porter wrote several books about how to earn money and how to spend it borrow it and save it.

8. Last summer I read *The Lucky Stone Barrio Boy* and *A Wrinkle in Time*.

9. Tony saw the flames called 911 and waited for help.

10. Who decides when money is too old to use or where it goes or how it is replaced?

Chapter 13: Punctuation

Using Commas B

Use a comma to separate two or more adjectives that come before a noun.

Stockholm is a large, beautiful city.

If the final adjective in a series is closely linked to the noun, do not use a comma before the final adjective.

Stockholm is the large, beautiful capital city of Sweden.

Use a comma before *and, but, or, nor, for, so,* or *yet* when it joins independent clauses.

The children must go to bed early, or they will be tired in the morning.

The sky was dark and cloudy, but the sun was still out.

When the independent clauses are very short, the comma before *and, but,* or *or* may be omitted.

I'm ready but Paul isn't.

Exercise A: Proofreading   Add commas (⌃) where they are needed in the following sentences.

EXAMPLE: 1. A squat⌃dark wood-burning stove stood in one corner.

1. They made a clubhouse in the empty unused storage shed.

2. We looked at the old faded photographs in the scrapbook.

3. What a lovely haunting melody that song has!

4. The city plans to build a modern convenient recreation building.

5. The delicate colorful wings of the hummingbird vibrate up to two hundred times each second.

Exercise B: Proofreading   Add commas (⌃) where they are needed in the following paragraph.

EXAMPLE: [1] Have you read *The Song of Hiawatha*⌃or do you want me to tell you about it?

[1] Henry Wadsworth Longfellow's narrative poem was published in 1855 and it has

been popular ever since. [2] Hiawatha is left without a mother and he is raised by his

grandmother Nokomis. [3] Hiawatha's father, the West Wind, is powerful yet Hiawatha

battles him. [4] Many readers admire Hiawatha for he is skillful and brave. [5] I have read

the poem but Sarah hasn't.

Name _____ Date _____ Class _____

WORKSHEET 4 *Using Commas C*

Use commas to set off a nonessential participial phrase or a nonessential subordinate clause.

A **nonessential** (or **nonrestrictive**) phrase or clause adds information that isn't needed to understand the meaning of the sentence. Such a phrase or clause can be omitted without changing the main idea of the sentence.

> NONESSENTIAL PHRASE: Our nation**, made up mostly of immigrants,** is one of the
> largest in the world.

> NONESSENTIAL CLAUSE: The mix of ideas and cultures**, which comes from all over
> the world,** has helped to make us great.

Do not set off an **essential** (or **restrictive**) phrase or clause. Since such a phrase or clause tells *which one(s)*, it cannot be omitted without changing the meaning of the sentence.

> ESSENTIAL PHRASE: The contributions **made by newcomers** have included
> inventions and business ideas. [Which contributions?]

> ESSENTIAL CLAUSE: One group **that has helped make our country great** is
> Hispanic Americans. [Which group?]

Exercise: Proofreading   Add commas (‸) to the following sentences as needed. If a sentence is correct, write *C* on the line provided.

> EXAMPLE: _____ 1. Gloria Estefan‸whom I once met‸is my favorite
> singer.

_____ 1. Estefan badly injured in a bus accident in 1990 made a remarkable comeback
the following year.

_____ 2. The accident which occurred on March 20, 1990 shattered one of her
vertebrae and almost severed her spinal cord.

_____ 3. The months of physical therapy required after the accident were painful.

_____ 4. Yet less than a year later performing in public for the first time since the
accident she sang on the American Music Awards telecast January 28, 1991.

_____ 5. On March 1 of that year launching a yearlong tour of Japan, Europe, and the
United States she and the band gave a concert in Miami.

_____ 6. Estefan who was born in Cuba came to the United States when she was two
years old.

_____ 7. Her family fleeing the Castro revolution settled in Miami where she now
lives with her husband, Emilio, and their son, Nayib.

_____ 8. The album released to mark her successful comeback is titled *Into the Light*.

_____ 9. It contains twelve songs including the first one written by the singer after the
accident.

_____10. Appropriately, that song inspired by a fragment that Emilio wrote as Gloria
was being taken to surgery is titled "Coming Out of the Dark."

Chapter 13: Punctuation

Using Commas D

Use commas to set off an appositive or an appositive phrase that is nonessential.

NONESSENTIAL APPOSITIVE: My best friend**, Ramona Suarez,** came here from Mexico.

NONESSENTIAL APPOSITIVE PHRASE: The city of Houston**, home of the Astrodome,** is her home, too.

Do not set off an appositive that tells *which one(s)* about the word it identifies. Such an appositive is essential to the meaning of the sentence.

My brother **Samuel** is the only one of my brothers who came. [Which brother?]

Use commas to set off words used in direct address.

Sylvia, will you please get the mail?

Have you heard**, Derek,** who will be on the debating team?

Use commas to set off a parenthetical expression, such as *after all, for example, on the other hand, I believe,* or *however.*

We do want to catch the train**, after all.**

The tennis team**, however,** did not win the tournament.

Exercise: Proofreading   Add commas (⌄) where they are needed in the following sentences.

EXAMPLE: 1. The dog⌄a boxer⌄is named Brindle⌄I think.

1. Mavis the composer Mozart wrote five short piano pieces when he was only six years old.

2. Katy Jurado the actress has appeared in many fine films.

3. Maya Angelou author of *I Know Why the Caged Bird Sings* is from Arkansas.

4. The card game canasta of course comes from mah-jongg an ancient Chinese game.

5. Jupiter the fifth planet from the sun is so large that all the other planets in our solar system would fit inside it.

6. The main character in many of Agatha Christie's mystery novels class is the detective Hercule Poirot.

7. The writing of Elizabeth Bowen an Irish novelist shows her keen, witty observations of life.

8. Charlemagne the king of the Franks in the eighth and ninth centuries became emperor of the Holy Roman Empire.

9. Chuck Yeager an American pilot broke the sound barrier in 1947 I think.

10. Artist Effie Tybrec a Sioux from South Dakota decorates plain sneakers with elaborate beadwork.

MECHANICS

Chapter 13: Punctuation

WORKSHEET 6 *Using Commas E*

Use a comma after certain introductory elements.

(1) Use a comma after *yes, no,* or any mild exclamation such as *well* or *why* at the beginning of a sentence.

Yes, the library has that book on Egypt.

(2) Use a comma after an introductory prepositional phrase if the phrase is long or if two or more phrases appear together.

On the shores of the Nile, a great civilization was born.

(3) Use a comma after a participial phrase or an infinitive phrase that introduces a sentence.

Concerned with the afterlife, Egyptian rulers built great tombs for themselves.

To provide world peace, all nations of the world must cooperate.

(4) Use a comma after an introductory adverb clause.

When the artists painted, they followed several rules.

Use commas to separate items in dates and addresses, but do not use a comma between the state and ZIP Code.

On December 17, 1903, in Kitty Hawk, North Carolina, modern aviation was born.

The pilot's address is 12 Sky Lane, Rocketville, Indiana 46208.

Use a comma after the salutation of a friendly letter and after the closing of any letter.

Dear Andrea,   Yours truly,

Exercise A: Proofreading   Add commas (⌃) where they are needed in the following sentences.

EXAMPLE: 1. No͵ the Egyptians were not just farmers.

1. Believing in an afterlife Egyptians prepared for it.

2. Built for monarchs and nobles stone tombs held supplies for use in the afterlife.

3. When he was still living the king had his picture painted.

4. On the wall of his tomb a picture shows the king hunting.

5. Well it shows how the king once hunted.

Exercise B: Proofreading   Add commas (⌃) to the following items as needed.

EXAMPLE: 1. on Tuesday͵ October 15͵ 1948

1. Dear Emma

2. from January 2 1993 to January 2 1994

3. 2309 Market Avenue Fort Worth Texas 76106

4. Yours truly

5. in Orlando Florida next week

Name _____ Date _____ Class _____

 **WORKSHEET 7** *Using Semicolons*

A **semicolon** separates complete thoughts as a period does and items within a sentence as a comma does.

Use a semicolon instead of a comma between independent clauses when they are not joined by *and, but, or, nor, for, so,* or *yet.*

One important crop in the South is cotton; it is grown for its fibers.

Use a semicolon rather than a period between independent clauses only when the ideas in the clauses are closely related.

Once cotton was king in the South; now the United States imports much cotton.

Use a semicolon between independent clauses joined by a conjunctive adverb or a transitional expression.

Commonly Used Conjunctive Adverbs

accordingly	furthermore	instead	nevertheless
besides	however	meanwhile	otherwise
consequently	indeed	moreover	therefore

Commonly Used Transitional Expressions

as a result	for example	for instance	that is
in addition	in spite of	in conclusion	in fact

Cotton could not be planted in the same fields each year; **as a result,** crops were rotated.

A semicolon rather than a comma may be needed to separate clauses joined by a coordinating conjunction when there are commas within the clauses.

Cotton is a low, bushy plant; and its fibers are a fuzzy mass, attached to the seeds, which are contained in a "boll."

Exercise: Proofreading Add semicolons (;) and commas (,) where necessary in the following sentences.

EXAMPLE: 1. I wanted to know more about wool therefore I looked the subject up in an encyclopedia.

1. Wool is a great fabric for cold weather wool keeps you warm even when it is wet.

2. My wool sweater is soft, warm, and comfortable it was hand-knitted in Norway.

3. Wool must be cut from the sheep, combed, spun, and dyed but the result is worth the effort.

4. I like to wear wool for skating, sledding, and hiking but my sister, who is allergic to wool, can't wear it at all.

5. I wear other fabrics nevertheless I prefer wool, especially in cold weather.

Chapter 13: Punctuation

 **Using Colons**

Use a colon before a list of items, especially after expressions like *as follows* or *the following*.

> The list of the world's endangered animals includes the following species: the American crocodile, the bald eagle, the polar bear, and the African elephant.

NOTE: Never use a colon directly after a verb or a preposition.

Use a colon before a statement that explains or clarifies a preceding statement.

> Alba made this statement: Always tell the truth and you'll be content.

Use a colon between the hour and the minute and between chapter and verse in referring to passages from the Bible.

> 11:05 A.M.   8:30 P.M.   John 3:16   Psalms 23:6

Use a colon after the salutation of a business letter.

> Dear Ms. Acevedo: To Whom It May Concern:

Exercise A: Proofreading   Add colons (:) where necessary in the following sentences.

> EXAMPLE: 1. Mr. Burkhardt said he would call me at 4:30 P.M.

1. He told me something important We must save the elephants.

2. He also told me the following items are valued by some people elephant meat, elephant tusks, and elephant hides and hair.

3. I read this fact The elephant is on the endangered species list.

4. Is the elephant mentioned in Genesis 1 26?

5. A *National Geographic* special about elephants will be shown at 7 30 P.M.

Exercise B: Proofreading   Proofread the following short letter, adding colons and correcting other errors in punctuation where necessary.

To Whom It May Concern

I am worried about the fate of the African elephant. The facts are as follows The herds are disappearing illegal killing is continuing and the rural people of Africa still need these elephants to survive.

One problem is the value of ivory. One pound is worth about $100, this is five times what most East Africans earn each month. If the African elephant is to be saved more steps must be taken to improve the lives of the East African people.

Sincerely

Teresa Scala

Chapter 13: Punctuation

WORKSHEET 9 *Review*

Exercise A: Proofreading   Add end marks and commas where they are needed in the following paragraph.

> EXAMPLE: [1] Have you ever played chess*?*

[1] To beginners and experts alike chess is a complex demanding game [2] It requires mental self-discipline intense concentration and dedication to long hours of practice [3] Displaying those qualities the Raging Rooks of Harlem tied for first place at the 1991 National Junior High Chess Championship which was held in Dearborn Michigan [4] Competing against the Rooks were sixty teams from all across the country [5] The thirteen- and fourteen-year-old Rooks attended New York City's Public School 43 [6] When they returned to New York after the tournament they were greeted by Mayor David Dinkins [7] As instant celebrities they appeared on television and were interviewed by local newspapers and national news services [8] Imagine how proud of them their friends and families must have been [9] The Rooks' coach Maurice Ashley wasn't surprised that the team did so well in the tournament [10] After all the twenty-five-year-old Ashley is a senior master of the game and his goal is to become the first African American grandmaster

Exercise B: Proofreading   Add end marks, commas, semicolons, and colons where they are needed in the following paragraph.

> EXAMPLE: [1] Acadiana*,*Louisiana*,*isn't a town*;*it's a region*.*

[1] Known as Cajun Country the region includes the twenty-two southernmost parishes of Louisiana [2] Did you know that the word *Cajun* is a shortened form of *Acadian* [3] Cajuns are descended from French colonists who settled along the Bay of Fundy in what is now eastern Canada they named their colony Acadie [4] After the British took over the area they deported nearly two thirds of the Acadians in 1755 consequently many families were separated [5] Some Acadians took refuge in southern Louisiana's isolated swamps and bayous [6] It's clear that they didn't remain isolated however the Cajun dialect blends elements of the following languages French English Spanish German and a variety of African and Native American languages [7] In 1847 the American poet Henry Wadsworth Longfellow described the uprooting of the Acadians in *Evangeline* a long narrative poem that inspired Joseph Rusling Meeker to paint *The Land of Evangeline* which is owned by the St Louis Art Museum [8] Today most people associate Cajun culture with hot spicy foods

and many people are familiar with lively rhythmic Cajun fiddle and accordion music

[9] Remembering their tragic history Cajuns sum up their outlook on life in a marvelous

saying *Lâche pas la patate* ("Don't let go of the potato") [10] What a great way to tell people

not to lose their grip

Exercise C: Proofreading   Add or delete periods, commas, semicolons, and colons in
the following items as needed. If an item is correct, write *C* on the line provided.

EXAMPLE: _____   1. Lakeway Ave,Kalamazoo, Mich, 49001

_____   1. Sincerely yours

_____   2. at the Rand Corp at 1 30 P M

_____   3. Dear Mother,

_____   4. Isaiah 40 31

_____   5. Dear Mr Landers

_____   6. Needham, Massachusetts, 02192

_____   7. March 15 1995

_____   8. Well I don't know.

_____   9. To Whom It May Concern;

_____ 10. Yours truly:

Chapter 14: Punctuation

Underlining (Italics)

Use underlining (italics) for titles of books, plays, periodicals, works of art, films, television programs, recordings, long musical compositions, trains, ships, aircraft, and spacecraft.

BOOKS:	*Sounder*
PLAYS:	*Hamlet*
WORKS OF ART:	*Mona Lisa*
FILMS:	*Citizen Kane*
PERIODICALS:	*Reader's Digest*
RECORDINGS, LONG MUSICAL COMPOSITIONS:	*The Nutcracker Suite*
SHIPS, TRAINS, AIRCRAFT, SPACECRAFT:	*Apollo 11*

NOTE: The article *the* before the title of a magazine or a newspaper is italicized and capitalized only when it is part of the official title of the publication.

Use underlining (italics) for words, letters, and figures referred to as such.

The *s* is doubled twice in the word *Mississippi*.

Is that a *3* or an *8*?

Exercise A: Proofreading Underline the words and phrases that should be underlined (italicized) in the following sentences.

EXAMPLE: 1. Have you read the latest issue of <u>Sports Illustrated</u>?

1. Parts of the wreck of the Titanic were found.

2. Do you spell the word traveling with one l or two?

3. One of my favorite paintings is Christina's World by Andrew Wyeth.

4. Chicago Tribune was the first newspaper to tell that story.

5. Aaron Copland's composition Appalachian Spring has become a classic.

Exercise B: Proofreading In the following paragraph, underline any words that should be underlined (italicized).

EXAMPLE: [1] Lorraine Hansberry is an American playwright best known for her play <u>A Raisin in the Sun</u>.

[1] With the production of A Raisin in the Sun in 1959, Hansberry became the youngest American and first African American playwright to win the Best Play Award from the New York Drama Critics Circle. [2] In 1974, the play was made into a musical called Raisin, which won a Tony Award for best musical. [3] A Raisin in the Sun has also been made into two movies. [4] Two of Hansberry's other plays, Les Blancs and To Be Young, Gifted and Black, were produced after her death in 1965.

MECHANICS

Chapter 14: Punctuation

WORKSHEET 2

Direct and Indirect Quotations

Use quotation marks to enclose a **direct quotation**—a person's exact words.

Be sure to place quotation marks both before and after a person's exact words.
"Did you go to the baseball game?" Tim asked.

Do not use quotation marks for an **indirect quotation**—a rewording of a direct quotation.
Tim asked whether I had gone to the baseball game.

A direct quotation begins with a capital letter.
Rosalinda said, "**Please lock that door.**"

Exercise A   On the lines provided, write *DQ* for each sentence that contains a direct quotation. Write *IQ* for each sentence that contains an indirect quotation.

EXAMPLE: __DQ__ 1. "Water is our most precious resource," quoted
Duncan.

_____ 1. Marie reminded me to conserve water.

_____ 2. The pamphlet said, "Only about one percent of the world's water is good
enough to drink."

_____ 3. "You can save four gallons of water a day," Nora said.

_____ 4. I asked her how I could do that.

_____ 5. She explained, "You can save four gallons for every minute less you spend
showering."

Exercise B: Revising   On the lines provided, revise the following sentences by supplying capital letters and punctuation marks as needed. If a sentence is correct, write *C.*

EXAMPLE: 1. Please come to the cookout with us, Felipe said.
"Please come to the cookout with us," Felipe said.

1. Ella exclaimed, this helmet mask is one of the most amazing things I've ever seen!

_____

2. Mr. Faulkner told the class that the mask weighs eighty pounds and is five feet tall.

_____

3. Don't you think that the figures must have been difficult to carve? asked Earl.

_____

4. Marcia said, just look at all the detail!

_____

5. Lou explained that the mask was designed to honor the Yoruba people.

_____

Chapter 14: Punctuation

Setting Off Direct Quotations

When the expression identifying the speaker interrupts a quoted sentence, the second part of the quotation begins with a small letter. Each part of a divided quotation is enclosed in a set of quotation marks. In addition, the interrupting expression is followed by a comma.

"Where," asked Charles, "can I find a pen like that?"

When the second part of a divided quotation is a full sentence, the interrupting expression ends with a period, and the second part of the quotation begins with a capital letter.

"This game is bound to be good," said Elena. "Both the Bucks and the Stallions are undefeated."

A direct quotation is set off from the rest of the sentence by a comma, a question mark, or an exclamation point, but not by a period.

"I'm so tired of this," said Wenona.

"Was that your sister?" Rosa asked.

"What a great backpack that is!" Evan said.

A period or a comma is always placed inside the closing quotation marks.

Pierce said, "Friday is always my best day."

"Monday is definitely my best day," said Toyoko.

Exercise: Proofreading   Add quotation marks and other punctuation where needed in the following sentences. Circle each letter that should be capitalized.

EXAMPLE: 1. "Today is Friday," said Miss Palumbo. "It's time to check our experiments."

1. Look at mine Wyatt said it's beginning to grow a new leaf

2. Yours said Miss Palumbo is looking great

3. What happened to mine asked Robert didn't it get enough light

4. I'm not sure said Velma that I gave mine enough water

5. Miss Palumbo Clinton asked will we be ready for the science fair

6. We have two weeks answered Miss Palumbo that should be enough time

7. Is it possible asked Robert for me to start a new plant

8. You don't need to said Micah I see a green shoot under the dead leaf

9. Wow exclaimed Robert I guess it's not dead after all

10. Maybe said Miss Palumbo you'd better help it along with some light

Chapter 14: Punctuation

WORKSHEET 4 *Punctuating Dialogue*

A question mark or an exclamation point is placed inside the closing quotation marks when the quotation itself is a question or an exclamation. Otherwise, it is placed outside.

"Who is the mayor of Chicago**?**" Renaldo asked. [The quotation is a question.]

Did you hear him say, "This is my country, too"**?** [The sentence, not the quotation, is a question.]

When you write dialogue, begin a new paragraph each time you change speakers.

"I'm not sure which containers I can take to the recycling center. Will the recyclers take plastics marked 5 and 6?" I asked.

"I think," Suellen replied, "they take only those marked 1 through 4."

When a quotation consists of several sentences, place quotation marks at the beginning and at the end of the whole quotation.

"The recital begins promptly at seven. Bring your costumes, but don't change until you're told. Bring juice and a snack if you need to," said Mrs. Carusso.

Exercise: Revising   On the lines provided, rewrite the following dialogue, correcting any errors in paragraph indentation, punctuation, and capitalization.

> EXAMPLE: Did I tell you that when we met our guide at the hiking trail he said I hope you are prepared for a strenuous hike?
>
> *Did I tell you that when we met our guide at the hiking trail he said, "I hope you are prepared for a strenuous hike"?*

The trail guide said watch for the blue markers. Where can we find them? Kristy asked. Usually you will find them on trees, he replied, but sometimes they are on rocks. It depends on the terrain. Just don't go very far without having one in view. If you're not sure where the next one is, go back to the previous one, and find the trail again. Are there any questions. Yes replied Angel do we have to go?

_____

_____

_____

_____

_____

_____

_____

Chapter 14: Punctuation

Other Uses of Quotation Marks

Use single quotation marks to enclose a quotation within a quotation.

Tamisha said, "I was thinking of that novel that begins 'It was the best of times, it was the worst of times.'"

Use quotation marks to enclose titles of short works such as short stories, poems, articles, songs, episodes of television programs, and chapters and other parts of books.

SHORT STORIES:	"Gimpel the Fool" "The Circular Ruins"
POEMS:	"Daddy" "Sunlight" "Channel Firing"
ARTICLES:	"Success with Fusion" "The Return of the Terns"
SONGS:	"Born in the U.S.A." "America the Beautiful"
EPISODES OF TELEVISION PROGRAMS:	"Pirate Revolt" "Trouble in El Paso"
CHAPTERS AND OTHER PARTS OF BOOKS:	"The Leaf, the Stem, and the Root" "A Trip to the Cottage"

Exercise A: Proofreading   Add quotation marks where necessary in the following sentences.

1. Jiro asked, Who wrote It is better to have loved and lost . . . ?

2. The doctor explained, The child says My stomach feels funny.

3. I like to see it lap the miles is a famous first line in poetry, Mr. Gómez remarked.

4. The principal said, Don't say another word, so I didn't, Max explained.

Exercise B: Proofreading   Add quotation marks where necessary in the following letter.

Dear Steve,

Thanks for your letter. Here are the answers to your questions.

My favorite song of all time is any one of the old blues tunes or Sittin' on the Dock of the Bay. I'm not sure about my favorite episode of a television program, but it is probably The Klingons Return.

Yes, I do read poetry, and Langston Hughes is my favorite poet. I especially like his poem Dream Deferred.

You might be interested in knowing that the October issue of *Ebony* includes a profile of me and a few other performing artists in an article called Starshine. The same article is going to be published as a chapter called Music Makers in *Musicians of the '90's.*

Take care,

Z. J.

MECHANICS

Name _____ Date _____ Class _____

 **Review**

Exercise A: Proofreading   Add underlining (italics), quotation marks, and other punctuation marks where necessary in the following sentences. Circle each letter that should be capitalized.

1. Todd asked can you tell me the answer to the fourth problem?

2. Diana said that she often confused the words affect and effect.

3. Pedro added my sister went to the all-state competition in Concord.

4. The article The Undersea War discusses the sinking of the Lusitania.

5. I saw that at the museum said Kathie it was next to Stuart Davis's painting Swing Landscape.

6. When you read the novel Hatchet asked Troy did you know how it would end?

7. Did Jeb shout I'm the winner! Zoe asked.

8. I saw that article about Apollo 17 in Smithsonian said Mamie.

9. Is the r doubled in occurring Phil and Aki asked we can't remember.

10. I'll be there for sure is what I thought she said said Lucía.

Exercise B: Revising   On the lines provided, rewrite the following sentences in proper paragraph form. Add capital letters and quotation marks, and add or change other punctuation where needed.

     My little sister loves puns and riddles. I don't know where she gets all of the things she asks me, but she always has something new. One day she asked where do fish keep their money? I don't know I said. Where? She answered in a riverbank, of course. Now, do you know what the largest pencil is. No, I answered, what is the largest pencil? She laughed and said it's Pennsylvania!

_____

_____

_____

_____

_____

_____

_____

_____

_____

_____

Chapter 15: Punctuation

Using Apostrophes to Show Possession

An **apostrophe** is used to form the *possessive case* of nouns and some pronouns.

The **possessive case** of a noun or a pronoun shows ownership or relationship.

    OWNERSHIP: **Emilio's** book   RELATIONSHIP: **Anne's** father

To form the possessive case of a singular noun, add an apostrophe and an *s*.

    a **day's** pay   **James's** bicycle   your **nickel's** worth

NOTE: A proper name ending in *s* may take only an apostrophe to form the possessive case if the addition of *'s* would make the name awkward to pronounce.

    Odysseus' journey   **Arkansas'** largest city

To form the possessive case of a plural noun ending in *s*, add only an apostrophe.

    the **Katzes'** house   the **students'** lockers   the **fans'** cheers

To form the possessive case of a plural noun that does not end in *s*, add an apostrophe and an *s*.

    men's clothing   **people's** rights   **women's** issues

Do not use an apostrophe with possessive personal pronouns.

    Is that paddleboat **theirs** or **ours**?

To form the possessive case of some indefinite pronouns, add an apostrophe and an *s*.

    somebody's boots   **everyone's** chance   **another's** idea

Exercise A   On the line provided, rewrite each of the following expressions by using the possessive case. Add apostrophes where necessary.

        EXAMPLE: 1. books of the library *the library's books*

1. ideas that you have _____

2. the melody of the woodwinds _____

3. the giraffe of the Pattersons _____

4. the backpack belonging to her _____

5. the lampshade of someone _____

Exercise B: Proofreading   Add apostrophes where necessary in the sentences below.

1. Have you been to the childrens museum in Indianapolis?

2. Mrs. Joness daughter works there as a guide.

3. The geeses home is nowhere near ours or yours.

4. The workers union expected fair wages for a days work.

5. Minneapolis cold weather is famous throughout the country.

MECHANICS

Chapter 15: Punctuation

Using Apostrophes in Contractions

A **contraction** is a shortened form of a word, a figure, or a group of words. To form a contraction, use an apostrophe to show where letters or numerals have been left out.

COMMON CONTRACTIONS

I am . . . I'm	1999 . . . '99
let us . . . let's	we are . . . we're
she is . . . she's	he will . . . he'll
I have . . . I've	she would . . . she'd
where is . . . where's	of the clock . . . o'clock

The word *not* can be shortened to *n't* and added to a verb, usually without any change in the spelling of the verb.

EXAMPLE: is not **isn't**   was not   **wasn't**
EXCEPTIONS: will not   **won't**   cannot   **can't**

Exercise A   On the line provided, rewrite each of the following groups of words as a contraction.

1. should not _____   6. she had _____

2. he is _____   7. were not _____

3. will not _____   8. I have _____

4. they are _____   9. who is _____

5. it is _____   10. you are _____

Exercise B: Proofreading   For each of the following sentences, add apostrophes where necessary.

EXAMPLE: 1. There's a book about otters on the round table in the library.

1. Lets plan a trip to the mountains in 96.

2. Wheres the window she said she couldnt open?

3. Ive got a plan to get back to the house at ten oclock.

4. He isnt sure who owns that bike, but hes sure it doesnt belong here.

5. Im not certain whether he cant come or he just wont come.

Name _____ Date _____ Class _____

Using Contractions and Possessive Pronouns

Do not confuse contractions with possessive pronouns.

Contractions	Possessive Pronouns
it's [*it is*]	its
it's [*it has*]	
who's [*who is*]	whose
who's [*who has*]	
you're [*you are*]	your
they're [*they are*]	their
there's [*there is, there has*]	theirs

Exercise A   On the line provided, write *CON* if the italicized word in each sentence below is a contraction or *PP* if the word is a possessive pronoun. Then insert apostrophes as needed.

EXAMPLE: __CON__   1. *They've* misplaced their tickets to the play.

_____ 1. Joel is not sure *whose* hat that is.

_____ 2. Was it your grandmother who knitted *your* sweater?

_____ 3. *Theres* the diner I was telling you about.

_____ 4. *Whos* in charge of the dues?

_____ 5. I fed the stray cat, but I didn't know *its* name.

_____ 6. He was wondering whether *youre* his friend or not.

_____ 7. The best entry in the contest was *theirs*.

_____ 8. Look outside to see whether *its* raining.

_____ 9. Was it *their* cat that was missing?

_____10. *Theyre* not going to the dance on Saturday.

Exercise B   Look at the italicized word in each sentence below. If the word is incorrect, write the correct form on the line provided. If the word is correct, write *C*.

EXAMPLE: 1. It's *you're* turn to do the dishes. _*your*_

1. This set of encyclopedias is *their's*.   _____

2. *Who's* been giving you those lovely flowers?   _____

3. *Your* name is not on the list of candidates.   _____

4. *Its* taken a long time to find the right gift.   _____

5. *Whose* the owner of that little brown car?   _____

MECHANICS

Chapter 15: Punctuation

 **WORSHEET 4** *Using Apostrophes in Plurals*

Use an apostrophe and an *s* to form the plurals of letters, numerals, and signs, and of words referred to as words.

The word has four *s*'s in it.

Enrico's *F*'s looked like 7's.

Rap music became popular in the 1980's.

Sharon uses too many *and*'s to join ideas in her writing; sometimes she uses +'s.

Exercise: Proofreading Add apostrophes as needed in the sentences below.

EXAMPLE: 1. It will be strange to live in the 2000's instead of the 1900's.

1. When *&*s appear in company names, you should write *&*s instead of *and*s.

2. When you are proofreading, look for all the *very*s, *nice*s, and *good*s, and try to replace them with more-specific words.

3. The 1940s was an era of big bands and dance music.

4. He said that only 7s and 5s were in his telephone number.

5. I always think there are two *c*s in *vacuum*, but there is only one.

6. Does the child know his ABCs yet?

7. The teacher told them to mind their *p*s and *q*s.

8. Do many newspaper writers begin sentences with *Or*s or *But*s?

9. The young child confused his *s*s and *z*s.

10. He adds extra loops to the tops and bottoms of his *3*s.

11. Sitcoms were very popular on television during the 1950s.

12. Mr. Ramírez asked the student to stop giving him *maybe*s.

13. *Cancelled* can be spelled with two *l*s or one.

14. He sometimes uses +s when he should be writing *and*s.

15. Look for *so*s in your writing, and check to be sure you should not be writing *therefore*s or other words instead.

16. Television miniseries became popular during the 1970s.

17. Can you count to 100 by 2s?

18. Many compromises were made between the North and the South during the 1840s and 1850s.

19. Young children sometimes confuse 6s and 9s.

20. Always cross your *t*s and dot your *i*s.

Name _____ Date _____ Class _____

 **WORKSHEET 5** *Using Hyphens*

Use a **hyphen** to divide a word at the end of a line. When dividing a word at the end of a line, remember the following rules:

(1) Divide the word only between syllables.

    INCORRECT: wonde-
          rful

    CORRECT: **wonder-**
          ful

(2) Do not divide a one-syllable word.

    INCORRECT: jump-
          ed

    CORRECT: **jumped**

(3) Divide an already hyphenated word at a hyphen.

    INCORRECT: sis-
          ter-in-law

    CORRECT: **sister-**
          in-law

(4) Do not divide a word so that one letter stands alone.

    INCORRECT: a-
          nonymous

    CORRECT: **anony-**
          mous

Use a hyphen with compound numbers from *twenty-one* to *ninety-nine* and with fractions used as adjectives.

    fifty-seven cars   **one-third** cup of water *but* **one third** of the class

Exercise: Proofreading   On the lines provided, rewrite the following sentences, correcting hyphen use as needed. If a sentence is correct, write C.

1. When I turned twenty one, my mom paid for me to go to New Mexico.

_____

2. There I visited my relative Tia Consuelo, my uncle's mot-
her-in-law.

_____

_____

3. She told me about a well-known New Mexico writer, Juan A. A. Sedillo, a law
yer, judge, and newspaper columnist.

_____

_____

4. That summer I read his short story "Gentleman of Río en Medio" and enjoyed it greatly, because it was based on real life.

_____

_____

5. While I was in New Mexico, I spent one fourth of my time reading.

_____

MECHANICS

Chapter 15: Punctuation

Using Parentheses and Dashes

Use **parentheses** to enclose material that is added to a sentence but is not considered of major importance.

Nina Otero (1882–1965) wrote about Hispanic folklore.

Otero (ō té rō) also told stories about her own family.

Material enclosed in parentheses may range from a single word to a short sentence. A short sentence in parentheses may stand by itself or be contained within another sentence.

Read Otero's story "Asking for the Bride." (It is very short.)

Many words and phrases are used *parenthetically;* that is, they break into the main thought of a sentence. Most parenthetical elements are set off by commas or parentheses.

The winner was Elaine, not Ellen.

The decision (whether to drive or fly) was a difficult one.

Sometimes parenthetical elements demand a stronger emphasis. In such instances, a *dash* is used.

Use a **dash** to indicate an abrupt break in thought or speech.

Her horse—I don't see it now—is beautiful.

"The price is—but I can tell you don't really want to know," the salesclerk said.

Exercise: Proofreading   Add parentheses or dashes where needed in each of the following sentences.

EXAMPLE: 1. Mr. Layle—he's going onstage right now—will be the speaker.

1. That house it was once a hotel is the largest private home in town.

2. Author Mary O'Hara 1885–1980 wrote wonderful books about horses.

3. If you'll step over here oh, excuse me, Ms. Samos you can see the view.

4. The Buffalo River a short but scenic river is in Arkansas.

5. Zane Grey author, adventurer, outdoorsman wrote books about the American West.

6. The Mississippi River the longest river in North America flooded extensively in 1993.

7. Hills and valleys called ridges and hollows in the Ozarks are geographic features of Northwest Arkansas and Southwest Missouri.

8. Many an American elm tree *Ulmus americana* has died from Dutch elm disease.

9. As we climb these steps oops, I almost slipped we can see how they were carved by hand into the cliff.

10. John Hancock he's a famous signer of the Declaration of Independence had a unique signature.

Chapter 15: Punctuation

 **Review**

WORKSHEET 7

Exercise A   On the lines provided, form the singular possessive and the plural possessive of each of the following nouns.

		Singular Possessive	Plural Possessive
EXAMPLE:	1. citizen	citizen's	citizens'
	1. book	_____	_____
	2. puppy	_____	_____
	3. donkey	_____	_____
	4. mouse	_____	_____
	5. calf	_____	_____
	6. hero	_____	_____
	7. elephant	_____	_____
	8. tooth	_____	_____
	9. school	_____	_____
	10. rally	_____	_____

Exercise B   On the lines provided, form the possessives of the following pronouns.

EXAMPLE: 1. someone _someone's_

1. they   _____
2. everybody   _____
3. I   _____

4. it   _____
5. who   _____

Exercise C   On the line provided, form a contraction of each of the following pairs of words.

1. will not   _____
2. there is   _____
3. who will   _____
4. they are   _____
5. who is   _____

6. are not   _____
7. it is   _____
8. should not   _____
9. let us   _____
10. I have   _____

Exercise D   Underline the correct word in parentheses in each sentence.

EXAMPLE: 1. (Whose, <u>Who's</u>) going to pick apples when we get to the orchard?

1. All the people on the tour must carry (they're, their) own luggage.

2. (Your, You're) going to be early if you leave now.

3. She doesn't think (its, it's) fair for him to always do the laundry.

4. (They're, Their) going to a movie at seven o'clock.

5. The kitten can't find (its, it's) toys.

Exercise E: Proofreading   On the lines provided, rewrite the following sentences, adding, deleting, or changing the positions of apostrophes and hyphens as necessary.

EXAMPLE: 1. Are there two *t*s or two *r*s in the word *carrot*?

Are there two *t*'s or two *r*'s in the word *carrot*?

1. The suspect had sped off in a dark green car, which the witness t-hought was a Dodge.

_____

_____

2. Sometimes Jessas *3*s look more like *5*s on her math papers.

_____

3. Jorge said, "I dont know who is coming and who isnt coming to my moth-er-in-laws house for her birthday party (sh'ell be fifty five)."

_____

_____

4. Now that the new law isnt going into effect, no ones quite sure what to do about yard was-tes in the 90s.

_____

_____

5. Alexs full name has five *a*s and three *e*s in it.

_____

Exercise F: Proofreading   In each of the following sentences, insert parentheses or dashes as needed.

EXAMPLE: 1. I'm waiting for the plumber—well, here she is at last—to install my new dishwasher.

1. Gabriela Mistral 1889–1957 was a Chilean poet who often wrote about children.

2. His violin it was Mozart's first musical instrument is on display in Salzburg.

3. The Sears Tower the tallest building in the United States is in Chicago.

4. The formulas for the worksheet oh no, I forgot to copy them from the chalkboard would have made our homework easier.

5. The common raven *Corvus corax* is not very common anymore because it has been killed off in many areas by humans.

Name _____ Date _____ Class _____

Improving Your Spelling

The following techniques can help you spell words correctly.

Pronounce words correctly. Pronouncing words carefully can often help you spell them correctly.

    interest: in•ter•est [*not* in•trest]

Spell by syllables. When you have trouble spelling long words, divide them into syllables. A **syllable** is a word part that can be pronounced by itself.

    fair [one syllable]

    dis•miss [two syllables]

    par•a•dise [three syllables]

Use a dictionary. When you are not sure about the spelling of a word, look in a dictionary. A dictionary will also tell you the correct pronunciations and syllable divisions of words.

Keep a spelling notebook. The best way to master words that give you difficulty is to list the words and review them frequently. Divide each page into four columns.

        COLUMN 1: Correctly spell the words you frequently misspell.

        COLUMN 2: Write the words again, dividing them into syllables and marking accents. (Use a dictionary if necessary.)

        COLUMN 3: Write the words again, circling the parts that give you trouble.

        COLUMN 4: Jot down any comments that may help you remember the correct spelling.

Proofread for careless spelling errors. By slowly rereading what you have written, you can correct careless errors.

Exercise Look up the following words in a dictionary. On the line provided, divide each word into syllables, using hyphens between syllables. Pronounce each syllable correctly, and learn to spell the word by syllables.

        EXAMPLE: 1. souvenir *sou-ve-nir*

1. advertisement _____
2. business _____
3. criticize _____
4. doctrine _____
5. embarrass _____

6. laboratory _____
7. opinion _____
8. similar _____
9. temperament _____
10. variety _____

Chapter 16: Spelling and Vocabulary

WORKSHEET 2 *Roots*

Many English words are made up of various word parts. Learning to spell the most frequently used parts can help you spell many words correctly.

The **root** is the part of the word that carries the word's core meaning. Many English word roots come from ancient Latin and Greek words. Sometimes a root has more than one form.

Word Root	Meaning	Example
–dict–	speak	dictator
–duc–, –duct–	lead	induce
–ject–	throw	project
–ped–	foot	pedestal
–pend–	hang, weigh	pendulum
–port–	carry, bear	import
–spec–	look	speculate
–struct–	build	construction
–vid–, –vis–	see	vision
–voc–	call	vocalize

Exercise A   For each of the following words, underline the root that you find in the above chart. Then, on the line provided, use the meaning of the root and your own knowledge to write a definition of each word. Check your definition in a dictionary.

EXAMPLE: 1. transp**ort** *to carry across*

1. conduct *(verb)* _____

2. instruct _____

3. television _____

4. vocational _____

5. spectacular _____

Exercise B   On the lines provided, write five sentences using the words that you defined in Exercise A.

EXAMPLE: 1. *We found a way to transport the couch from the store to our house.*

1. _____

2. _____

3. _____

4. _____

5. _____

Chapter 16: Spelling and Vocabulary

WORKSHEET 3 | *Prefixes*

A **prefix** is one or more than one letter or syllable added to the beginning of a word to create a new word with a different meaning.

COMMONLY USED PREFIXES

Prefix	Meaning	Example
anti–	against	antifreeze
bi–	two	biweekly
co–	with, together	coauthor
de–	away, from, off, down	decrease
dis–	away, from, opposing	disfavor
in–	not	incoherent
inter–	between, among	international
mis–	badly, not, wrongly	mistake
over–	above, extremely	overdone
post–	after, following	postscript
pre–	before	predate
re–	back, again	revisit
semi–	half, partly	semicircle
sub–	under, beneath	submerge
un–	not, opposite	unknown

Exercise   Underline the prefix in each of the following words. Then use the meanings of the prefix and the root and your own knowledge to write a definition of each word. Check your definition in a dictionary.

EXAMPLE: 1. <u>mis</u>direct *to direct wrongly or badly*

1. semiofficial _____

2. reschedule _____

3. preregister _____

4. bilingual _____

5. misunderstand _____

6. unleash _____

7. demystify _____

8. disengage _____

9. inability _____

10. overtime _____

Name _____ Date _____ Class _____

 **WORKSHEET 4** *Suffixes*

A **suffix** is a word part that is added after a root. Often, adding a suffix changes both a word's part of speech and its meaning. Here are some common suffixes.

COMMONLY USED SUFFIXES

Suffix	Meaning	Example
–able	able, likely	enjoyable
–en	make, become	wooden
–ful	full of, characteristic of	soulful
–ible	able, likely	destructible
–ity	state, condition	mobility
–ize	make, cause to be	finalize
–ly	characteristic of	brightly
–ment	result, action	enjoyment
–or	one who	sailor
–ous	characterized by	poisonous
–tion	action, condition	concentration
–ty	quality, state	realty
–y	condition, quality	thrifty

Exercise   Read the following paragraph. On the lines provided, write the suffix and the meaning of each underlined word. Use a dictionary if necessary.

During the 1960's, movie executives began to <u>realize</u> that the <u>popularity</u> of musicals could bring commercial success. Robert Wise, the <u>director</u> of *The Sound of Music*, was no <u>exception</u>. He created an <u>immensely</u> <u>successful</u> film; his <u>investment</u> really paid off. The <u>likeable</u> governess in the movie, Julie Andrews, <u>instantly</u> became the <u>golden</u> girl of the silver screen.

1. realize _____

2. popularity _____

3. director _____

4. exception _____

5. immensely _____

6. successful _____

7. investment _____

8. likeable _____

9. instantly _____

10. golden _____

Name _____ Date _____ Class _____

Spelling Rules A

One way to improve your spelling is to memorize some important rules.

Except after *c*, write *ie* when the sound is long *e*. Some exceptions: *either, neither, leisure, weird.*

Write *ei* when the sound is not long *e*, especially when the sound is long *a*. Some exceptions: *friend, mischief, view, ancient.*

NOTE: These rules apply only when the *i* and the *e* are in the same syllable.

The only word ending in *–sede* is *supersede*. The only words ending in *–ceed* are *exceed, proceed,* and *succeed*. All other words with this sound end in *–cede.*

Exercise A   The following paragraph contains ten words with missing letters. Add the letters *ie* or *ei* to spell each numbered word correctly.

EXAMPLE: Many people know [1] th ___*ei*___ r signs in the Chinese zodiac.

My [1] n _____ ghbor, Mrs. Yee, told me about the Chinese zodiac signs. Not all

Chinese people [2] bel _____ ve in the zodiac. My parents don't, and [3] n _____ ther do

I, but I do think it's interesting. The Chinese zodiac is an [4] anc _____ nt set of twelve-

year cycles named after different animals. According to Mrs. Yee, the [5] ch _____ f traits

in your personality come from your animal sign. At first, I thought this notion was a bit

[6] w _____ rd, but it's not hard to understand. For example, a tiger is supposed to

[7] s _____ ze opportunities [8] f _____ rcely. That description perfectly fits my brother's

[9] fr _____ nd Mike Chen, who was born in 1974. Mrs. Yee showed me a zodiac chart so

that I could figure out the signs of all [10] _____ ght members of my family.

Exercise B: Proofreading   Identify the spelling errors of words ending in *–cede, –ceed,* and *–sede* in the following sentences. Cross out the error. Then write the correct spelling on the line provided. If a sentence is correct, write *C*.

EXAMPLE: 1. Edgar Allan Poe ~~succeded~~ in creating a memorable
atmosphere of tension in "The Tell-Tale Heart." *succeeded*

1. "The Tell-Tale Heart" has superceded "The Gold Bug" as my
favorite Poe short story.   _____

2. The narrator says that he is not mad, but then prosedes to outline
plans to harm an old man.   _____

3. As the story unfolds, the narrator certainly exceeds the bounds of
normal, rational behavior.   _____

4. You must consede that the narrator is mad.   _____

5. Unfortunately, no one interceeds to save the old man.   _____

Chapter 16: Spelling and Vocabulary

WORKSHEET 6 | *Spelling Rules B*

When adding a prefix to a word, do not change the spelling of the word itself. Some commonly used prefixes are *mis–*, *re–*, *un–*, *in–*, *pre–*, *dis–*, and *over–*.

Use the following rules to add a suffix to a word.

1. When adding the suffix *–ly* or *–ness*, do not change the spelling of the word itself. Exceptions: For words that end in *y* and have more than one syllable, change the *y* to *i* before adding *–ly* or *–ness*.

2. Drop the final silent *e* before a suffix beginning with a vowel. Exceptions: words ending in *ce* or *ge* before a suffix beginning with *a* or *o* and the words *dyeing*, *singeing*, and *mileage*.

   NOTE: When adding *–ing* to words ending in *ie*, drop the *e* and change the *i* to *y*.

3. Keep the final silent *e* before a suffix beginning with a consonant. Some exceptions: *argument*, *judgment*, *awful*, *truly*, and *ninth*.

4. For words ending in *y* preceded by a consonant, change the *y* to *i* before any suffix that does not begin with *i*.

5. For words ending in *y* preceded by a vowel, keep the *y* when adding a suffix. Some exceptions: *daily*, *laid*, *paid*, and *said*.

6. Double the final consonant before a suffix beginning with a vowel if the word (a) has only one syllable or has the accent on the last syllable *and* (b) ends in a single consonant preceded by a single vowel. Examples: *sitting*, *forbidden*. Some exceptions are words ending in *w* or *x*: *bowing*, *boxing*.

Exercise A   On the lines provided, spell each of the following words with the given prefix.

EXAMPLE: 1. un + even *uneven*

1. mis + understand   _____

2. pre + wash   _____

3. re + adjust   _____

4. over + cook   _____

5. in + appropriate   _____

Exercise B   On the lines provided, spell each of the following words with the given suffix.

EXAMPLE: 1. win + er *winner*

1. kindly + ness _____

2. courage + ous _____

3. destroy + ing _____

4. confine + ment _____

5. begin + er _____

6. adore + able   _____

7. day + ly   _____

8. tie + ing   _____

9. sure + ly   _____

10. pity + ful   _____

Chapter 16: Spelling and Vocabulary

 **WORKSHEET 7** *Plurals of Nouns A*

For most nouns you simply add –*s* to form the plural.

SINGULAR: tortilla   PLURAL: tortillas

Use the following rules to form the plurals of other nouns.

1. For nouns ending in *s*, *x*, *z*, *ch*, or *sh*, add –*es*.

    SINGULAR: bench   PLURAL: benches

2. For nouns ending in *y* preceded by a vowel, add –*s*.

    SINGULAR: Sunday   PLURAL: Sundays

3. For nouns ending in *y* preceded by a consonant, change the *y* to *i* and add –*es*.

    SINGULAR: navy   PLURAL: navies

    EXCEPTIONS: For proper nouns, add –*s*.

4. For some nouns ending in *f* or *fe*, add –*s*. For others, change the *f* or *fe* to *v* and add –*es*.

    SINGULAR: wife   PLURAL: wives

5. For nouns ending in *o* preceded by a vowel, add –*s*.

    SINGULAR: rodeo   PLURAL: rodeos

6. For nouns ending in *o* preceded by a consonant, add –*es*.

    SINGULAR: potato   PLURAL: potatoes

    EXCEPTIONS: proper nouns (*Eskimos*) and some other nouns (*altos, silos*)

NOTE: Some nouns that end in *o* preceded by a consonant have two plural forms (*heros* or *heroes*).

Exercise A   On the lines provided, spell the plural form of each of the following nouns.

EXAMPLE: 1. right *rights*

1. monkey   _____
2. trophy   _____
3. dish   _____

4. tax   _____
5. radio   _____

Exercise B: Proofreading   The following paragraph contains five spelling errors. Cross out each error. Then write the word correctly on the line provided.

EXAMPLE: [1] Three ~~freinds~~, Linda Dunlap and Sally and Rob Grady, went to Canada's Prince Edward Island. 1. *friends*

[1] The Gradies said they loved the island's rugged seashore. [2] Seeing the island fulfilled several of their fondest wishs. [3] They visited the farmhouse that's the setting for the novel *Anne of Green Gables* and walked the pathwaies around the house. [4] They saw many farms, which are famous for potatos. [5] They also spent time in Charlottetown, the largest of the island's citys.

1. _____   2. _____   3. _____

4. _____   5. _____

Chapter 16: Spelling and Vocabulary

WORKSHEET 8 *Plurals of Nouns B*

Use the following rules to form the plurals of nouns.

1. A few nouns, such as *children, oxen, geese, feet, teeth, women,* and *mice,* form the plural irregularly.
2. For most compound nouns, form the plural of the last word in the compound.

    SINGULAR: horseshoe   PLURAL: horseshoes

3. For compound nouns in which one of the words is modified by the other word or words, form the plural of the word modified.

    SINGULAR: sister-in-law   PLURAL: sisters-in-law

4. For some nouns, such as *Chinese* and *sheep,* the singular and plural forms are the same.
5. For numbers, letters, symbols, and words used as words, it is best always to add an apostrophe and *–s.*

    if's   *t*'s   *&*'s   1960's (also written 1960s)

Exercise A   On the line provided, spell the plural form of each of the following nouns. (Note: Italics indicate words used as words or letters used as letters.)

EXAMPLE: 1. *B*   *B's*

1. *7*   _____
2. Sioux   _____
3. *oh*   _____
4. man   _____
5. basketball   _____
6. son-in-law   _____
7. major general   _____
8. handful   _____
9. editor in chief   _____
10. 1990   _____

Exercise B   On the lines provided, write the plural forms of the following four pairs of words. Then use words with similar consonant sounds to create tongue twisters or hard-to-say sentences. Your tongue-twisting sentences can be silly or serious.

EXAMPLE: 1. sheep—sea serpent *sheep—sea serpents*

Six shy sheep and seven salty sea serpents sang silly songs.

1. lady-in-waiting—louse _____

    _____

2. moose—man _____

    _____

3. trout—treehouse _____

    _____

4. tooth—ten-year-old _____

    _____

Chapter 16: Spelling and Vocabulary

 **WORKSHEET 9** *Spelling Numbers*

Observe the following rules for spelling numbers.

1. Spell out a number that begins a sentence.

   Five hundred students signed the petition.

2. Within a sentence, spell out numbers that can be written in one or two words. Use numerals for other numbers.

   Did you say **five hundred** students?

   She said **5,500** students.

   NOTE: If you use several numbers, some short and some long, write them all the same way. Usually, it is better to write them all as numerals.

   There are **500** students in the school, not **5,500**.

3. Spell out numbers used to indicate order.

   That is the **second** [*not* 2nd] petition that I have signed.

Exercise: Proofreading   Each of the following sentences contains an error in writing a number. Correct the error on the line provided.

> EXAMPLE: 1. 500 students were in last year's graduating class.
> *Five hundred*

1. There are four hundred and fifty people in our class this year.   _____

2. The girl who spoke at graduation was 1st in the class academically.   _____

3. 30 minutes is a long time to speak; however, she spoke that long on the subject "Our Future."   _____

4. There were 1,000 people in attendance at the ceremony.   _____

5. The graduation ceremony was the 3rd one I had attended.   _____

6. I wonder if some high schools are so big that they have to hold 2 graduation ceremonies.   _____

7. Sitting with my parents were 21 other relatives from all over the country.   _____

8. One of my aunts drove nine hundred miles to be at the graduation, and my grandparents flew 2,500 miles.   _____

9. Following graduation, we had a reception attended by 65 people at our house.   _____

10. We probably won't see some of the relatives again until my brother, who is in the 8th grade, graduates.   _____

Chapter 16: Spelling and Vocabulary

WORKSHEET 10 *Using Context Clues A*

The **context** of a word consists of the words that surround it in a sentence and the whole situation in which the word is used. The context gives you clues to the meaning of a word. Two types of context clues are *definitions and restatements*, and *examples*.

Definitions and restatements are clues that define the term or restate it in other words.

The *conifer*, **a type of tree that bears cones**, thrives in cold climates.

Examples used in context may also reveal the meaning of an unfamiliar word.

Most *conifers*—such as **pine, spruce,** and **sequoia**—grow far from the equator.

Exercise   For each italicized word in the sentences below, write on the line provided the letter of the definition that is closest in meaning.

a. command	b. clear	c. destruction	d. solve	e. knowledge
f. dissolver	g. respect	h. skill	i. aloneness	j. public

_____ 1. The code was complicated, but she eventually managed to *decipher* it, or break it.

_____ 2. The puppy raced around the room, scattering cushions, banging into furniture—just creating *havoc.*

_____ 3. The sympathetic teacher discussed our problems with considerable *perception* and understanding.

_____ 4. One of the ways the soldiers showed *deference* to the emperor was to bow.

_____ 5. Luke finds it extremely difficult to make friends because he has lived the greater part of his life in *isolation*, apart from other children.

_____ 6. Throwing the English tea overboard into Boston Harbor was an *overt* act of rebellion.

_____ 7. One example of the gymnast's *dexterity* was her somersaults on the balance beam.

_____ 8. The one *mandate* my parents tell me I must remember is that I should never lie to them.

_____ 9. Clear scales over a snake's eyes act like *transparent* eyelids that keep out dirt.

_____ 10. Do not spill any *solvent*, such as turpentine, alcohol, or acid, on this table.

Name _____ Date _____ Class _____

 ## *Using Context Clues B*

The **context** of a word is the words that surround it in a sentence. The context gives you clues to the meaning of a word. Three types of context clues are *synonyms, contrast,* and *cause and effect.*

Synonyms are clues that indicate that an unfamiliar word is the same as or similar to a familiar word or phrase.

The seventeenth-century *pewter* was like tarnished **silver**.

Contrast clues indicate that an unfamiliar word is opposite in meaning to a familiar word or phrase.

Fred Astaire was quite *debonair,* whereas Jerry Lewis was known for his **clumsiness**.

Cause-and-effect clues indicate that an unfamiliar word is related to the cause or the result of an action, feeling, or idea.

Because Mozart was a *prodigy,* **he got far more public attention than most small children**.

Exercise For each italicized word in the sentences below, write on the line provided the letter of the definition that is closest in meaning.

a. made loud noise	b. avoid	c. longingly	d. force	e. in disguise
f. imaginary	g. scolded	h. excess	i. noticeably	j. not in harmony

_____ 1. Even though they had just arrived in India, they were already thinking *wistfully* of their family at home.

_____ 2. Because her puppy chewed on the phone cord, Chela sharply *reprimanded* it.

_____ 3. Movie stars sometimes travel *incognito* so that they will not be recognized.

_____ 4. Although the sale items were *prominently* displayed in the store, I did not see them.

_____ 5. Even though he *clamored* for attention, we tried to ignore the mischievous boy.

_____ 6. Harold has a *fictitious* playmate like a character in a play or story.

_____ 7. People should not attempt to *evade* their duties as citizens like children avoiding their chores.

_____ 8. I will allow you to make your own choice about whether or not to go; I certainly won't *coerce* you.

_____ 9. Sid always used a *plethora* of words, although one or two words would do.

_____10. The *dissonant* sounds made by the school orchestra tuning up for the evening show were like the howls and screeches in a pet shop.

Chapter 16: Spelling and Vocabulary

WORKSHEET 12 *Choosing the Right Word*

A **synonym** is a word that means nearly the same thing as another word. However, words that are synonyms rarely have exactly the same meaning. Two words may have the same **denotation,** or dictionary definition, but a different **connotation,** or suggested meaning. For example, *sly* has the same denotation as *clever,* but the words have very different connotations. The connotation of *sly* is "sneaky," whereas the suggested meaning of *clever* is "smart." An **antonym** is a word that has nearly the opposite meaning of another word. For example, *light* has an opposite meaning to *heavy.*

Homographs are words that are spelled the same but have different meanings. Although the words look the same, they may not be pronounced the same. Use context clues to help you discover the meaning of a homograph in a sentence. Examples: the *bow* of a ship, a pretty *bow* on a package.

Exercise A   For each of the italicized words below, write the letter of the word or phrase that has the same meaning. Underline each italicized word that has a negative connotation. Use a dictionary if necessary.

_____ 1. How do you *abbreviate* the title <u>Prime Minister</u>?
    a. shorten   b. change   c. eliminate

_____ 2. Fortunately, heavy rains are *transitory* in this region.
    a. damaging   b. accurately reported   c. lasting a short time

_____ 3. The child often tried to *shirk* his chores so he could play.
    a. discuss   b. avoid   c. begin

_____ 4. Rufino's singing voice is *shrill.*
    a. piercing   b. deep   c. loud

Exercise B   For every italicized word, write the letter of its antonym from the list.
    a. useless   b. motionless   c. polished   d. slender

_____ 1. "This exercise program is *beneficial,*" encouraged the doctor.

_____ 2. The cabin was built of roughly hewn logs and looked very *rustic.*

_____ 3. The robot can walk, swing its arms, and turn its head. In fact, all of its parts are *mobile.*

_____ 4. We need a good *stout* beam to support this roof.

Exercise C   Each of the following sentences contains a pair of homographs. On the lines provided, write a meaning for each homograph. You may use a dictionary to find exact meanings.

1. The cave guide told the people not to *bat* at a *bat* should they see one.

_____

2. As we *wind* through the forest, we can hear the *wind* in the trees.

_____

Name _____ Date _____ Class _____

 **WORKSHEET 13** *Review*

Exercise A On the line provided, write each word syllable-by-syllable, using hyphens between syllables. Use a dictionary if you are unsure.

EXAMPLE: 1. country *coun-try*

1. friend _____   4. ignorance _____

2. trouble _____   5. tradition _____

3. accommodate _____

Exercise B Underline the root in each of the following words. Then, on the line provided, use the meaning of the root and your own knowledge to write a definition of each word. Check your definition in a dictionary.

EXAMPLE: 1. <u>ped</u>al *a lever operated by the foot*

1. diction _____

2. video _____

3. constructive _____

4. education _____

5. export _____

Exercise C On the line provided, add the prefix in parentheses to the word that follows it. Then give the meanings of the prefix and of the whole word. Use a dictionary if needed.

EXAMPLE: 1. (bi–) annual *biannual; two; twice a year*

1. (anti–) viral _____

2. (de–) form _____

3. (inter–) state _____

4. (post–) natal _____

5. (sub–) normal _____

Exercise D On the line provided, add the suffix in parentheses to the word that precedes it. Then give the meaning of the new word, and identify its part of speech. Use a dictionary if necessary.

EXAMPLE: 1. beauty (–fy) *beautify—to adorn or make beautiful, verb*

1. appease (–ment) _____

2. change (–able) _____

3. defense (–ible) _____

4. envy (–ous) _____

5. employ (–able) _____

MECHANICS

Chapter 16, Worksheet 13, continued

Exercise E: Proofreading   Each of the following sentences contains a spelling error. Identify and correct each error.

EXAMPLE: 1. William Goyens was a certifyed Texas hero. *certified*

1. Goyens was an industryous blacksmith.   _____

2. In 1820, he moved to Texas, where he succeded in business.   _____

3. Goyens acheived his greatest fame as a negotiator with the Comanche and the Cherokee peoples.   _____

4. Because of Goyens's efforts, the Comanches and the Cherokees agreed to remain on peaceful terms with the settlers.   _____

5. In addition to negotiating peace treaties, Goyens studied law to protect his own and others' freedoms.   _____

Exercise F   In each item below, a plural word is misspelled or a number is not written properly. On the line provided, write the word or number correctly.

EXAMPLE: 1. trains, bookscase, boys, teeth *bookcases*

1. ninth-graders, doorknobs, Eskimos, knifes   _____

2. ways, rodeoes, Japanese, mice   _____

3. Eight dogs bark. 9 cats meow. It sounds like 150 animals.   _____

4. tomatos, #'s, Johnsons, sons-in-law   _____

5. pencils, benches, *b*'s, 5th place, gravies   _____

Exercise G   Follow the directions below, and write sentences on the lines provided. Use a dictionary if necessary.

1. Write a sentence containing either an example or a definition context clue for the word *legacy*.

   _____

2. Write a sentence containing one of the following types of context clues for the word *natural*: synonym, contrast, or cause and effect.

   _____

3. In a sentence, use a synonym of the word *big* that has a pleasant connotation.

   _____

4. In a sentence, use an antonym for the word *indifferent*.

   _____

5. Use the homographs *desert* (des´•ert) and *desert* (des•ert´) in a sentence.

   _____

Chapter 17: The Writing Process

WORKSHEET 1 | *Freewriting*

Freewriting is a technique for gathering ideas for writing. In freewriting, you write whatever comes into your mind, without worrying about grammar, usage, mechanics, or organization. To freewrite, set a time limit of three to five minutes. Start with a subject that's important to you, and keep writing until the time is up. If you get stuck, just write anything. The important thing is to keep your pen moving. **Focused freewriting,** or **looping,** means taking a word or phrase from freewriting you've already done and starting to freewrite again.

Exercise A   Choose a subject from the list below. On the lines provided, freewrite on this subject for three or four minutes. Simply put your pen or pencil to the paper and write whatever comes into your mind about the subject. Don't worry about grammar, spelling, or mechanics.

the old West   baseball   African American history and culture   polar bears

_____

_____

_____

_____

_____

_____

_____

_____

_____

_____

Exercise B   Choose one word or phrase from your freewriting in Exercise A. Write that word or phrase below. Then, on the lines provided, do focused freewriting for three or four minutes.

Word or phrase: _____

_____

_____

_____

_____

_____

_____

_____

_____

COMPOSITION

Chapter 17: The Writing Process

WORKSHEET 2 | *Brainstorming*

Brainstorming is a technique for gathering ideas for writing. In brainstorming, you say whatever comes to mind in response to a word. You can brainstorm alone or with a group or partner. To brainstorm, write any subject at the top of a sheet of paper or on the chalkboard. List every idea about the subject that comes to your mind. (In a group, have one person list the ideas.) Keep going until you run out of ideas.

Exercise A   Choose one of the following general subjects. Brainstorm about the subject alone or with a few classmates. On the lines below, write all the ideas that you can think of about that subject.

mountain bikes	musical instruments	iguanas
recycling	soccer	comic book collecting

Subject you chose: _____

Brainstorming notes:

_____   _____

_____   _____

_____   _____

_____   _____

_____   _____

_____   _____

_____   _____

_____   _____

Exercise B   Choose one of the ideas you listed in your brainstorming notes for Exercise A. On the lines provided, explain why that idea would be a good topic to write about.

Idea you chose: _____

Explanation: _____

_____

_____

_____

_____

_____

_____

Chapter 17: The Writing Process

WORKSHEET 3 *Clustering*

Clustering is a way to explore a subject. To cluster, write your subject on your paper, and circle the subject. Around the subject, write whatever ideas about it occur to you. Circle these ideas. Draw lines connecting them with the subject. When an idea in one of your circles makes you think of related ideas, you can do further clustering around that idea.

Exercise Choose one of the following topics, and write it in the center circle below. Make a cluster chart that shows at least four specific details related to the subject. Then show at least two ideas related to each of two of the clustered ideas. Draw additional circles and lines if needed.

    sculpture   bicycling   cat care   cloning   the future

COMPOSITION

Chapter 17: The Writing Process

Asking Questions

Try asking yourself questions to find facts and ideas for writing. The *5W-How?* **questions** are *Who? What? Where? When? Why?* and *How?*

Imagining gives you creative ideas for writing. Trigger your imagination by asking **"What if?" questions,** such as *What if snow had dollar value?* and *What if I could hear conversations from two miles away?*

Exercise A   You are going to interview a classmate who has lived in India. Write six questions beginning with the words *Who, What, Where, When, Why,* and *How.*

1. _____
   _____ ?

2. _____
   _____ ?

3. _____
   _____ ?

4. _____
   _____ ?

5. _____
   _____ ?

6. _____
   _____ ?

Exercise B   You are writing an essay about science. You are thinking about dinosaurs. Write four "What if?" questions that will help you to develop your ideas.

1. What if _____
   _____ ?

2. What if _____
   _____ ?

3. What if _____
   _____ ?

4. What if _____
   _____ ?

Name _____ Date _____ Class _____

WORKSHEET 5   *Reading and Listening*

Reading and *listening* are ways to gather ideas and information for your writing. **Reading** sources include books, magazines, newspapers, and brochures. Here are some tips for finding specific information.

- Check the tables of contents and indexes to find the exact pages you need to read.
- Skim the pages until you find something about your topic.
- Slow down to take notes on the main ideas and important details.

By **listening,** you can get a lot of information from speeches, radio and TV programs, interviews, audiotapes, or videotapes. Before you listen, make a list of questions about your topic. While you listen, take notes on the main ideas and important details.

Exercise A   Which of the following American Indian nations interests you most: Mohawk, Seminole, Navajo, Dakota, or Nez Perce? Look in an encyclopedia or other book to find the answers to the following questions. Write your answers on the lines provided.

1. In what part of the continent did this nation originally live?

   _____

2. What form of housing or shelter did they traditionally use?

   _____

3. How many members have survived and live in the United States today?

   _____

4. Do the members now live primarily on reservations or in urban areas?

   _____

5. Are they known for some kind of art, such as beadwork, pottery, or basket making?

   _____

Exercise B   Listen to a radio broadcast of the top songs of the week (pop, rock, country, or gospel). Then answer the following questions.

1. Of the songs you heard, which two do you like best?

   _____

2. Who recorded each of these two songs?

   _____

3. What number in the countdown is each?

   _____

4. Who wrote each of these songs?

   _____

COMPOSITION

Chapter 17: The Writing Process

WORKSHEET 6 | *Purpose and Audience*

Before you write, always ask yourself, *Why am I writing?* You write in many different forms, but you have one or more basic **purposes**: to express your feelings, as you might in a journal or a letter; to be creative, as in a short story or a poem; to explain or inform, as in an essay or a news story; and to persuade, as in a letter to the editor or a political speech.

Before you write, also ask yourself, *Who will read my writing?* Consider your **audience**—the readers. Ask yourself these questions.

- Why is my audience reading my writing? Do they expect to be entertained, informed, or persuaded?
- What does my audience already know about my topic?
- What does my audience want or need to know about my topic?
- What vocabulary and type of language should I use?

Exercise The following paragraph was written for students your age. Rewrite the paragraph to make it appropriate for students in elementary school. Use shorter sentences and simpler words. Add details to provide background information that your audience may not know. For example, you might explain where India is located.

> In 1948, soon after India became an independent nation, Indians had both cause to celebrate and cause to mourn. They had cause to celebrate because they were now free to rule themselves, having thrown off rule by Great Britain. They had cause to mourn because Mohandas K. Gandhi, the leader of the Indian revolution against Great Britain, had been assassinated.

_____

_____

_____

_____

_____

_____

_____

_____

_____

_____

_____

_____

_____

Chapter 17: The Writing Process

 **WORKSHEET 7** *Arranging Ideas*

After gathering ideas for a piece of writing, you need to put your ideas in order. There are four common ways to order ideas.

- **Chronological order** presents events as they happen in time. You use chronological order in narration—for example, in stories, narrative poems, explanations of processes, history, biography, and drama.
- Using **spatial order,** you describe objects in order by location—near to far, left to right, top to bottom, and so on. Description may be used in any type of writing.
- When arranging ideas in **order of importance,** you give details from least to most important, or the reverse. Use this type of order in persuasive writing, description, explanation, and evaluative writing.
- Use **logical order** to relate items to the groups they belong in. You order logically when you classify, define, or compare and contrast.

Exercise A Arrange the list of ideas below in chronological order by numbering the ideas from 1 to 5.

_____ Poet Vachel Lindsay dined at the hotel.

_____ Hughes's literary career then took off!

_____ In 1925, Langston Hughes worked in a Washington, D.C., hotel dining room.

_____ That night Lindsay read Hughes's poems to his audience.

_____ Hughes left three of his poems by Lindsay's plate.

Exercise B Think of at least three reasons for exercising, and list them below in order of importance.

1. _____

2. _____

3. _____

Exercise C Think of two books, songs, or movies that you like. On the lines provided, list two ways in which they are similar and two ways in which they are different.

Similar: 1. _____

2. _____

Different: 1. _____

2. _____

COMPOSITION

Name _____ Date _____ Class _____

 **WORKSHEET 8**   *Using Visuals A*

Visuals can help you bring order to your prewriting notes. Two types of **visuals** are *charts* and *Venn diagrams*. A **chart** allows you to list ideas in columns and rows. Headings for columns and rows identify the information in the body of the chart.

A **Venn diagram** uses overlapping circles to show how subjects are similar and different. If you are comparing (and contrasting) two subjects, draw two overlapping circles, one for each subject. In the overlapping section, record details shared by both subjects. In the parts that don't overlap, write details that make these subjects different.

Exercise A With a little practice, charts become easy to create. Try your hand at it. In the space provided below, make a chart to organize the following notes about the advantages and disadvantages of having school year-round. You can add other advantages and disadvantages to your chart.

Students wouldn't be as likely to forget skills over long summer vacation.

Students couldn't take long vacations in the summer.

Students could learn more.

Students couldn't earn money at summer jobs.

Kids couldn't go to summer camps.

School schedules could more nearly match parents' work schedules.

School buildings could be used year-round.

Students wouldn't have as much free time to experience life outside school.

Chapter 17, Worksheet 8, continued

Exercise B Use the Venn diagram below to show how cats and dogs are similar and how they are different. Write a heading above each circle.

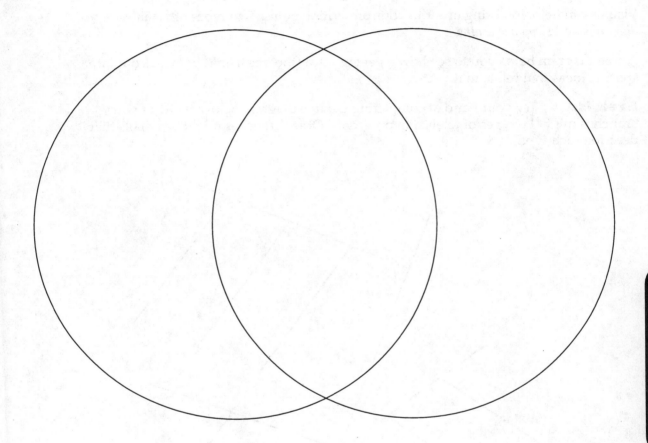

COMPOSITION

Chapter 17: The Writing Process

Using Visuals B

Visuals can help you bring order to your prewriting notes. Two types of visuals are *tree diagrams* and *sequence chains*.

A **tree diagram** helps you to see how a general idea (the tree trunk) branches out into specific ideas that relate to it.

Exercise A   Try your hand at completing the tree diagram below. Some of your branches might be types of television programs. Other branches might be details that describe each type.

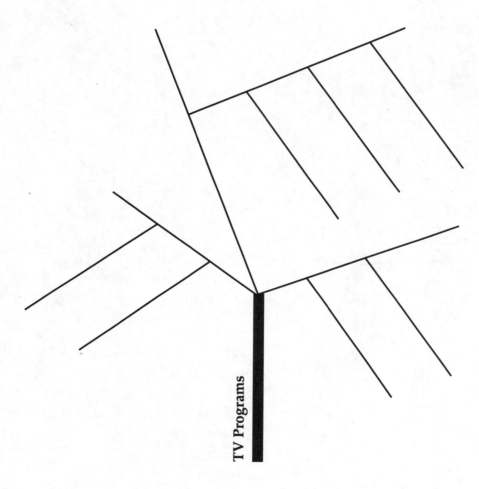

Chapter 17, Worksheet 9, *continued*

A **sequence chain** can help you organize events in chronological order. You can use a sequence chain to show the steps in a process or the main events in a story. Write down a brief sketch of the first event or step, draw a box around it, and draw an arrow pointing to the next box. Follow this procedure until all events or steps are recorded.

Exercise B   Read a newspaper or magazine article about an event. Then briefly record the main events in the sequence chain below. You can add more boxes to the chain if necessary.

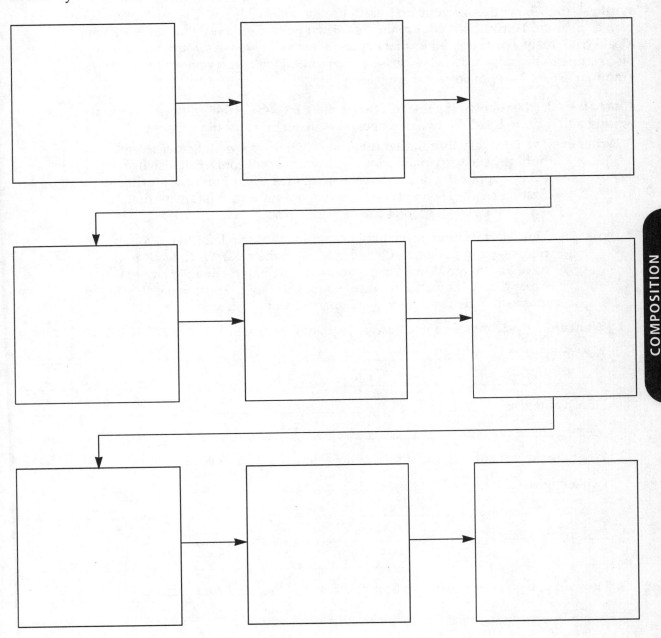

COMPOSITION

Name _____ Date _____ Class _____

 **WORKSHEET 10**

Writing a First Draft

After you have planned a piece of writing, it's time to write a **first draft**. There are no precise rules for writing a first draft. Whether people write their first drafts quickly or slowly, they are all creating something new from separate parts. This process is called **synthesizing**. To synthesize your first draft, use the following tips: Use your prewriting plan as a guide. Think about your main idea. Then write a sentence that states this main idea. Write freely. Focus on details that express your main idea. As you write, you may discover new ideas. Include these ideas in your draft. Don't worry about spelling and grammar errors. You can correct them later.

Exercise   In the following passages, two writers talk about their different ways of writing a first draft. Read the two passages, and answer the questions below.

Writer 1:   I write a very thorough outline based on my prewriting ideas. The outline lists every main idea that my draft will contain. It also lists every supporting detail for each main idea. After I outline, I write my first sentence. Then I revise that sentence until I am happy with it. Then I write my second sentence, and so on.

Writer 2:   I just start writing everything I can think of that relates to my topic, purpose, and audience. One idea leads to the next, which leads to the next, and so on. When I come across something really interesting, I expand on it. Sometimes I throw out everything except that one interesting part and rewrite that part several times until I like it.

1. What are the advantages and disadvantages of working like Writer 1?

   Advantages: _____

   _____

   Disadvantages: _____

   _____

2. What are the advantages and disadvantages of working like Writer 2?

   Advantages: _____

   _____

   Disadvantages: _____

   _____

3. How do you go about writing a first draft? Briefly describe your method.

   _____

   _____

   _____

   _____

Name _____ Date _____ Class _____

Chapter 17: The Writing Process

WORKSHEET 11 *Self-Evaluation*

When you **evaluate** something, you examine its strengths and weaknesses. One way to evaluate something is to think about what makes it good. Suppose, for example, that you wanted to evaluate a pair of running shoes. You would ask yourself such questions as *What qualities would a good pair of running shoes have?*

These techniques can help you evaluate your own writing.

- **Read carefully.** Read your paper more than once. First, read for *content* (what you say), then for *organization* (how you order ideas), and then for *style* (how you use words and sentences).
- **Listen carefully.** Read your paper aloud. *Listen* to what you've said. You may notice that the ideas don't flow smoothly or that some sentences sound awkward.
- **Take time.** Set your draft aside. Come back to it later and read through it. You'll find it's easier to be objective after a little time away from your writing.

Exercise   Do you like true-life adventure stories? Read the following paragraph. Then, on the lines provided, write your evaluation of the writing. In evaluating the writing, ask yourself these questions: Is the writing interesting? Does it grab and hold your attention? Does the writing have a clear main idea? Is the main idea supported with details? Does the order of the ideas make sense? Do the ideas flow smoothly?

Can you imagine being lost? That's what happened to Steven Callahan, and he wrote about it in the book *Adrift*. He was finally rescued by some fishers. Callahan's boat sank in the Atlantic Ocean, and he survived in an inflatable raft. He was lost at sea for seventy-six days. He survived storms, shark sightings, and a diet of raw fish. And, oh yes, there's something I need to tell you. He spotted ships, but they passed him by. No one else ever survived so long at sea in an inflatable raft. His story is a great one.

_____
_____
_____
_____
_____
_____
_____
_____
_____
_____

COMPOSITION

Chapter 17: The Writing Process

 **Peer Evaluation**

Peer evaluation is a review of one writer's work by another writer. Here are some guidelines for the writer whose work is being evaluated: Make a list of questions for the peer evaluators. Which parts of your paper worry you? Keep an open mind. Don't take your evaluators' suggestions as personal criticism.

Here are some guidelines for the peer evaluator: Tell the writer what's good about the paper. Give the writer some encouragement. Focus on content and organization. The writer will catch spelling and grammar errors when proofreading. Be sensitive to the writer's feelings. State your suggestions as questions, such as "What does this mean?" and "Can you give an example?"

Exercise   Read the following paragraph. Then read the negative comments made about it below. Rewrite each negative comment by making specific suggestions for improving the paragraph.

> Black lava covers the soil. Volcanoes are mountains with holes in their tops. Steam rises from the hot melted rock. The land is burnt and useless. Lava is boiling rock that comes from deep within the earth.

1. The paragraph makes no sense. I can't tell what the writer's point is. _____

   _____

   _____

2. The statements don't seem connected. _____

   _____

   _____

3. The order of the sentences doesn't make sense. _____

   _____

   _____

4. The sentences are choppy. _____

   _____

   _____

Chapter 17: The Writing Process

WORKSHEET 13 *Revising*

When you **revise,** you make changes to improve your paper. There are four main ways to revise:

- You can **add** new information to help your audience understand your main idea. Add words, phrases, sentences, or whole paragraphs.
- You can **cut** or take out repeated or unnecessary information and unrelated ideas.
- You can **replace** weak or awkward wording with more precise words or details.
- You can **reorder** or move information, sentences, and paragraphs for logical order.

Exercise A Study the revisions made to the following paragraph. Then answer the questions below.

Most boys and girls in Canada and ~~Mexico~~ *Latin America* learn to play soccer. Soccer is popular with young people around the globe because it's fun to play, it's easy to learn, and it doesn't take much special equipment. *All one really needs is a soccer ball, a field, and some players.* ~~Basketball is the most popular sport in the United States.~~ *So do* Boys and girls in Europe and the United Kingdom ~~also learn to play soccer.~~

1. Why did the writer add the sentence "All one really needs is a soccer ball, a field, and some players"?

   _____

   _____

2. Why did the writer replace *Mexico* with *Latin America*?

   _____

   _____

3. Why did the writer move the sentence about boys and girls in Europe?

   _____

   _____

4. Why did the writer cut the sentence about basketball?

   _____

   _____

COMPOSITION

Exercise B: Revising   The following paragraph can be improved by revision. On the lines below, rewrite the paragraph, using the techniques explained on Worksheet 13. You may also find it helpful to combine two short sentences by making a compound sentence. Pay special attention to adding transitional words and phrases to make the paragraph flow smoothly.

[1] Ever since *The Wonderful Wizard of Oz* was read to me when I was little, I had wanted to see a tornado. [2] I also liked books about dinosaurs. [3] Maybe I thought that a tornado would take me to some magical place. [4] Tornados are violent circular windstorms that have winds that whirl around and around. [5] When I was eleven, I visited my aunt and uncle in Texas. [6] They live in Texas. [7] We saw black clouds swirling in the sky. [8] It ripped up some big trees. [9] A tornado dropped down out of the clouds and started coming toward the house. [10] It really scared all of us. [11] We were very lucky. [12] It went back up into the clouds before it damaged any buildings. [13] I've seen a tornado. [14] I never want to see another one! [15] No one was hurt, either.

_____

_____

_____

_____

_____

_____

_____

_____

_____

_____

_____

_____

_____

_____

_____

_____

_____

_____

_____

_____

_____

Chapter 17: The Writing Process

WORKSHEET 14 Proofreading and Publishing

When you **proofread,** you carefully reread your paper. You correct mistakes in grammar, usage, capitalization, spelling, and punctuation. One way to proofread is to use the following guidelines.

1. Is every sentence a complete sentence, not a fragment?
2. Does every sentence begin with a capital letter and end with the correct punctuation mark?
3. Do plural verbs have plural subjects? Do singular verbs have singular subjects?
4. Are verbs in the right form? Are verbs in the right tense?
5. Are adjective and adverb forms used correctly in making comparisons?
6. Are the forms of personal pronouns used correctly?
7. Does every pronoun agree with its antecedent (the word it refers to) in number and in gender?
8. Are all words spelled correctly? Are the plural forms of nouns correct?

After you proofread, you're ready to **publish,** or share your writing. Some ways to publish your work include reading what you've written to your classmates or to a group of friends, displaying your work on a school bulletin board or in the library, keeping a folder of your writing to share with family and friends, and sending your writing to a newspaper or magazine.

Exercise A: Proofreading   Use the checklist above to proofread the following paragraph. Correct the errors in grammar, usage, spelling, punctuation, and capitalization. Use a dictionary and the handbook to help you.

Even after the english brought pianoes to India. The indian people prefer their own keyboard instrument. They called it the harmonium. The harmonium has a voice like a sad pipe organ, but it looks like an accordion? you sit on the floor to play it. One hand plays the melody on the keyboard. The others press the bellows to make the sownd. Indian music sounds best on the harmonium than on the piano.

Exercise B   On the lines below, list two suitable ways in which you might publish an essay on your views about the advantages or disadvantages of year-round school.

1. _____

   _____

2. _____

   _____

COMPOSITION

Chapter 17: The Writing Process

WORKSHEET 15

The Aim and Process of Writing

Aim—The "Why" of Writing

WHY PEOPLE WRITE	
To express themselves	To get to know themselves, to find meaning in their own lives
To share information	To give other people information that they need or want; to share some special knowledge
To persuade	To convince other people to do something or believe something
To create literature	To be creative, to say something in a unique way

Process—The "How" of Writing

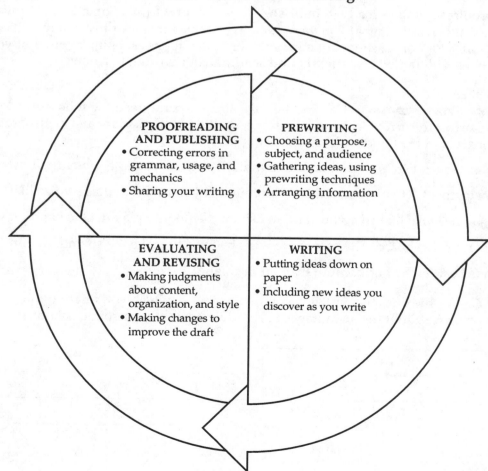

PROOFREADING AND PUBLISHING
• Correcting errors in grammar, usage, and mechanics
• Sharing your writing

PREWRITING
• Choosing a purpose, subject, and audience
• Gathering ideas, using prewriting techniques
• Arranging information

EVALUATING AND REVISING
• Making judgments about content, organization, and style
• Making changes to improve the draft

WRITING
• Putting ideas down on paper
• Including new ideas you discover as you write

Chapter 18: Paragraph and Composition Structure

WORKSHEET 1   *The Paragraph's Main Idea*

Every paragraph must contain a *main idea*. The **main idea** is the idea around which the entire paragraph is organized. It is what the paragraph is about.

Exercise   On the line provided, write the main idea of each paragraph below.

1. Summertime is coming, and the work is plentiful for teenagers. Surveying local newspapers and business owners, I've discovered that there will be a wide variety of jobs available for young workers. Teens who like to work around food should check the ice cream parlors and the sandwich shops. Those who want to be outdoors should try lawn-care services and recreational facilities. Some gift stores need help, too. Of course, grocery stores always need sackers and stock people. Check local newspaper listings daily!

Main idea: _____

2. You take pay phones for granted, but until recently they've been impossible to use for persons with serious hearing impairments. How can a person with a serious hearing impairment call a cab or call home when he or she is traveling? In a year-long experiment, pay phones with TDD's (telecommunication devices for the deaf) have been placed in Gallaudet University and in train stations and airports in Washington, D.C., and Baltimore. A TDD has a small screen and a computer-like keyboard that lets users type messages and receive responses. If the experiment is a success, pay phones equipped with TDD's will make life much easier for more than twenty-two million Americans with hearing impairments.

Main idea: _____

3. Fantasies can come true. Ever since she was in junior high school and started thinking about college, Alexandra had dreamed about taking a course in writing poetry. She loved poetry and wrote poems constantly. She had imagined handing her college poetry teacher the first assigned poem. The teacher would read the poem and say, "That's the best beginning student poem that I've ever read! You should be in my advanced poetry writing class!" Well, Alexandra finished middle school and high school, writing poetry all the time, and began college. She enrolled in a beginning poetry writing class. She gave the teacher her first poem, and—you guessed it!—he said, "That's the best beginning student poem that I've ever read! Would you like to be in the advanced class?"

Main idea: _____

4. The ancient Mayan and Aztec peoples marked their calendars, too. Each civilization had 365-day calendars, divided into periods of 18 months. The calendars of both peoples also contained yearly ritual schedules that formed 52-year cycles. Yes, it sounds complicated compared to our way of calculating the calendar.

Main idea: _____

COMPOSITION

Chapter 18: Paragraph and Composition Structure

| WORKSHEET 2 | *The Topic Sentence* |

The **topic sentence** states the main idea of a paragraph. It can occur anywhere in a paragraph. Often it is either the first or second sentence. Sometimes a paragraph has no topic sentence, especially if it is a narrative paragraph that tells about a series of events. The reader has to add up the details to figure out what the main idea is.

Exercise Underline the topic sentence in each of the following paragraphs.

1. Reports of fabulous, unbelievable creatures have occurred throughout human history. The ancient Egyptians and Greeks told of a bird called the phoenix. They believed that this bird could burst into flames and then grow again from its own ashes. In the Middle Ages, books were written containing pictures of unicorns and dragons. During the Renaissance, sailors reported sighting sea serpents and mermaids. In our own century, people have reported seeing such fantastic creatures as the Loch Ness monster, Bigfoot, the Abominable Snowman, and the Ape Man of China.

2. In "Rumpelstiltskin," a young woman is given three chances to guess the title character's name. In "The White Snake," the hero has to perform three tasks in order to win the hand of a princess. In "Cinderella," the main character has three evil stepsisters. In the story of "Aladdin's Lamp," a genie gives Aladdin three wishes. As these examples show, the number three plays an important role in many traditional folk tales and fairy tales.

3. A computer recently defeated the world champion chess player. Computers can now imitate speech. They can also control robots that assemble cars in factories. In short, computers are now capable of doing many things that only humans could do in the past. No one knows what computers might be capable of in the future.

4. A chilly wind blew through the valley. Overhead, flocks of geese were winging their way south. The leaves on the trees had begun to change, flecking the mountainsides with red and orange, yellow and brown. On the forest floor, squirrels hurriedly gathered acorns for the coming winter. The calendar still said "summer," but nature was whispering "fall."

5. Watching public television is a great way to add to the education you get at school. The Public Broadcasting Service (PBS) is a nationwide network of local TV stations supported by gifts from businesses, other organizations, and ordinary citizens. PBS airs programs that make science, history, geography, music, and art both informative and fun to watch for the whole family. If you've never seen *Where in the World Is Carmen Sandiego?* and *Nature*, give them a try.

Chapter 18: Paragraph and Composition Structure

Using Sensory Details

Supporting sentences give specific details that explain or prove the main idea of the paragraph. One way to support a main idea is to use *sensory details*. These are words that appeal to one of the five senses—sight, hearing, smell, touch, and taste. Vivid sensory details help your reader clearly imagine what you're writing about.

Exercise A   Read the following paragraph. Then complete the chart below, listing at least two details from the paragraph that appeal to each of the five senses.

When the Rotary Club held its annual summer picnic, our whole town turned out. The bandstand in the park was decorated with colorful banners and balloons. On the stage, a bluegrass band played traditional square-dance tunes to the beat of an old washtub bass. Celia Winthrow, the town's mayor, called out dance steps. In front of the bandstand, dancers hugged their partners and whirled them around. Tables on the lawn were piled high with food, and the breeze carried wonderful aromas—spicy sweet-potato pie, barbequed chicken, and roasted vegetables. People milled about or sat sipping lemonade on the grass, laughing, talking, fanning themselves against the heat, and swatting at flies.

Sight	
Hearing	
Touch	
Taste	
Smell	

Exercise B   Choose one of the following topics or one of your own. Write the topic on the line provided. Then complete the chart with sensory details related to the topic. Include two details for each of the five senses.

POSSIBLE TOPICS: the most exciting football game I've ever attended

my favorite holiday   kindergarten memories

Topic: _____

	Detail 1	Detail 2
Sight		
Hearing		
Touch		
Taste		
Smell		

COMPOSITION

Chapter 18: Paragraph and Composition Structure

WORKSHEET 4 | *Using Facts and Examples*

The main idea in a paragraph can be supported by *facts* or *examples*. A **fact** is a statement that can be proved true by directly observing or by checking a reliable reference source.

FACT: There are six official languages used at the United Nations: Arabic, Chinese, English, French, Russian, and Spanish.

OPINION: French is the most beautiful of those languages. [An opinion, like the one expressed in this statement, can't be proved.]

Examples are specific instances or illustrations of a general idea.

Cedar, fir, hemlock, pine, spruce, and yew are examples of evergreen trees.

Exercise A Read the following prewriting notes for a paragraph about other planets in our solar system. Cross out any facts that do not support the main idea. Then write a topic sentence to introduce the paragraph.

Mercury's surface temperature ranges from 801 degrees to –279 degrees Fahrenheit.

The atmosphere of Venus contains deadly sulfuric acid, and the surface is hot enough to melt lead.

At the equator, the temperature on Mars may occasionally rise to 63 degrees Fahrenheit.

Jupiter, Saturn, Neptune, Uranus, and Pluto are too cold for life as we know it.

Mars was named after the Roman god of war.

The Viking space probes were launched in an effort to find life on Mars.

Topic sentence: _____

_____

Exercise B For each set of examples below, write a topic sentence that shows how the examples are related.

1. Zaire, in central Africa, received its independence in 1960. So did Somalia, in East Africa; Senegal, in West Africa; and Chad, in North Central Africa.

_____

_____

2. Corn, a type of grass, is eaten throughout North, Central, and South America. Rice, another grass, is a basic food throughout most of Asia. Oats, barley, millet, and wheat— all grasses—have been central to the European diet for tens of thousands of years.

_____

_____

Name _____ Date _____ Class _____

 **WORKSHEET 5** ## *Unity in Paragraphs*

A paragraph has **unity** when all of its sentences are related to the main idea. Notice how the unrelated idea (which has been crossed out) destroys the unity of the following paragraph.

> Before 1786, many sailors drowned because their lifeboats could not survive rough seas. Then Lionel Lukin, a London coach builder, decided to build an unsinkable boat for rescue purposes. ~~Of course, coaches and carriages have now been replaced by the automobile.~~ Lukin invented a small boat with a hollow, watertight compartment. Today Lukin's basic concepts are used in building lifeboats, as well as pleasure boats, around the world.

Exercise   In each of the following paragraphs, one sentence should make you say, "What's *that* doing there?" Find and cross through the sentence that destroys the unity of each paragraph. [Remember: In a unified paragraph, all details are directly related to the main idea or the sequence of actions.]

1. The disappearance of Amelia Earhart remains a mystery. Earhart, who was the first female pilot to fly across the Atlantic Ocean, crashed in the Pacific while attempting to fly around the world. She was born in Atchison, Kansas, in 1897. Some searchers believe that she survived the crash into the Pacific, because radio distress calls were received. An intensive search for the source of the signals was made. Searchers were not able to find her, however. Finally, the distress signals ceased. In spite of continued searches by airplane and ship, no clue to what became of Amelia Earhart has yet been found.

2. One reason the mountain bike is popular is that it's built to help the rider keep control even when riding it off paved roads. The extra-wide handlebars improve the rider's balance. Jeremy has a mountain bike, but he only rides on city streets. With its wide tires the mountain bike will roll right over small obstacles that would trip up the skinny tires of a racer. And because the tires are knobby, riders can keep going even if the ground is muddy or sandy. Most importantly, wide tires help riders keep their balance. Because of these features, mountain bike riders can go almost anywhere.

3. Helicopters can do a number of unusual things. For example, they can fly straight down. They can hover in one spot. They can fly backward, forward, and even sideways. Nicknames for helicopters include "whirlybirds" and "choppers." Helicopters can also fly in and out of small places.

4. Over the years the Loch Ness monster has been hunted in a number of ways. Once several men cruised the bottom of the loch, or lake, in a yellow submarine. Submarines are also used to explore the world's oceans. Another time a pilot repeatedly flew a tiny aircraft over the loch. A number of scientists searched for the monster from a raft equipped with lights and cameras.

Name _____ Date _____ Class _____

Coherence in Paragraphs A

A paragraph has **coherence** when a reader can easily see how its ideas are connected or related. **Transitional words and phrases** help to connect ideas. The following chart lists some common transitions.

Comparing Ideas/Classification and Definition		
also	another	similarly
and	moreover	too
Contrasting Ideas/Classification and Definition		
although	however	nevertheless
but	instead	on the other hand
Showing Cause and Effect/Narration		
as a result	consequently	so that
because	since	therefore

Exercise Choose appropriate transitional words and phrases from the above list to connect the ideas in the following sentences.

1. Ludwig van Beethoven lost his hearing in his later years. _____ , despite his hearing impairment, he continued to compose great music.

2. Many of the plants of the Brazilian rain forest may be useful for manufacturing medicines.

   _____ , the rain forest should be preserved.

3. In Washington, D.C., you can visit the American Museum of Natural History.

   You _____ can visit the National Air and Space Museum.

4. The inspectors missed a crack in the body of the airplane. _____ , part of the plane flew off in midair, forcing an emergency landing.

5. The color pictures you see on a television screen are made up of tiny red, blue, and green

   dots. _____ , the colors in a magazine are made up of tiny red, yellow,

   blue, and black dots.

Name _____ Date _____ Class _____

 **WORKSHEET 7**   *Coherence in Paragraphs B*

A paragraph has **coherence** when a reader can easily see how ideas are connected or related. **Transitional words and phrases** help to connect ideas. Following are some common transitions.

Showing Time/Narration		
at last	meanwhile	then
eventually	next	thereafter
Showing Place/Description		
above	beyond	inside
behind	here	next to
Showing Importance/Evaluation		
first	mainly	then
last	more important	to begin with

Exercise   Choose appropriate transitional words and phrases from the above list to connect the following ideas.

1. As you write a first draft, don't worry about spelling and punctuation. Get

   your thoughts out _____ , and check your work later.

2. A shepherd boy stumbled on a cave. _____ the cave he found ancient writings that are now known as the Dead Sea Scrolls.

3. Edison tried many different materials in his electric lamp. _____ , he found one that would last more than a few hours.

4. In 1991, the Native Arts Institute offered the painter a position as an artist in

   residence. _____ she was able to devote herself full time to painting.

5. Directly in front of me was the forest. _____ the forest lay the mountains.

COMPOSITION

Chapter 18: Paragraph and Composition Structure

WORKSHEET 8

Description: Using Spatial Order

When you want to tell in your writing what something is like or what it looks like, you use **description**. In a description, sensory details provide effective support. Often, you'll use **spatial order**—the order in which items are arranged in space. The following example is a description that uses spatial order.

> Near the entrance to the botanical gardens stood a greenhouse. The greenhouse was divided into two areas. One was a dry, desert area full of cactuses. The other was a wet, tropical area full of orchids. Alongside the greenhouse ran a brick pathway that led into a rose garden and then through a wooden archway to an open, grassy field. Through the field ran a stream, one part of which was dammed up to form an artificial pond. The pond mirrored the blue sky and clouds above. In this pond swam a few painted turtles, with red and blue necks, and hundreds of large, ornamental carp—orange, white, yellow, and red fish with long whiskers. On either side of the pond grew exotic trees—magnolias, ginkgoes, tamarinds, persimmons, and papayas.

Exercise A Read the description of the botanical gardens again. Then, on the lines below, list the following details in the order of their distance from the entrance to the gardens. The last detail has been filled in.

DETAILS: rose garden   grassy field   greenhouse
      brick pathway   archway   pond   trees

1. _____

2. _____

3. _____

4. _____

5. _____

6. _____

7. *trees* _____

Exercise B You and a friend from your photography club arrange to shoot some pictures at the botanical gardens. Your friend has never been to the gardens and asks you for directions to your meeting place near the pond. On the lines below, jot down directions that will make it easy for your friend to find the spot. Or, if you wish, draw a map. Make your directions or map as clear as possible, without copying the paragraph above.

_____

_____

_____

Chapter 18: Paragraph and Composition Structure

WORKSHEET 9

Narration: Using Chronological Order

In **narration,** you tell how a person or a situation changes over a period of time. You may use narration to tell a story or incident, to explain a process, or to explain causes or effects. Often, you'll use **chronological order**—the order in which events occur.

Exercise   When you tell a joke, you start at the beginning and tell what happens next until you get to the punch line. Read the directions and then, on the lines provided, use narration to develop each of the following items. (Circle the letter of each chosen topic.)

1. Write a brief narrative paragraph about one of the following subjects (include at least three events).

   A. the funniest thing that ever happened to me (Make up a story, if you like.)

   B. what happened at the Boston Tea Party (Check a history book.)

   _____

   _____

   _____

   _____

   _____

2. Choose one of the following subjects and list at least four steps in the process.

   A. how to wash a car (or a dog or a cat)

   B. how to ask someone for a date

   _____

   _____

   _____

   _____

   _____

3. Write a brief cause-and-effect explanation of something that has happened to you. Tell the sequence of events in chronological order, showing how one event caused another, how the second event caused something else to happen, and so on. Give at least four events in all.

   _____

   _____

   _____

   _____

   _____

COMPOSITION

Chapter 18: Paragraph and Composition Structure

WORKSHEET 10

Classification: Using Logical Order

When you **classify,** you tell how a specific subject relates to other subjects that belong to the same group. You classify by defining or by comparing and contrasting. Usually, writers use **logical order**—grouping related ideas—in paragraphs that classify.

Exercise A   Read the following paragraph, which compares and contrasts two legendary figures from British history. Then, on the lines provided, list similarities and differences of the two figures.

> Almost everyone has heard of King Arthur, the legendary ruler of Camelot, in ancient Britain. Arthur and his Knights of the Round Table are well known because of a book written about them long ago by Sir Thomas Malory. Less well known to Americans is another legendary figure from British history, Boadicea (bō´•ad•ə•sē´•ə). Like Arthur, Boadicea was a ruler. She was a queen who ruled over a group of ancient British tribes known as the Celts. She led the Celts in a rebellion against the Romans who had invaded and conquered Britain. Both Arthur and Boadicea were famous British rulers. However, there is one really important difference between them: Boadicea is an actual historical figure. Arthur may or may not have actually existed.

Similarities:	**Differences:**
_____	_____
_____	_____
_____	_____
_____	_____

Exercise B   On the lines provided, use the classification strategy of defining to tell about Saint Bernards. First, explain what a Saint Bernard is by telling its general class. Then, list all the characteristics that distinguish it from other breeds of dogs. (If you need some information about the animal, use an encyclopedia, or talk to an owner.)

_____

_____

_____

_____

_____

_____

_____

Chapter 18: Paragraph and Composition Structure

WORKSHEET 11

Evaluation: Using Order of Importance

Evaluating is the process of judging something's value, deciding whether something is good or bad. You have to give reasons, or support, for your opinion. A good way to arrange your reasons is by **order of importance**. You can emphasize one reason by putting it first or last in the paragraph.

Exercise   What's your evaluation—good, bad, or somewhere in between? What are your reasons for your evaluation? Pick three of the following topics, and write a sentence expressing your evaluation. Then give two or three reasons to support your opinion. List the reasons in order of importance from most to least important. Use the lines provided.

EXAMPLE: **Topic:** *a veggie pizza*

Evaluation: *This veggie pizza is delicious.*

Reasons: (1) *It has homemade sauce.*

(2) *It has a crisp, crunchy crust.*

(3) *There are lots of fresh toppings.*

1. a recent recording you've listened to or a concert you've attended
2. last week's episode of your favorite TV series or a movie you've seen
3. a sporting event you attended or watched on TV
4. a new fad or fashion for teenagers
5. life in your city, community, neighborhood

Topic 1: _____

Evaluation: _____

Reasons: (1) _____

(2) _____

(3) _____

Topic 2: _____

Evaluation: _____

Reasons: (1) _____

(2) _____

(3) _____

Topic 3: _____

Evaluation: _____

Reasons: (1) _____

(2) _____

(3) _____

COMPOSITION

Chapter 18: Paragraph and Composition Structure

WORKSHEET 12 ***Planning a Composition***

The main idea of your composition is the major point you want to make about your topic. Every detail and each paragraph you write will tie into this main idea.

Exercise A   For each of the following topics, write a sentence that states a main idea that would be appropriate for a brief composition.

1. professional musicians _____

_____

2. health and nutrition for athletes _____

_____

3. summer activities _____

_____

4. traditional American Indian homes _____

_____

5. the importance of space exploration _____

_____

Exercise B   One sentence in each of the following pairs states a main idea, and one gives a supporting detail. On the line provided, write the letter of the sentence that states a main idea.

EXAMPLE: 1. a. For example, I was always wondering whether
I remembered to lock my bicycle.
b. I used to worry about everything.   _*b*_

1. a. A soil analysis is recommended before landscaping.
   b. The test will reveal the deficiencies in the soil.   _____

2. a. Ms. Pérez was the one who taught me the most.
   b. I have had some outstanding piano teachers.   _____

3. a. Science fiction can take the reader out of ordinary life.
   b. The main character in H. G. Wells's *The Time Machine*
   is propelled into the future.   _____

4. a. Newspapers, tapes, magazines, records, and films are all
   available for public use.
   b. The public library has more than just books.   _____

5. a. The food processor makes cooking easier and faster.
   b. It can knead bread dough easily and quickly.   _____

Chapter 18: Paragraph and Composition Structure

 **WORKSHEET 13** *Early Plans*

An **early plan,** also called an **informal outline,** is one way of sorting your ideas to make your job of writing easier. You put items in groups and then arrange your groups in order. Follow these steps to group ideas.

- Group items that have something in common with each other.
- Write a heading for each group to show how the items in it are related.
- Set aside any items that don't seem to fit. You can delete them or fit them in later.

Then you can order the ideas in each group. Here are some common ways to order ideas: *chronological* (time) *order, order of importance, logical order,* and *spatial* (space or location) *order.*

Exercise Here are two sets of details about scuba diving. First, write the kind of order or arrangement that you would use if you were including these details in a composition. Then, number the details in each set from 1 to 5. Use the number *1* to indicate the detail you would put first and the number *5* to indicate the detail you would put last.

Group 1

Kind of order: _____

_____ In the 1980's, thousands of people learned to dive.

_____ Books and movies popularized diving in the 1950's and 1960's.

_____ Jacques Cousteau and a friend invented the aqua-lung in the 1940's.

_____ Diving became very popular in the 1970's.

_____ Before the 1940's, people studied undersea life from underwater vessels with windows.

Group 2

Kind of order: _____

_____ air tank worn on back

_____ weight belt worn around waist

_____ fins worn on feet

_____ regulator for breathing held in mouth

_____ goggles worn over eyes

COMPOSITION

Chapter 18: Paragraph and Composition Structure

 **Formal Outlines**

A **formal outline** uses letters and numbers to show the relationships of ideas. A **topic outline** states ideas in words or brief phrases. A **sentence outline** states ideas in complete sentences.

Exercise   There are four blank spaces in the formal topic outline below. Use each of the four ideas below to complete the outline.

Located mostly north of the equator in the western Pacific

Early 1980's—establishes independent government

Strategic location—military importance

Equatorial climate

Title: Micronesia: Island Nation

Main idea: A Pacific island chain joins the independent nations of the world.

  I. History

     A. Nineteenth century—Spain sells islands to Germany

     B. Twentieth century—Occupied by Japan and then by the United States

     C. _____

  II. Geography

     A. About two thousand volcanic islands and atolls

     B. _____

     C. _____

  III. Importance to the world

     A. Resources—fish, tropical fruits

     B. Industry—crafts, boating, tourism

     C. _____

Chapter 18: Paragraph and Composition Structure

 **The Introduction**

A good **introduction** captures the reader's interest and presents the main idea of the composition. Three ways of capturing a reader's attention are

- asking a question
- telling an anecdote (a short, interesting story)
- stating an intriguing or startling fact

Exercise   Read the following introductions. Tell what method is used in each introduction to grab the reader's attention. Notice that the last sentence of each introduction introduces the main idea of the composition.

1. "Who do you think you are, the Queen of Sheba?" If you've heard this expression, you may have wondered who the Queen of Sheba was. She was the legendary mother of the first emperor of Ethiopia. Her life story is one of the most fascinating of all African legends.

_____

2. Several years ago I decided I wanted a cat, so I visited my local Humane Society shelter. One of the shelter's employees pointed out a cat that would have to be destroyed soon unless someone took him. So I took the cat and paid for his shots and neutering. As I left with Ziggy, I started thinking about the stray-animal problem. This problem has worsened in the United States, but there are simple steps that can be taken to end it.

_____

3. Why don't penguins' feet get frostbite from the cold? Why are snowshoe hares and polar bears white? Why are walruses, seals, and whales so fat? At the American Museum of Natural History, an exhibit answers all these questions and more.

_____

4. According to David Suzuki, professor of Zoology at the University of British Columbia, it is estimated that more than one hundred species of animals and plants become extinct every day. Most of these extinctions are assumed to be taking place in the rain forests of Brazil. People are burning and clearing these forests to grow crops or to graze cattle. There are several reasons that the rest of the world should put a stop to the destruction of the rain forests.

_____

COMPOSITION

Chapter 18: Paragraph and Composition Structure

WORKSHEET 16 | *The Body*

The **body** of a composition develops the main idea with paragraphs. Each paragraph supports or proves a main point by developing it with supporting details.

The body of a composition should have unity and coherence. When a composition has **unity,** the separate paragraphs work together to support the main idea of the introduction. When a composition has **coherence,** the ideas are easy to follow. The ideas are arranged in an order the reader will understand. The reader can easily see how your ideas are connected. Transitional words and phrases such as *next, first, however, in addition to,* and *finally* help readers connect the ideas in a composition.

Exercise A   In each numbered item below, the first sentence gives the main idea for a composition; the second sentence provides one major supporting idea. For each item, write at least one additional supporting idea.

1. Daily exercise can make people's lives better. Daily exercise gives a person a feeling of well-being and a more positive outlook on life.

    _____

2. There are many varieties of pollution in our society. Toxic chemicals are dumped into rivers.

    _____

Exercise B   Read the four pairs of sentences that show the end of one paragraph and the beginning of the next. On the line provided, write the transitional word or phrase that best ties together the two paragraphs. Some pairs might have more than one right answer.

   Next   Otherwise   Furthermore   However   First of all

1. Of all the annoying people on earth, my little brother leads the list.

    _____ , he uses his age to get his way.

2. Chen didn't listen to the music. He concentrated on counting the nails in the floor backstage.

    _____ , he knew he'd get so nervous that he'd never be able to play his recital piece.

3. When you ask your parents to let you stay out past curfew, explain your reasons carefully.

    _____ , be prepared to answer any objections they might have.

4. I was convinced that all Mexican food was too spicy for me to enjoy.

    _____ , after eating at Luisa's house, I discovered that Mexican food is delicious and fun to eat.

Chapter 18: Paragraph and Composition Structure

WORKSHEET 17

Unity and Coherence in a Composition

As you revise your composition, you will want to look for ways to give it *unity* and *coherence*. Your paper has **unity** when all your body paragraphs develop a point about the main idea in your introduction. Your paper has **coherence** when every sentence and paragraph leads to the next sentence or paragraph.

Exercise   Read the following composition. Then answer the questions below.

[1] *The Joy Luck Club* is a novel about a Chinese family who have become Americans in one generation. Amy Tan, the book's author, was born to Chinese immigrants who escaped China during wartime. One of the characters in the book, Jing Mei Woo, is a Chinese American girl born in San Francisco. At the beginning of the story, Jing Mei has just been asked to take her mother's place in a social club called the Joy Luck Club. Her mother has just died, and Jing Mei is at the beginning of her search for understanding of her culture.

[2] Jing Mei really comes to understand herself for the first time when she travels to China as an adult. She visits the daughter her mother lost in China during the war. She comes to love the native Chinese culture, and she gains a new pride in her ethnic heritage. Chinatown today is one of San Francisco's most popular tourist attractions.

[3] During the Second World War, many Asians were put in prison camps. Many people believed that Japanese Americans sympathized with the Japanese and should be treated like enemies. Japanese American people lost their property and their freedom during that period. They were discriminated against because it was easy to see from their features that they were of Asian descent.

[4] Jing Mei both admires and fears the members of the Joy Luck Club. These people are from her mother's generation, and they come from a different world. Jing Mei was raised in San Francisco during the 1950's. The Joy Luck Club members were raised in China during the 1930's and immigrated to America.

1. What is the main idea of this composition? _____

    _____

2. What sentence in paragraph two is unrelated and should be deleted? _____

    _____

3. Why should the last paragraph be moved so that it comes right after paragraph one?

    _____

    _____

4. Which paragraph destroys the unity of the composition because it is not related to the main

    idea? _____

    _____

COMPOSITION

Chapter 18: Paragraph and Composition Structure

WORKSHEET 18 | *The Conclusion*

A **conclusion** helps readers know that your composition has come to an end. Here are some ways you can conclude your paper.

- Refer to your introduction.
- Restate the main idea.
- Close with a final idea.

Exercise   Read the following composition. Then write an appropriate conclusion for it. Tell whether your conclusion refers to something in the introduction, restates the main idea in different words, or closes with a final idea that pulls the composition together.

Have you ever wondered if there really is a Bigfoot or a Sasquatch? If you have, you're not alone. People have always wondered about mysterious creatures like these. However, stories of monsters and magical creatures are often exaggerations. The following examples point out that some monsters or magical creatures later turned out to be fairly ordinary beings.

There are many stories in Europe about the unicorn. The unicorn is a single-horned horse with the legs of a deer and the tail of a lion. We don't see unicorns. But we do see rhinoceroses. The rhinoceros has a single horn on its head, and it looks kind of like an overweight horse. Perhaps a European traveler in Africa once saw a rhinoceros and called it a unicorn.

Another magical creature is the centaur. It is said to be half man and half horse. In ancient times, invaders from Mongolia went to the Mediterranean. People there had never seen anyone ride on horseback. It's possible that they mistook the Mongolians for centaurs.

Sea monsters were drawn on maps of the world until a few hundred years ago. Of course, no one knew very much about large water animals. So maybe a frightened sailor saw a beached whale and turned it into a dragon in his mind.

_____

_____

_____

_____

_____

_____

_____

_____

_____

_____

_____

Chapter 19: The Research Report

WORKSHEET 1

Choosing a Subject

Research reports give information about a subject, use print and nonprint sources, and provide lists of sources for the information. In planning a research report, you first must choose a subject. Ask these questions to help you decide on a subject.

- What do I wonder about?
- What's important to me?
- What have I read or seen lately that I'd like to know more about?

Exercise   You can find excellent subjects by skimming magazine or newspaper articles and by looking through reference works such as encyclopedias and dictionaries. Think about what interests you and what you want to know more about. Follow the directions below.

1. **Using a Dictionary.** Often you can find good subject ideas in a dictionary. Open a large dictionary, and start looking through it at random until you find a word that names something that interests you. Write that topic on the line below.

   _____

2. **Using an Encyclopedia.** Encyclopedias are also good sources of subject ideas. Skim through a couple of volumes of an encyclopedia. Write two possible subjects that you find there.

   _____

   _____

3. **Using Magazines.** Look at some magazines at home or in your school or public library. Find an article on a subject that would be good for a research report. Write that subject below.

   _____

4. **Using Newspapers.** Newspapers are also good sources of topic ideas. Glance through some copies of your local newspaper or a national paper. Write two possible subject ideas that you find in these newspapers.

   _____

   _____

5. **Using Television News.** Watch a television news program, or think about one that you've seen in the past. Write a possible subject based on that program.

   _____

Think about the subjects you listed above. Which do you think would be the most interesting for a research report? Write that subject on the line below.

   _____

Name _____ Date _____ Class _____

 **Narrowing a Subject**

After deciding on a general subject for a research report, you need to narrow your subject. You need to focus on just one topic, that is, on one part of the subject. Each subject contains many topics. Before deciding on a topic, ask yourself these questions.

- Can I find enough facts about this topic? Where?
- Is my topic too broad for a short report? Or is the topic too narrow? (If the topic is too narrow, you will have trouble finding enough information.)
- Do I have time to get the information I need? (If you have to send away for information, how long will it take to get?)
- Is the topic interesting enough to hold my attention? (You'll be more willing to put extra time and effort into a topic you like.)

One way to narrow a subject is to make a cluster chart. Write your subject in the middle of a piece of paper, and circle the subject. Think of related ideas, write them down, and circle them. Draw lines to connect circles. Continue until you have filled your page. Here is a sample cluster chart on oceans.

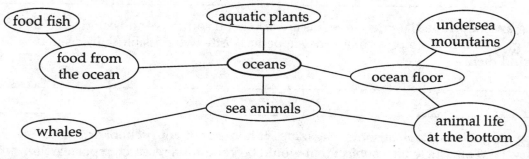

Exercise Use the space below to make a cluster chart about city life or country life, or choose a subject of your own. Begin by writing the subject in the center circle. After you have finished your cluster chart, study it to find a narrow topic. Write your topic at the bottom of this page.

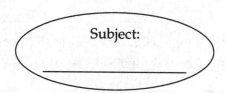

Topic: _____

Chapter 19: The Research Report

Thinking About Audience and Purpose

The main **purpose** of your research report is to give information to your readers. The information consists mostly of facts and the opinions of experts. Your first **audience** probably will be your teacher and classmates, but reports might be for different audiences. Don't bore your audience by telling them what they already know. But don't confuse them by not telling them enough, either. Explain or define ideas or words they may not understand.

Exercise A   Think about the audience for a report on your hobby, or choose another topic. To help you get started, answer these questions on the lines provided.

1. What does my audience probably already know about the subject?

_____

_____

_____

2. What new or unusual information might interest and surprise my audience?

_____

_____

_____

Exercise B   You're planning a report on killer whales to read to your class. Here are some sentences about whales. Which information would you use in your report? On the line under each sentence, state whether or not you would use the information in your report. Explain why each piece of information does or does not suit your purpose and your audience.

1. Whales live in water.

_____

2. Killer whales are the fastest members of the dolphin family and can swim for short distances at 25 knots.

_____

3. A knot is a measure of speed, equal to 1.15 miles per hour.

_____

4. A friend of mine saw a killer whale in a marine park.

_____

5. Killer whales travel in groups called pods.

_____

COMPOSITION

Chapter 19: The Research Report

Making an Early Plan and Asking Questions

Your **early plan,** or informal outline, for your report will list the main ideas that you want to cover. To find the information for your early plan, ask yourself questions. You can start with the *5W-How?* questions: *Who? What? When? Where? Why? How?* The questions will help guide your research and keep you focused on your topic.

Exercise   On the lines provided, write six questions about your research report topic. If you haven't chosen a topic, ask questions about modern moviemaking.

Topic: _____

Question 1: Who _____

_____

_____ ?

Question 2: What _____

_____

_____ ?

Question 3: When _____

_____

_____ ?

Question 4: Where _____

_____

_____ ?

Question 5: Why _____

_____

_____ ?

Question 6: How _____

_____

_____ ?

Name _____ Date _____ Class _____

Chapter 19: The Research Report

Finding and Evaluating Sources

Your library and your community contain many valuable sources of information for research papers. The following chart lists some of the sources that are available.

Library Resources	Community Resources
Encyclopedias	Museums
Books	Supermarkets
Magazines	Wildlife parks
Newspapers	Hospitals or clinics
Booklets and pamphlets	Colleges
Videotapes and audiotapes	Government offices
Slides	Interviews with experts

When you're researching a topic, you need to *evaluate* the sources of information. To **evaluate** means to determine something's strengths and weaknesses. Not all of your sources will be equally useful. Here are some questions that will help you evaluate, or judge, the usefulness of a source.

- **Is the source nonfiction?** Remember, you're looking for facts.
- **Can you trust your sources?** Are the sources respected and reliable?
- **Is the information current?** You need the latest available information.
- **Is the information objective?** Be sure all sides of a topic are presented.

Exercise Evaluate the sources for each topic by circling the letter of the best source in the middle column. Use the four evaluation questions above. In the right-hand column, explain why the sources in the middle column should or should not be used.

Topic	Sources
1. Harmful and helpful spiders	a. *Arachnophobia*, a movie about spiders that invade a town
	b. an article about spiders in the latest edition of *The World Book Encyclopedia*
	c. a book, written by a medical doctor in 1915, on the treatment of spider bites
2. Recent trends in video games	a. an article on video games in the latest issue of *Scientific American*
	b. a TV interview with the inventor of a video game
	c. an article in a newspaper on sale at the supermarket checkout counter about someone who was captured by a video game and taken to Mars

COMPOSITION

Chapter 19: The Research Report

Listing Sources and Taking Notes

Keep track of your sources by making **source cards** on index cards or sheets of notebook paper divided in half. Write the name of each source on a separate card, and give each card a source number. Write the source number in the upper right corner of the card.

When taking notes, let your early plan and questions about your topic guide you. Scan through the sources for information that relates to your headings and your questions. The tips below can help you take efficient notes.

- Use a separate 4" × 6" **note card** or half a sheet of paper for each source and for each note.
- Use abbreviations and short phrases.
- Use your own words. If you copy someone's exact words, put quotation marks around the words.
- Label each card by writing at the top left a key word or phrase that tells what the card is about.
- Put the source number at the top right of each card.
- At the bottom of each card, write the number of the page where you found the information.
- Take notes from each of your sources.

Exercise A   Below are the Modern Language Association (MLA) guidelines for listing sources from a book.

Books: List author, title, city of publication, publisher, and copyright year, punctuated as in the following example. (Use a shortened form of the publisher's name.)

Ventura, Piero. *Clothing.* Boston: Houghton, 1993.

On the lines below, write information correctly for a source card on a book that *you* have written with the title *Great Research Reports,* published in 1995 by Myown Press, New York City.

_____

_____

Exercise B   On an index card or half a sheet of paper, use your own words, short phrases, and abbreviations to take notes from the following paragraph.

   Not all writers and teachers live far from reality in those "ivory towers." Ernesto Galarza (1905–1984), for example, was a writer and teacher who was also an activist. Galarza did indeed write successful books, such as his autobiography *Barrio Boy,* and he had a Doctor of Philosophy degree from Columbia University. But Galarza was also a notable labor leader. Once a young farm worker himself, Galarza worked to make conditions better for poor Mexican field hands. He led strikes of tomato pickers and cantaloupe pickers in the 1950's.

Chapter 19: The Research Report

Organizing and Outlining Information

After gathering most of your information, you need to organize it. Separate your note cards into stacks with the same or similar labels. Think of a heading to identify each stack. Decide on the order of your main headings—perhaps order of importance or chronological (time) order. Then sort the cards in each stack to make subheadings for your outline.

Next, create an outline from your main headings and subheadings. A **formal outline** uses letters and numbers to show the relationships of ideas. Here is a framework for the beginning of such an outline, which serves as a table of contents for the reader.

      I. Major heading
        A. Subheading
          1. Detail
          2. Detail
        B. Subheading

Exercise   You have gathered information for a report on "Animals in American Folklore." Now you are ready to write your formal outline. Following is your list of headings and subheadings. Figure out an appropriate order, and place them in the outline form below.

Brer Rabbit	Uncle Remus stories	Songs about cattle
Songs about horses	Folk songs	The eagle in American
Animal tales	A blue ox named Babe	Indian songs
Cowboy songs	Brer Fox	

      Animals in American Folklore

       I. _____

         A. _____

         B. _____

           1. _____

           2. _____

      II. _____

         A. _____

         B. _____

           1. _____

           2. _____

COMPOSITION

Chapter 19: The Research Report

Writing a First Draft

Below are some notes you have taken for a report on Arlington National Cemetery in Arlington, Virginia. Both notes are exact quotations. The first is from an interview with a history teacher. The second is from a book on Civil War history.

Origins of the cemetery	1

"When the Union Army captured Lee's plantation, they decided it would serve Lee right if they buried their dead there. So that's what they did. They turned the land around Lee's home into a cemetery for the soldiers killed by Lee's armies."

Origins of the cemetery	2

"On the banks of the Potomac River, across from the White House and the Washington Monument, lies Arlington National Cemetery, a place of burial for hundreds of thousands of U.S. soldiers. The land that became the cemetery once belonged to Robert E. Lee—the same Lee who became commander of the Grand Army of the Confederacy. Lee's house still stands in the middle of the cemetery. From Lee's front porch modern-day visitors are treated to a breathtaking view of the nation's capital across the river."

p. 12

Exercise On a separate sheet of paper, use both notes above to write a paragraph for your report. Paraphrase, or state in your own words, at least one of the notes. Be sure that the paragraph has a topic sentence, is well organized, and is relatively free of errors. [Note: In your final draft of an actual report, you would include proper documentation for all sources cited. For this paragraph, write in parentheses the source-card number and page number, if any, after citing information from a source. Insert the citation in parentheses just before the end mark of the sentence in which you have used that source's information.]

Chapter 19: The Research Report

 **WORKSHEET 9** *Evaluating and Revising*

Evaluating a report means determining its strengths and weaknesses. **Revising** a report means making changes to improve it. If the answer to any of the following questions is no, your report may need revisions such as adding sources or facts. You could also replace or reorder information.

- Does the report use several different sources? Does the report consist of facts and the opinions of experts?
- Is the report in the writer's own words? If someone else's words are used, are the words in quotation marks?
- Is the information well organized?
- Is the introduction interesting, and does it tell what the report is about? Does the conclusion bring the report to a close?
- Is the list of sources in correct form on a separate sheet at the end?

Exercise   Here are the changes the writer made in one paragraph while revising a research report titled "From Crew Cut to Flattop." Look at the changes carefully. Then, on the lines below, answer the questions that follow.

In the eighties and early nineties, trendsetters wanted to look different from everyone else. The *more outrageous* ~~funnier~~ the better, they thought. (Neon colors emphasized the effect.) One unisex style, called the buzz or flattop, had closely cut or shaved sides like a Mohawk. ~~It's my favorite style.~~ However, the top hair of a flattop was clipped into a geometric shape and stood up straight *—like Bart Simpson's hair.*

1. Why did the writer replace the word *funnier* with the words *more outrageous* in the second

   sentence? [Hint: Which word expresses the correct fact?] _____

   _____

2. Why did the writer move (reorder) the third sentence to the end of the paragraph? How

   does this change help the organization of the paragraph? _____

   _____

3. Why did the writer cut the sentence *It's my favorite style*? _____

   _____

4. Why did the writer add *like Bart Simpson's hair* to the last sentence? _____

   _____

COMPOSITION

Name _____ Date _____ Class _____

 **WORKSHEET 10** # Proofreading and Publishing

Proofreading is reading carefully for mistakes in spelling, capitalization, usage, and punctuation, and then correcting them. **Publishing** is sharing your report with others.

Exercise A: Proofreading   The following paragraphs are part of a research report. Proofread for errors in spelling, punctuation, usage, and capitalization.

What are the most important forces in Arab society today. "Today is no different than past generations. Arab society is molded now, as it has been for hundreds of years, by family and religion. It has been and always will be thus." (Evans and Smith, 21) Scholars who watch the Arab world agrees that anyone who wants to understand Arab society must understand the force of family and religion.

In arab society, the family continues to be the basic unit. People in Arab countries, in fact, for the most part is known by their individual family units and by their tribal affiliations (a tribe is a group of familys). Within these family units, men remain the dominant figures. Fathers or husbands have authority over women. Parents usually arrange for they're children's marriages.

The people's religion, Islam, is a powerful force in Arab soceity. Even the justice system operates according to Islamic law. The religion is based on the Koran, Islams holy book. Islamic religion is very strict, and almost unchangeable. Why? it rests on the writings of Muhammad, Islam's founder. To Muslims, revelation ended with Muhammad's death in A.D. 632; therefore, Islam's leaders consider the law final

Exercise B   You've written a research report on Arab society. Think of five specific ways to publish your report. List your ideas on the lines provided.

1. _____

2. _____

3. _____

4. _____

5. _____

Name _____ Date _____ Class _____

WORKSHEET 1 **The Dewey Decimal System**

Every book in your library is labeled with a number and letter code to help you to find the book. That label is the book's **call number**.

The **Dewey decimal system** is a method for organizing nonfiction books in libraries. It has ten general numerical subject classifications. They are listed below.

> 000–099 General Works (encyclopedias, periodicals, etc.)
> 100–199 Philosophy (includes psychology, conduct, etc.)
> 200–299 Religion (includes mythology)
> 300–399 Social Sciences (economics, government, law, etc.)
> 400–499 Languages (dictionaries, grammars, etc.)
> 500–599 Science (mathematics, chemistry, physics, etc.)
> 600–699 Technology (agriculture, engineering, aviation, etc.)
> 700–799 The Arts (sculpture, painting, music, photography, sports, etc.)
> 800–899 Literature (poetry, plays, orations, etc.)
> 900–999 History (includes travel and biography)

Fiction books are shelved in alphabetical order by authors' last names. If the author has written more than one book, the books are shelved in alphabetical order by the first word of their titles (not counting *A, An,* or *The*).

Exercise A Write the general subject area of books with the following call numbers.

1. 930.6 _____
2. 001.5 _____
3. 534.0 _____
4. 768.5 _____
5. 601.3 _____

6. 222.4 _____
7. 459.6 _____
8. 159.5 _____
9. 862.4 _____
10. 324.5 _____

Exercise B Look at each of the descriptions of books below. On the line provided, write N for each nonfiction book and F for each fiction book.

_____ 1. A history book by J. Frank Dobie

_____ 2. A short story by Toni Cade Bambara

_____ 3. A book about recycling

_____ 4. A novel by Madeleine L'Engle

_____ 5. *On Writing Well*, a book about writing by William Zinsser

Name _____ Date _____ Class _____

 **The Card Catalog**

To find the call number of any book you're looking for, use the *card catalog*. The **card catalog** is a cabinet of drawers containing alphabetically arranged cards. Fiction call numbers can be found in either the *author cards* or the *title cards*. Nonfiction call numbers can be found in author cards, title cards, or *subject cards*. Sometimes a card contains a "see also" note. This cross-reference directs you to another section of the card catalog that has more information on the same subject. An **on-line catalog** is a computerized version of the card catalog.

Exercise A   Each item below gives you some information about a book. On the line, write which card file you would look in to find the book's call number (*author, title,* or *subject* file). (Note: Authors are listed last name first. Titles of books are italicized.)

1. *The Adventures of Tom Sawyer* _____

2. honeybees _____

3. Abraham Lincoln _____

4. Keller, Helen _____

5. *The Diary of a Young Girl* _____

6. Thurber, James _____

7. famous pianists _____

8. computers _____

9. *Death Be Not Proud* _____

10. Bontemps, Arna _____

Exercise B   Go to your library and use the card catalog to find three books on space travel. Write their call numbers and titles. Then find two books by Isaac Asimov, and write their call numbers and titles.

1. _____

2. _____

3. _____

4. _____

5. _____

Resources

The Parts of a Book

Most nonfiction books contain the nine parts listed below.

JACKET: description of book and author

TITLE PAGE: full title, author, publisher, and place of publication

COPYRIGHT PAGE: date and place of first publication and any revisions

TABLE OF CONTENTS: titles of chapters or sections with their page numbers

LIST OF ILLUSTRATIONS: pictures, charts, maps, diagrams, and their page numbers

APPENDIX: additional information about subjects in book

GLOSSARY: definitions of difficult words

BIBLIOGRAPHY: names of books used as references by the author

INDEX: topics in the book with page numbers where they can be found

Exercise   Write where in a book you would check to find the following information.

1. page number(s) on which a particular topic is covered

   _____

2. additional information about a subject

   _____

3. page number on which a particular chart can be found

   _____

4. biographical information about the author

   _____

5. date of the last revision of the book

   _____

6. page number on which a particular chapter begins

   _____

7. books the author used as references

   _____

8. place of publication

   _____

9. page number on which a particular section begins

   _____

10. definition of a difficult word

   _____

RESOURCES

Name _____ Date _____ Class _____

 **WORKSHEET 4**   *Using Reference Materials*

The following list describes special reference sources and the kinds of materials and information they contain.

VERTICAL FILE: up-to-date subject file containing pamphlets and newspaper clippings with government, business, and educational information

MICROFORMS: pages from newspapers and magazines that are reduced for viewing on a screen

ENCYCLOPEDIAS: multiple volumes of articles on general subjects

BIOGRAPHICAL REFERENCES: information about outstanding people

SPECIAL BIOGRAPHICAL REFERENCES: information about outstanding people in particular fields or groups (e.g., *Biographical Dictionary of American Sports*)

ATLASES: maps and geographical information

ALMANACS: up-to-date information about current events, statistics, and dates

BOOKS OF QUOTATIONS: famous quotations indexed by subject

BOOKS OF SYNONYMS: lists of words that are synonyms

REFERENCE BOOKS ABOUT LITERATURE: information about various works of literature

READERS' GUIDE TO PERIODICAL LITERATURE: index of articles of more than one hundred magazines

Exercise   Write the reference or references you might use to find the following information.

1. a famous quotation about economic hardship _____

2. the name of the team that won the first World Series _____

3. another word that has the same meaning as *soft* _____

4. the location of Lubbock, Texas _____

5. the author of the poem "Preaching Blues" _____

6. number of sisters and/or brothers Thomas Jefferson had _____

7. a list of magazine articles on new developments in plastics _____

8. the headline of a newspaper from December 1920 _____

9. biographical information on Irish Americans who have held political office

_____

10. a pamphlet on water safety _____

Name _____ Date _____ Class _____

WORKSHEET 5   *Using the Newspaper*

A daily newspaper has a variety of reading materials in its various sections. The following chart shows contents that you may find in a typical newspaper.

WHAT'S IN A NEWSPAPER?		
WRITER'S PURPOSE/ TYPE OF WRITING	READER'S PURPOSE	READING TECHNIQUE

to inform
   news stories
   sports
	to gain knowledge or information	Ask yourself the *5W-How?* questions.

to persuade
   editorials
   cartoons
   reviews
   ads
	to gain knowledge, to make decisions, or to be entertained	Identify points you agree or disagree with. Find facts or reasons the writer uses.

to be creative or expressive
   comics
   newspaper columns
	to be entertained	Identify ways the writer interests you or gives you a new viewpoint or ideas.

Exercise   Using a copy of a Sunday newspaper from home or your library, answer the following questions on the lines below.

1. What part of the newspaper do you read first? Why? _____

    _____

2. Find one article that gives you information about a local event. In this article, find the answers to the *5W-How?* questions and list them briefly below.

    _____

    _____

    _____

3. Find a review of a movie, book, or play. Tell the writer's opinion, and briefly list the evidence the writer provides to back up that opinion.

    _____

    _____

    _____

4. Briefly describe a part of the paper that is meant to be expressive or creative.

    _____

    _____

    _____

Name _____ Date _____ Class _____

WORKSHEET 6 ***Using the Dictionary A***

Dictionaries differ in the amount and kinds of information that they contain. An **unabridged dictionary** of English is very large and may contain around 460,000 words. A **college** or **abridged dictionary** is shorter and contains perhaps 160,000 words. There are also smaller **school dictionaries** for students and **paperback dictionaries**.

The words listed in a dictionary are called **entries**. Entries are listed in alphabetical order. Each page of entries has a pair of **guide words** at the top. The first guide word is the first entry on the page; the second guide word is the last entry on the page.

Generally speaking, the larger a dictionary is, the more information it contains. Consider, for example, the words found between *yak* and *yam* in two dictionaries.

Webster's New World Dictionary:
Student's Edition
yak[1]
yak[2]
Yalu
yam

Webster's New World Dictionary:
Third College Edition
yak[1]
yak[2]
Yakima
Yakima
yakitori
Yakut
Yakutsk
Yale (lock)
Yalow, Rosalyn Sussman
Yalta
Yalu
yam

The student dictionary has four entries, whereas the college dictionary has twelve.

Exercise Use a college or unabridged dictionary to answer the following questions.

1. Who met at the city of **Yalta** in 1945, and where is this city located?

   _____

2. What would you be eating if you had **yakitori** for dinner?

   _____

3. What does **Rosalyn Sussman Yalow** do for a living?

   _____

4. The **Yalu** river runs between Manchuria, in China, and what other country?

   _____

5. What language is spoken by the **Yakima** people of Washington state?

   _____

Resources

WORSHEET 7 ***Using the Dictionary B***

Information found in dictionaries includes

- **Entry word**. The entry word shows how the word is spelled and how it is divided into syllables. The entry word may also show capitalization and alternate spellings.

- **Pronunciation**. The pronunciation, which follows the entry word, is shown by the use of *accent marks, phonetic symbols,* or *diacritical marks*. **Accent marks** show which syllables of a word are said more forcefully. **Phonetic symbols** represent specific sounds. **Diacritical marks** are special symbols placed above the letters to show how they sound. A **pronunciation key** explains the sounds represented by these symbols.

- **Part-of-speech labels**. These labels indicate how the entry word should be used in a sentence. Some words may be used as more than one part of speech.

- **Other forms**. These spellings may show plural forms of nouns, tenses of verbs, or the comparative forms of adjectives and adverbs.

Exercise A   Use your dictionary to find an alternate spelling for each of the following words. On the line provided, give the alternate spelling.

1. abridgment _____   3. savior _____

2. likable _____   4. ameba _____

Exercise B   Use the pronunciations given in the dictionary to answer the following questions.

1. Which letters are silent in the word *corps*?   _____

2. Is there a *b* sound in the word *subtle*?   _____

3. Should the final *e* be pronounced in the word *finale*? If so, how should it be pronounced?   _____

4. Is there a *d* sound in the word *handkerchief*?   _____

Exercise C   Look up each of the following words in a dictionary. On the line provided, give all the parts of speech listed for each word.

1. fuss _____   3. smooth _____

2. incline _____   4. smirk _____

Exercise D   Use a dictionary to help you write the following words.

1. the plural form of *tally*   _____

2. the plural form of *volcano*   _____

3. the past tense of *lay*   _____

4. the comparative forms of *good*   _____

RESOURCES

Resources

| WORKSHEET 8 | *Using the Dictionary C* |

The **etymology** of a word tells its origin and history. Usually, the etymology appears in brackets right after the pronunciation. As you can see, etymologies use many abbreviations. Here is a sample etymology for the word *amateur*.

[< F < L *amator*, lover = ptp. of *amare*, to love]

This etymology tells you that the word *amateur* is derived from a French (F) word. The French word came from the Latin (L) word *amator*, which means "lover." The Latin word *amator* in turn came from the past participle (ptp.) of the Latin verb *amare*, which means "to love." Understanding a word's etymology can help you remember the meaning of a word and other words like it.

Most dictionaries contain a list of abbreviations that you can refer to when reading etymologies. The list usually appears at the beginning or end of the dictionary.

Exercise Look up the following words in a dictionary, and study their etymologies. Then explain in your own words the origin of each word.

1. Fahrenheit _____

_____

2. money _____

_____

3. Thursday _____

_____

4. mamba _____

_____

5. chortle _____

_____

6. polecat _____

_____

7. liberty _____

_____

8. odd _____

_____

9. rhythm _____

_____

10. Mardi Gras _____

_____

Resources

WORKSHEET 9   *Using the Dictionary D*

Contents of a dictionary entry include

- **Examples**. Phrases or sentences may demonstrate how the defined word is used.
- **Definitions**. If there is more than one meaning, definitions are numbered or lettered.
- **Special usage labels**. These labels identify words that have special meaning or are used in special ways in certain fields.
- **Related word forms**. These various forms of the entry word are usually created by adding suffixes or prefixes.
- **Synonyms and antonyms**. Sometimes **synonyms,** words that are similar in meaning, and **antonyms,** words that are opposite in meaning, appear at the end of a word entry.

Exercise A   If your college or unabridged dictionary lists special usage labels for entry words, look up the following words. On the line provided, write the usage label(s) given for each word or for any of its meanings. If your dictionary has no labels, write *none*.

1. noise _____

2. glitzy _____

3. quarter _____

4. mixture _____

5. dude _____

Exercise B   Use an unabridged or college dictionary to answer the following questions. Use the lines provided.

1. What is one usage of the word *get* and an example sentence?

_____

2. How many numbered definitions do you find for the word *loop*?

_____

3. What are some related forms of the word *logical*?

_____

4. How many numbered definitions do you find for the word *free*?

_____

5. What is a synonym for the word *perplex*?

_____

Resources

WORKSHEET 10 | **Personal Letters**

A **personal letter,** sometimes called a *friendly letter,* is often a good way to communicate with a friend or relative. Like a conversation, a friendly letter contains a specific, personal message from you to the person you're communicating with. The purpose of a personal letter is to express emotions and ideas.

Exercise A   On the lines provided, write a personal letter to a friend on a topic of interest to both of you. For example, you may write about a band that you both like or about a hobby that you share.

Dear _____ ,

_____

_____

_____

_____

_____

_____

_____

_____

Your friend,

_____

Exercise B   On the lines provided, write a friendly letter to a relative on a topic of interest to both of you.

Dear _____ ,

_____

_____

_____

_____

_____

_____

_____

_____

Love,

_____

Name _____ Date _____ Class _____

Social Letters

A **social letter** is a courteous announcement or response concerning a particular event. Social letters may include **thank-you letters, invitations,** or **letters of regret**. In a thank-you letter, try to say something specific about the kindness that the person has done for you. In an invitation, include specific information about the occasion, the time and the place, and any other special details your guest might need to know. In a letter of regret, let someone know that you will not be able to accept an invitation. If the letters *R.S.V.P.* (an abbreviation for "please reply" in French) appear on the invitation, it's especially important to send a written reply.

Exercise A   On the lines provided, write the body of a thank-you letter to a friend who brought you your homework assignments while you recovered from the flu.

_____

_____

_____

_____

_____

_____

Exercise B   On the lines provided, write an invitation to a surprise birthday party for your best friend. Include all the information your guests will need to know.

_____

_____

_____

_____

_____

_____

Exercise C   On the lines provided, write the body of a letter expressing your regret at not being able to attend a classmate's going-away party.

_____

_____

_____

_____

_____

_____

Resources

The Parts of a Business Letter

There are six parts of a business letter. The **heading** includes your address and the date of the letter. The **inside address** contains the name and the address of the person to whom you are writing. The **salutation** is the greeting. It is almost always *Dear* and then the person's name. The **body** is the main part of the letter. The **closing** is the polite ending. *Yours truly, Sincerely,* and *Sincerely yours* often are used as closings. The **signature** is handwritten directly below the closing. Beneath the signature, type or print your name.

The two forms of a business letter are *block form* and *modified block form*. When you use **block form**, every part of the letter begins at the left margin, and paragraphs are not indented. When you use **modified block form**, the heading, the closing, and your signature each start to the right of the center of the page. The first line of each paragraph is indented.

Exercise A   Each statement below refers to one of the six parts of a business letter described above. Write *H* if the statement refers to the heading, *I* if it refers to the inside address, *S* if it refers to the salutation, *B* if it refers to the body, *C* if it refers to the closing, or *SI* if it refers to the signature.

_____ 1. It is the greeting.

_____ 2. It is the polite ending.

_____ 3. It contains the name and the address of the person to whom you are writing.

_____ 4. It contains the date of the letter.

_____ 5. It contains the main message.

Exercise B   On the given lines, label each part of the business letter shown below in block form.

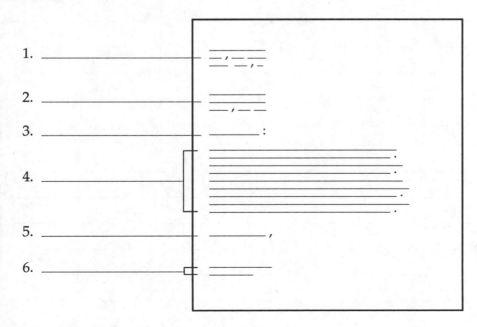

Name _____ Date _____ Class _____

 **WORKSHEET 13** ***Types of Business Letters***

In a **request letter,** you ask for information about a product or service or request sample materials. In an **order letter**, you ask for something specific, such as a free brochure advertised in a magazine or an item of merchandise that is listed in a catalog with no printed form. In a **complaint** or **adjustment letter,** you report an error or state that you have a complaint. When writing such letters, register your complaint as soon as possible, be sure to mention specifics (such as how to solve the problem), and keep the tone of your letter calm and courteous. In an **appreciation** or **commendation letter,** you express your gratitude or praise for a person, group, or organization. State exactly why you are pleased.

Exercise On the lines below, write a business letter for one of the following situations. Make up any information you need to have a complete letter.

1. Inquire about a video game from an imaginary company (make up the name of the game and the name and address of the company). The catalog description of the game is too brief, and you want a complete description before you place an order.

2. Write a letter to the editor of your local newspaper complaining about the lack of news coverage about a recent community event. Explain why you think the newspaper should have covered the event and how this problem can be avoided in the future.

3. Write a letter of appreciation or commendation to a school official or community leader, expressing your thanks for a job well done.

_____

_____

_____

_____

_____

_____

_____

_____

_____

_____

_____

_____

_____

_____

Resources

WORKSHEET 14

Addressing Envelopes and Completing Printed Forms

Follow these guidelines to address an envelope: (1) Place your complete return address in the top left-hand corner of the envelope. (2) Center the name and address of the person or organization to whom you are writing on the envelope. For a business letter, the name and address to which the letter is being sent should exactly match the inside address of the letter. (3) Use standard two-letter postal abbreviations for state names, and include ZIP Codes.

Follow these guidelines to complete printed forms: (1) Look over the entire form before you begin. (2) Take note of any special instructions, such as "Please print clearly" or "Use a pencil." (3) Read each item carefully. (4) Supply all the information requested. You can use a dash or the symbol *N/A*, which means "not applicable," to indicate that some information does not apply to you. (5) Proofread your completed form. Make sure you have given all requested information. Check for errors, and correct them neatly.

Exercise A Suppose you need to send a letter to someone you know. Write the necessary information on the envelope drawn below.

```
 _____

 _____

 _____



                    _____

                    _____

                    _____

                    _____
```

Exercise B Complete the form below, following the guidelines given above.

```
                    Application for Health Club

 Name    _____     Age: _____

 Address _____     Height: _____

         _____     Weight: _____

 Swimmer: Yes _____ No _____     Lifesaving Certification: Yes _____ No _____

 Type of Membership Requested:  Full _____   Health Club Only _____   Pool Only _____
```

Resources

 **WORKSHEET 15** | *Manuscript Style A*

A **manuscript** is any typed or handwritten composition. Use the following guidelines as you make a final copy of your paper.

Handwritten Papers: Use regular 8 ½" × 11" lined paper and blue or black ink. Write legibly. Do not skip lines unless your teacher instructs you to.

Typewritten Papers: Use regular 8 ½" × 11" typing paper. Avoid very thin (onionskin) paper and erasable paper. Use a fresh black ribbon. Double-space between lines.

Word-processed Papers: Use letter-sized sheets or continuous-feed paper that separates cleanly along the edges. Make sure that the printer you use can produce clear, dark, letter-quality type. Check with your teacher to be sure that the typeface you plan to use is acceptable. Double-space between lines.

Whether your paper is handwritten, typed, or word-processed, use the following format.

- Use only one side of a sheet of paper.
- Leave one-inch margins at the top, sides, and bottom of each page.
- Indent the first line of each paragraph five spaces from the left margin.
- Number all pages (except the first page) in the upper right-hand corner, one-half inch from the top.
- Follow your teacher's instructions for placement of your name, the date, your class, and the title of your paper.
- Make corrections neatly. To insert a word or a short phrase, use a caret mark (∧) and add the word(s) immediately above it.

Exercise On the lines provided, write *C* for correct or *I* for incorrect next to each statement about the preparation of a manuscript.

_____ 1. Number all pages.

_____ 2. Indent the first line of each paragraph five spaces from the left margin.

_____ 3. Use both sides of a sheet of paper if your paper is handwritten.

_____ 4. Typewritten papers should be single-spaced.

_____ 5. Leave side margins of one inch only on word-processed papers.

_____ 6. Use blue or green ink for handwritten papers.

_____ 7. Double-space between lines of word-processed papers.

_____ 8. Use 8 ½" × 11" lined paper for handwritten papers.

_____ 9. Always place your name and the title of your paper at the top of your first page.

_____10. It is acceptable to use erasable paper if manuscript is typed.

RESOURCES

Resources

WORKSHEET 16   *Manuscript Style B*

Few **abbreviations,** shortened forms of words or phrases, are appropriate in a formal paper. Many may be used in tables, notes, and bibliographies.

Certain abbreviations such as *Mr., Mrs., Sr., Jr., Dr.,* and *Sen.* are acceptable when used with a person's name. If they do not accompany a name, spell out the words.

    Is **Dr.** Saperstein in?   Yes, the **doctor** is available.

    Sen. Dale Bumpers   What is your schedule, **Senator**?

Abbreviate given names only if the person is most commonly known that way. Leave a space between two such initials, but not between three or more.

    E. M. Forster   **I. M.** Pei   **W.E.B.** Du Bois

The abbreviations A.M., P.M., A.D., and B.C. are acceptable when they are used with numbers.

    10:30 A.M.   8:30 P.M.   400 B.C.   A.D. 30

After spelling out the first use, abbreviate the names of agencies and organizations commonly known by their initials.

    FIRST USE: **National Education Association**   SECOND USE: **NEA**

In text, spell out the names of states whether the names stand alone or follow another geographical term. Use traditional abbreviations for state names in tables, notes, and bibliographies. Use the two-letter postal abbreviations only in addresses that include the ZIP Code.

    TEXT: **Wisconsin**   TABLES, ETC.: **Wis.**   WITH ZIP CODE: **WI**

Exercise: Proofreading   Rewrite the following sentences to correct manuscript style.

  1. President Bill Clinton is the former gov. of Ark.

    _____

  2. Maya Angelou was born in Stamps, AR, not far from Clinton's hometown of Hope.

    _____

  3. Mrs. Clark, a member of our Parent-Teacher Association, read two of Angelou's poems at the Parent-Teacher Association meeting.

    _____

    _____

  4. The meeting, which began at 8:30 P.M.—or was it earlier in the P.M.?—also included a reading from Angelou's book *I Know Why the Caged Bird Sings*.

    _____

    _____

Name _____ Date _____ Class _____

 **Manuscript Style C**

A number that states "how many" should be spelled out if it can be expressed in one or two words. Otherwise, use numerals.

seven forks   **eight thousand** customers

6,550 egg rolls   **thirty-nine** minutes

Spell out numbers that express order, such as *first* and *fourth*. If they represent the day of the month, use numerals only.

the **first** game   on July **4**

In your writing, use **nonsexist language**—language that applies to people in general, both male and female.

In the past, many skills and occupations excluded either men or women. Expressions showed these restrictions. Now that most jobs are held by both men and women, language is adjusting to reflect this change. When you are referring to humanity as a whole, use nonsexist expressions rather than gender-specific ones.

SEXIST: **fireman, housewife**   NONSEXIST: **firefighter, homemaker**

Sometimes the antecedent of a pronoun may be either masculine or feminine. In such a case, use both masculine and feminine pronouns to refer to it.

Each **student** should bring **his** or **her** notebooks.

You can often avoid the awkward *his or her* construction by substituting an article (*a, an,* or *the*) for the construction or by rephrasing the sentence.

Each **student** should bring **a** notebook.

Students should bring **their** notebooks.

Exercise: Proofreading   On the line provided, correct the manuscript style in each of the following sentences.

1. When she was young, she wanted to be a policeman.

   _____

2. The town's population is two thousand six hundred and nine.

   _____

3. The movie was really my 2nd choice, but I liked it very much.

   _____

4. There are 10,000 students at the college this year.

   _____

5. Anyone who expects to succeed must keep his attitude positive.

   _____

Resources

◇ **WORKSHEET 18** *Review*

Exercise A On the lines provided, answer the following questions to review your understanding of the library and its resources.

1. Which of the following fiction books would be shelved first: *Barrio Boy*, by Ernesto Galarza, or *Gorilla, My Love*, by Toni Cade Bambara?

   _____

2. Using the card catalog or on-line catalog, find a book about your favorite hobby. Write the title, the author's name, and the call number.

   _____

3. After locating a book on your favorite hobby, look in the book's table of contents. Copy the titles of at least two chapters or sections of the book.

   _____

   _____

4. Tell which reference materials you might use to find information about the climate and the landforms of Antarctica.

   _____

5. What is the Dewey Decimal System? Does it apply to fiction or nonfiction?

   _____

   _____

Exercise B Below are three items describing aims for writing. In the spaces following the items, name parts of a newspaper that are likely to meet these aims.

To inform   To persuade   To be creative or expressive

1. _____   3. _____   5. _____

2. _____   4. _____

Exercise C Use an unabridged or college dictionary to answer the following questions. Use the lines provided.

1. What are two correct pronunciations of *arctic*? _____

2. What two past tense forms does the verb *dive* have? _____

3. What is one usage of the word *due* and an example sentence? _____

   _____

Resources, Worksheet 18, continued

4. Is the term *hand-me-down* considered colloquial or slang?

_____

5. What are two synonyms for the word *delusion*?

_____

Exercise D   Write a letter to an aunt and uncle to thank them for a birthday present.
Make up necessary details for your letter. Include a salutation and a closing.

_____
_____
_____
_____
_____
_____

Exercise E   You ordered a poster enlargement of a photo of your softball team. When you
received it, part of the team had been cut out of the picture. In the space below, write a letter
of complaint to the photo store. Your letter should contain all six parts of a business letter.
Make up the name of the photo store and any details you may need to complete your letter.

_____
_____
_____
_____
_____
_____
_____
_____
_____
_____
_____
_____
_____
_____
_____

Resources, Worksheet 18, continued

Exercise F   On the line provided, write *C* for correct or *I* for incorrect next to each statement about addressing envelopes and completing order forms.

_____ 1. If a request for information does not apply to you, you should write *N/A* on the form.

_____ 2. Put your own address on the back of your envelope.

_____ 3. You will want to read each item of a form carefully before answering it.

_____ 4. Proper form does not require that the name and the address on the envelope match the inside address of the letter.

_____ 5. After you fill out a form, you should proofread your responses.

Exercise G   On the line provided, write *C* for correct or *I* for incorrect next to each statement about the preparation of a manuscript.

_____ 1. Double-space between lines of a typewritten paper.

_____ 2. Leave a two-inch margin at the bottom of each page.

_____ 3. For handwritten papers, use both sides of a sheet of paper.

_____ 4. Indent the first line of each paragraph five spaces from the left margin.

_____ 5. Single-space between lines of a word-processed paper.

Exercise H: Proofreading   On the line provided, correct the manuscript style in each of the following sentences. If a sentence is correct, write *C*.

1. B.J. Thomas was the 1st singer my parents saw at the theater.

_____

2. Here is a copy of the old American Medical Association guidelines, but the new American Medical Association guidelines have been misplaced.

_____

_____

3. Company foremen from all over Ariz. will meet on July Sixth at ten in the A.M.

_____

_____

4. The sen. said that any state resident who brings their letter can attend.

_____

_____

5. These statues, which date from B.C. 1000, weigh five thousand two hundred pounds.

_____

_____

Appendix: Diagraming Sentences

Diagraming Subjects and Verbs

A **sentence diagram** is a picture of how the parts of a sentence fit together.

To diagram a sentence, first find the simple subject and the simple predicate, or verb, and write them on a horizontal line. Then separate the subject and verb with a vertical line. Keep the capital letters, but leave out the punctuation marks, except in cases such as *Dr.* and *June 6, 1946.*

The dog barked all night long.

dog	barked

To diagram an imperative sentence, place the understood subject *you* in parentheses on the horizontal line.

Watch me, Rita!

(you)	Watch

To diagram a question, first make the question into a statement. Then diagram the sentence.

Will Dr. Ramírez perform the operation?

Dr. Ramírez	Will perform

Exercise   On a separate sheet of paper, diagram only the simple subjects and the verbs in the following sentences. Remember that simple subjects and verbs may consist of more than one word.

EXAMPLE: 1. Midas is a character in Greek mythology.

Midas	is

1. Midas ruled the kingdom of Phrygia.

2. One of the gods gave Midas the power to turn anything into gold.

3. Soon, this gift became a curse.

4. Do you know why?

5. Read the story of King Midas in a mythology book.

Appendix: Diagraming Sentences

Diagraming Compound Subjects and Compound Verbs

To diagram a compound subject, put the subjects on parallel lines. Then join them by a dotted line on which you write the connecting word (the conjunction).

Cardinals and **chickadees** come to our bird feeder.

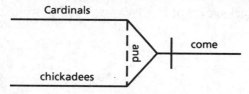

A compound verb is diagramed in the same way.

The engine **sputtered** and **died**.

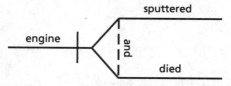

Alex **was shouting** and **waving** his arms.

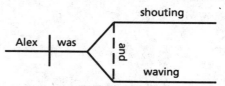

A sentence with both a compound subject and a compound verb combines the two patterns.

Camels and **donkeys can carry** huge loads and **are** still **used** as pack animals.

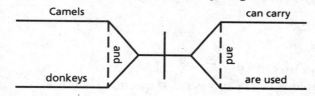

Exercise   On a separate sheet of paper, diagram the simple subjects and the verbs in the following sentences. Remember that the word *not* is never part of a verb phrase.

EXAMPLE: 1. Nikki and Chris chopped the cilantro and added it to the salsa.

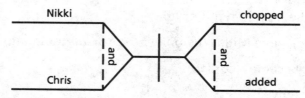

1. Mr. Carrington collects aluminum cans and returns them for recycling.

2. The students and the faculty combined their efforts and defeated the proposal.

3. The plane circled above the landing field but did not descend.

4. Pencil and paper are needed for tomorrow's math assignment.

5. Walking and jogging build leg muscles and make your heart and lungs strong.

Appendix: Diagraming Sentences

Diagraming Adjectives and Adverbs

Both adjectives and adverbs are written on slanted lines below the words they modify. Note that possessive pronouns are diagramed in the same way adjectives are.

ADJECTIVES: **mighty** warrior   **long, exciting** movie   **my final** offer

ADVERBS: answered **quickly**   may **possibly** happen   **never** plans **carefully**

When an adverb modifies an adjective or another adverb, it is placed on a line connected to the word it modifies.

a **dangerously sharp** curve   listened **quite intently**   the **nearly complete** book

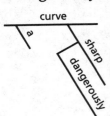 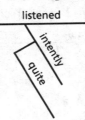 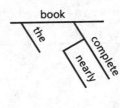

When a conjunction joins two modifiers, it is diagramed like this:

The **small** and **silky** kitten meowed **softly** but **insistently**.

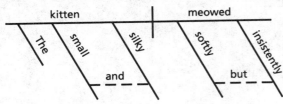

Exercise   On a separate sheet of paper, diagram the following sentences. Include all the words from each sentence in your diagrams.

1. The shutters rattled quite noisily.

2. They and the Reynolds are definitely leaving tomorrow.

3. The anxious and exhausted motorist drove much too far.

4. The new car had been slightly damaged.

5. The mission bells rang slowly and mournfully.

Appendix: Diagraming Sentences

Diagraming Direct Objects and Indirect Objects

A direct object is diagramed on the horizontal line with the subject and the verb. A vertical line separates the direct object from the verb. Notice that this vertical line does not cross the horizontal line. The second example below shows how to diagram a compound direct object.

Josh cleaned his **room**.

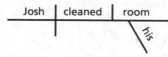

We invited **Marissa** and **Leon**.

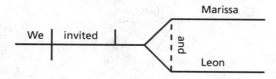

An indirect object is diagramed on a short horizontal line below the verb. Connect the indirect object to the verb by a slanted line. The example on the right shows how to diagram a compound indirect object.

Will you show **me** your sketch?   Give **Rex** and **Zippy** their dinner.

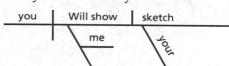   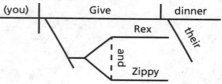

Exercise   On a separate sheet of paper, diagram the following sentences.

EXAMPLE: 1. Where did he find his cap?

1. Placido Domingo signed photographs and programs.

2. Snow gives motorists and pedestrians trouble.

3. The cashier handed the children balloons.

4. Her older sister taught Lynn the rules.

5. Did Rico give Ron and you a ride?

Name _____ Date _____ Class _____

Diagraming Subject Complements

A subject complement (predicate nominative or predicate adjective) is placed on the horizontal line with the simple subject and the verb. A line slanting toward the subject separates the subject complement from the verb. Some examples below show how to diagram compound subject complements.

PREDICATE NOMINATIVES: Is Freddie Jackson your favorite **singer**?

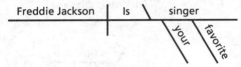

Sir Francis Drake was a **navigator** and a **buccaneer**.

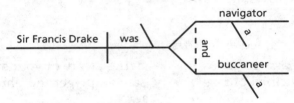

PREDICATE ADJECTIVES: The air grew **cold**.

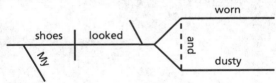

My shoes looked **worn** and **dusty**.

Exercise On a separate sheet of paper, diagram the following sentences.

EXAMPLE: 1. Is he ready?

1. Was her mother a motorcycle mechanic?

2. The Gypsies' origin remains mysterious and strange.

3. Be quiet!

4. My favorite Mexican foods are tamales and tacos.

5. The waterfall was small and peaceful.

Name _____ Date _____ Class _____

Diagraming Prepositional Phrases and Verbal Phrases

A prepositional phrase is diagramed below the word it modifies. Write the preposition on a slanting line below the modified word. Then write the object of the preposition on a horizontal line connected to the slanting line. The first example below shows a prepositional phrase with a compound object.

project **of Desmond and Jane**
[adjective phrase]

invited **to the celebration**
[adverb phrase]

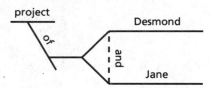

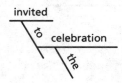

Verbal phrases are diagramed as follows:

Hearing a noise, Larry looked up suddenly. [participial phrase]

Being aware of your surroundings is a basic safety tip. [gerund phrase used as subject]

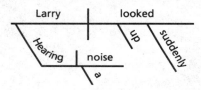

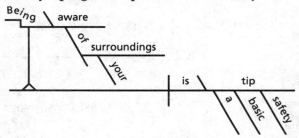

Her desire is **to go home**. [infinitive phrase used as predicate nominative]

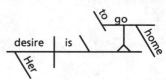

Infinitives and infinitive phrases used as modifiers are diagramed like prepositional phrases.

Exercise On a separate sheet of paper, diagram the following sentences.

1. Hundreds of animal species are being protected by concerned citizens.

2. Citrus fruits are grown in California and Florida.

3. Taking that shortcut will cut several minutes off the trip.

4. I want to watch *Nova* tonight.

5. That is my cat licking its paws.

Appendix: Diagraming Sentences

Diagraming Subordinate Clauses

Diagram an adjective clause by connecting it with a broken line to the word it modifies. Draw the broken line between the relative pronoun and the word that it relates to. [Note: The words *who, whom, whose, which,* and *that* are relative pronouns.]

The jeans **that I like** are black.

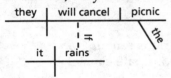

Students **who study** make better grades.

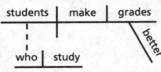

Diagram an adverb clause by connecting it with a broken line to the word it modifies. Place the subordinating conjunction that introduces the adverb clause on the broken line.

If it rains, they will cancel the picnic.

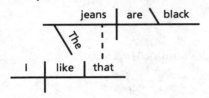

Yoshi runs faster **than I do.**

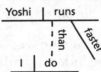

Diagram a noun clause by connecting it to the independent clause with a solid line.

What you think is important to me.

I will ask **what he wants.**

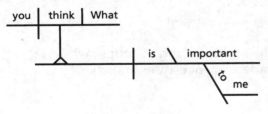

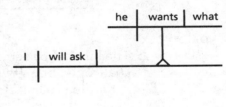

Exercise   On a separate sheet of paper, diagram the following sentences.

1. If I had not studied on Thursday night, I could not have answered half of the questions.

2. Our teacher announced what would be on the test.

3. Several friends of mine were not paying attention when the teacher gave the assignment.

4. My friends who did not listen are worried now about their grades.

5. I am hoping I made an A.

Appendix: Diagraming Sentences

Diagraming Sentences Classified by Structure

SIMPLE SENTENCE: A green light shone under the door. [one independent clause]

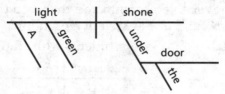

COMPOUND SENTENCE: I want a motorboat, but Jan prefers sailboats. [two independent clauses]

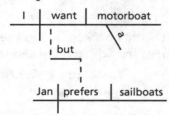

COMPLEX SENTENCE: The satellite will be launched if conditions remain good. [one independent clause and one subordinate clause]

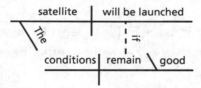

COMPOUND-COMPLEX SENTENCE: The knight boasted of his victories, and he fought whoever challenged him. [two independent clauses and one subordinate clause]

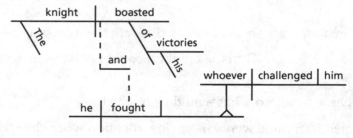

Exercise   On a separate sheet of paper, diagram the following sentences.

1. The bus stopped at the restaurant, and all of the passengers went inside.

2. Invite whomever you want.

3. Shall we meet you at the station, or will you take a taxi?

4. Alexander the Great conquered most of the known world, but he died when he was still a young man.